LIFEKEYS

Discover
Who You Are

————— LIFEKEYS —————

Discover Who You Are

Jane A.G. Kise
David Stark • Sandra Krebs Hirsh

BETHANY HOUSE
Minneapolis, Minnesota

Library of Congress Cataloging-in-Publication Data

Kise, Jane A. G.
    Lifekeys : discover who you are / Jane A. G. Kise, David Stark, Sandra Krebs Hirsh.—Rev. ed.
        p. cm.
    Summary: "A newly revised comprehensive guide to discovering your talents, spiritual gifts, passions, values, and personality—all that God made you to be. Engaging stories, inventories, self-tests, and other easy-to-use exercises make LifeKeys a one-of-a-kind tool. Perfect for churches and individuals, helping people discover who they are and where they fit best"—Provided by publisher.
    Includes bibliographical references.
    ISBN 0-7642-0075-5 (pbk.)
    1. Success—Religious aspects—Christianity. 2. Self-actualization (Psychology)—Religious aspects—Christianity. 3. Gifts, Spiritual. 4. Lay ministry. I. Stark, David, 1955– II. Hirsh, Sandra Krebs. III. Title.
        BV4598.3.K57   2005
        248.4—dc22   2005013062

To the people of Christ Presbyterian Church,
especially those who have participated in our classes
and enriched these pages through their insights,
experiences, and suggestions.

LIFEKEYS RESOURCES

LifeKeys: Discover Who You Are

LifeKeys Discovery Workbook

LifeKeys Leadership Resource

Find Your Fit: LifeKeys for Teens

Find Your Fit Discovery Workbook

Find Your Fit Leader's Guide

SoulTypes

Work It Out

Other Books From
LifeKeys Authors

Finding and Following God's Will
(by Jane A. G. Kise)

Growing People Through Small Groups
(by David Stark and Betty Veldman Wieland)

Christ-Based Leadership
(by David Stark)

For more information: *www.lifekeys.com*

JANE A. G. KISE, EdD, is a freelance writer and consultant, specializing in team building and school staff development. She also teaches seminars and speaks across North America on prayer, constructive use of differences, and unlocking our lives for God. She is the author or coauthor of more than a dozen books, including *Finding and Following God's Will, Did You Get What You Prayed For, Working With Purpose,* and *SoulTypes.* Kise is also a frequent contributor to *Guideposts* and other magazines. She holds a BA from Hamline University, an MBA from the University of Minnesota, and a doctorate in educational leadership from the University of St. Thomas. She and her family live in Minneapolis.

DAVID STARK is director of Changing Church Forum, a ministry of Prince of Peace Lutheran Church. He is also vice president of BusinessKeys International. He divides his time among three roles: pastor, business consultant, and trainer, and is coauthor of *LifeKeys, LifeDirections,* and author of *Christ-Based Leadership* and his own small group materials, *People Together* and *Growing People Through Small Groups.* Stark holds a BA in biology and an MDiv from Princeton Theological Seminary. He and his family reside in Minneapolis.

SANDRA KREBS HIRSH has authored or coauthored more than ten books on psychological type, including *LifeTypes* and *Introduction to Type in Organizations,* which has sold more than two million copies. She heads a management/organizational consulting firm, in addition to coaching individuals and writing, and is much in demand worldwide for her expertise in human resources and organizational development. Hirsh holds graduate degrees in American studies and industrial relations. She lives in Minneapolis.

ACKNOWLEDGMENTS

This project grew out of the efforts of a whole team of people. We would especially like to thank:

Richard N. Bolles, for reading the manuscript and providing us with key suggestions.

Judy Gentry, for her partnership with us in the early stages of developing these materials.

Charette Barta, for her encouragement in shepherding *LifeKeys* toward publication.

Reverend Judie Ritchie, for her help with spiritual direction for each personality type.

Terri Elton, for her energy and enthusiasm in convincing churches to try *LifeKeys*.

Kevin Johnson, for his editorial support.

Dorothy Cummings, Tom and Terri Gulliford, Victoria Manuel, and Laurel Schnabel—members of the original team at church.

And thanks to all the people whose stories are told anonymously in these pages for their willingness to enrich this book with their lives.

Contents

Note on the Second Edition 15
Note for *LifeKeys* Leaders............................. 19
Preface.. 21
1. *LifeKeys* to Discovering Who You Are, Why You're Here,
   and What You Do Best 27
2. Life Gifts—Doing What Comes Naturally.............. 37
3. Spiritual Gifts—God's Special Instruments 73
4. Personality Types—Melodies for Life 133
5. Values—Chords That Touch Your Soul 177
6. Passions—What God Puts in Your Heart............... 193
7. Life Choices—Orchestrating Your Priorities.......... 213
8. Service—For Whom Will You Play? 231
A Final Note of Encouragement........................ 245
Writing a Personal Mission Statement 251

LifeKeys Applications
   Volunteer and Service Opportunities.................. 255
   First Career Direction 263
   Midlife Transitions 269
   Retirement Planning................................ 277
Suggestions for Further Reading 283
My *LifeKeys* Notations............................... 286
Values Cards 289

NOTE ON THE SECOND EDITION

When we began working on *LifeKeys* more than a decade ago, we thought we were designing a class to help people understand who they were and what they might do for God. Since then we've had a lot of surprises, both in how people use the materials and in the ways the materials address issues we had not consciously surfaced. In this second edition, we've had a chance to address some specific needs as well as marvel at God's hand on our efforts. Here are a few of the surprises.

The depth of discovery. In our very first class, Sandra, who had led business-based career development workshops for years, was struck by the deep level at which people were tackling the materials. With the added faith perspective, people were more honest about their struggles to match who they were and what they might do.

Since then we've had people use *LifeKeys* in many ways. In this edition, we've developed separate exercises and reflection questions for the most common purposes. These *LifeKeys* applications are

- Volunteer and Service Opportunities
- First Career Direction
- Midlife Transitions
- Retirement Planning

In addition, the *LifeKeys Leadership Resource* contains ideas for team building, setting organizational direction, and other areas.

Affirmation of many ways to serve God. We could tell story after story of people who didn't think their interests could in any way be used by God. Or who felt that their career paths were separate from what God wanted them to do.

One woman who assumed her lack of college degree disqualified her from the kind of church work she hoped to pursue, decided to apply for a staff position after identifying her passion for children's ministry. She excelled in the position and soon was given even larger responsibilities.

Another *LifeKeys* attendee, a computer programmer, thought her job was totally disconnected from service to God. The class helped her dream about new ways to put her gifts to use. She soon took a new job at a hospital. That led to discovering a new passion—helping a children's hospital in Haiti. Soon she was fundraising and putting together teams and resources, effectively acting on what God had placed in her heart.

Still other attendees found affirmation of what they were already doing or found new ways to serve right where they were— at work, at home, at church, or in the community.

The inclusivity of our message. While we wrote *LifeKeys* from our own Christian perspective, presenting a biblical view of giftedness, mission, and true servanthood, we worked hard to honor the beliefs and needs of people with religious convictions different from our own. We are thankful that the first edition of *LifeKeys* has helped people of varying faiths. We have taught seminars with people present from several church denominations—as well as those who espouse Jewish, Baha'i, Unitarian, and other beliefs—all able to work with and appreciate our teachings. In writing, we tried to find universal places of agreement and found that *LifeKeys* touches universal needs. Occasionally someone tells us it's the first useful thing they've received from organized religion. Frequently when we teach a seminar, less than half of the attendees are members of the host church. Others come because they want to understand who they are and whether religion or faith can add meaning and value.

The power of empowered laypeople for the church of the twenty-first century. From the start *LifeKeys* was designed to help people dream about what they might do for God, not just fill places in church ministries, as important as that is. We believe the old rule of thumb that 20 percent of the people can handle about 80 percent of those positions. This leaves a huge group available for either work outside the church or new ministries of their own design. And because of cultural trends this is vital to the church's future.

In the last few decades the role the church plays has diminished in influencing the spiritual beliefs of the surrounding culture. No longer are we in a season of—to quote a famous film—"If you build it, they will come." Rather, people do not necessarily look to the institutional church for their spiritual needs. Therefore, the more the church can empower laypeople to go out and add value to the communities they live in, demonstrating the reality of the Gospel that they believe in, the more influence the church can have. The further we go into this new millennium, the more churches will need to turn outward. And *LifeKeys* helps people dream what they might do; at the church where *LifeKeys* started, a preponderance of outreaches and new ministries have been started by our "graduates."

Sometimes ministers shudder at the thought, saying, "But how will I fill my Sunday school rooms with teachers if I don't emphasize our volunteer needs?" We know how difficult it is at times to recruit volunteers. But we think God gave enough people with the gifts for teaching Sunday school, ushering, singing in the choir, and running church-based outreaches, if only they discovered who they were. *LifeKeys* is designed to motivate people to prioritize ministry in their lives. If that happens, you'll have more than enough people for inside-the-church ministries. *LifeKeys* requires trust on the part of church leadership that God knows their needs and is placing in people's hearts the desire to meet them.

LifeKeys can help your church's vision to grow big enough for people who aren't naturally excited by the same old programs. They can make a difference with their gifts and talents by reaching into the community, excited to be a part of something bigger than themselves. How can the church possibly do as Jesus asked— spreading the Gospel (Matthew 28:19) and reaching out to those who are hungry, homeless, sick, or imprisoned (Matthew 25:45)— unless its mission is to equip its members for service to a hurting, needy world? It is our prayer that *LifeKeys* will help people discover and develop the gifts God gave them so that the church can fulfill this role.

NOTE FOR *LifeKeys* LEADERS

If you are leading a group, large or small, through the *LifeKeys* process, several resources are available to help you both with planning and teaching *LifeKeys*.

- The *LifeKeys Discovery Workbook* provides basic information on each of the *LifeKeys* and presents the inventories in a concise format for ease of facilitation. We often use the *Workbook* in workshop settings and encourage participants to read the book later on their own.
- A basic leader's guide can be downloaded free of charge from *www.janekise.com*. The information it contains is an updated version of the "Help for *LifeKeys* Leaders" found in the first edition of *LifeKeys*. Included are basic exercises, brief lecture outlines, and format ideas.
- The *LifeKeys Leadership Resource* contains more background information, additional exercises, and more than one hundred reproducible masters that can be copied as handouts or made into overheads. A companion CD-ROM makes it easy to prepare handouts and overheads as well.
- The *Suggestions for Further Reading* section of this volume provides a list of excellent resources that can help you enrich the materials for your participants.

At least twice a year we also offer *LifeKeys* Train-the-Trainer clinics. The first half is a *LifeKeys* clinic taught by the authors. The second half prepares you to teach *LifeKeys* yourself. Check upcoming dates at *www.lifekeys.com, www.janekise.com,* or *www.changingchurch.org.* You are welcome to teach *LifeKeys* without attending the class, but the hundreds of participants we have taken through the course have informed us that their time with us was enlightening, enriching, and a great source of practical help in preparing to teach *LifeKeys*.

Whatever steps you take to teach *LifeKeys*, we pray that you'll find the experience spiritually rewarding as you assist others in discovering all God created them to be.

PREFACE

Have you discovered the keys to a fulfilling life?

Do the various roles you play or the work you do fit with who you are?

Does the life you lead give you a sense of purpose and meaning?

For a staggering number of people—even those who appear to have their act together—the answer to these questions is no.

This book grew out of our efforts to help members of our congregation identify *LifeKeys*—truths about who they are, why they are here, and what they do best that will add significance and direction to their lives. All around us people were saying:

"I'm curious about this notion of having a purpose in life. Is there anything to it?"

"There are more layoffs coming; I wonder if I should rethink my career goals."

"I feel pulled in another direction. Should I take a fresh look at my options?"

"I don't seem to fit in anywhere or have talents anyone wants."

We—Jane, David, and Sandra—believe that the best answers to these questions are spiritual answers. *LifeKeys* is our process for helping you find those answers. We'd like to tell you how it all began.

David: Being someone who tends toward large-scale dreams, I wanted to see the church become a place where people could discover and develop their God-given potential. In my early ministry experiences, I saw people change when they understood their gifts and their passions—in short, when they found their *LifeKeys*. They confidently stepped out in faith, believing that God was leading them. If we concentrate too much on our weaknesses, as all too often is done in the church, we miss discovering how each one of us was uniquely created for the work God wants done.

Through a series of serendipitous events, I was asked to teach a seminar on gift identification for the women's association at our church. The existing curriculum I used missed the emphasis I wanted. There wasn't enough information about the merits of each person's gifts, people needed more material to process what they learned about themselves, and they weren't convinced that God loved them enough to gift them. Even in our "healthy" church, people needed more.

I realized that creating a better approach was a bigger task than I wanted to tackle on my own—I needed a team of writers, organizers, and others with a heart for helping people discover what God could do through them.

Jane: I participated in that early women's class that David taught. Sitting in the seminar, I realized for the first time how unique my upbringing was. Coming from a family where my four brothers and I were encouraged to find out how and where we could be of service, the class confirmed much of what I already believed God had in mind for my mission. However, most of the other women at my table were disheartened. They felt dwarfed by the suggested standards of spirituality and giftedness. Somehow they lacked the foundational belief that out of love God had chosen the best for them, and so they were disappointed in what they discovered about themselves. I heard comments like "I don't like my gifts"; "I want to be someone else"; "I don't feel valuable to God."

When David asked for help with creating a richer spiritual gifts discovery process, I spontaneously put down my name. I was sure that this concept of finding *LifeKeys,* done correctly, could help people experience what my family had given me. I also knew that David needed an organizer—he readily admits to being a visionary, not an administrator! I could put his thoughts on paper and think through class arrangements.

As the project grew, so did my role, especially as we realized that people needed a notebook that included the teaching materials and self-discovery exercises. Years later I constantly hear from people—at church, on the phone, even at the State Fair—about the positive choices they have made as a result of understanding their own *LifeKeys.* It's amazing what happens when God puts a team together!

Sandra: While active in church throughout most of my life, I had also been deeply hurt by the actions of some religious people who had made me feel like the "unwashed among the washed." I became a soloist in my spiritual journey, helping others through my career in human resources consulting, but avoiding formal religious ties. However, close to the time I met David and Jane, my soul was longing for a more meaningful role. I again wanted to make church attendance a part of my life.

On a dreary November day while trying to find some papers, I looked out my office window and noticed a man dashing across the parking lot. He was obviously trying to get somewhere in a hurry. A few minutes later, as I prepared to leave, the same man stood outside my office door!

"Are you Sandra Hirsh—who works with personality type?" he asked breathlessly.

"Yes, and who are you?"

"I'm David Stark, a pastor at Christ Presbyterian Church," he stated, and went on to add more about *my* home church! He explained the course he wanted to develop and asked, "Would you be interested in advising us?"

I said, "I'd be glad to hear your teachings. I'll let you know if I can add anything of value." David claims that I later said he required a *great deal* of my help, but in truth I was impressed with his vision and eagerly joined the team.

This "chance" encounter led to what my soul was seeking—a community of faith and a chance to serve with others in a meaningful way that matched my gifts.

Through a lot of trial and error, prayer, and the contributions of dozens of people, we began to formulate first a class, then a notebook, and finally *LifeKeys* as you now see it. For us, the greatest joy is seeing the powerful impact this God-centered self-discovery process has on people. The three themes that play over and over again in our materials are:

- God created you and therefore values you highly.
- God created you uniquely and there is genuinely only one of you.
- God from the foundation of the world had good works in mind for you to do.

Hearing these themes releases people—ourselves included—in ways that we have seldom seen. We hope that as you work your way through this book, the uniqueness and value of your own life will begin to surface. Somewhere deep inside you are *LifeKeys* awaiting your discovery. Join us as we explore how your life gifts, spiritual gifts, personality, values, and passions provide the keys to a meaningful life. When you understand how you have been created, God's Spirit can honestly do far more than you could ask or even imagine.

LifeKey #1

God has an important part for you—yes, YOU—to play!

Chapter 1

LifeKeys to Discovering Who You Are, Why You're Here, and What You Do Best

I had been my whole life a bell, and never knew it until at that moment I was lifted and struck.[1]

—Annie Dillard

The school orchestra: that safe haven for a positive first experience with music. Even if you were tone-deaf and had trouble catching the beat, the director could still find a place for you. She might suggest another instrument: "Amber, with your strong lungs, I think the trombone might be a more suitable fit than the flute." Or, with encouragement, she'd build on your strengths: "Bill, you have the best sense of rhythm in the string section, but we're short of drummers—would you consider switching?"

When the director created this atmosphere, orchestra was great: a chance to get out of class, make as much noise as you wanted, and not have to worry about mistakes. What could be more fun? After all, there were twenty-nine flutes, eighteen clarinets, a host of cornets and saxophones—so many players that it was impossible to guess the source of any bad notes.

In this inclusive atmosphere, students could keep trying until they found an instrument that made them feel a part of the orchestra. Some stayed in the third row of clarinets through high school, supplying the low harmony that allowed the melody to shine. Some

---

[1]Annie Dillard, *Pilgrim at Tinker Creek* (New York: Harper & Row, 1974), 35.

switched to the unusual instruments—oboe or the baritone saxo-phone—balancing the sound of the group. Others played as well as they could, but more than anything contributed a fun-loving spirit. And in some way, everyone went on to be a star. Besides the drum-mer who now plays with a major symphony, one band produced:

- a pianist who uses her musical skills as an occupational thera-pist;
- two trumpet players who pass on their love of music to adoles-cents by conducting high school bands;
- a trombonist who found a career in sound-mixing;
- a flute player who put her talents to use on mission outreach trips;
- and many more who never played another note but gained from their orchestra experience a sense of the richness that music provides to life.

Whatever their path, young musicians who played under such an encouraging director had the experience of being a part of something bigger than themselves, of learning to harmonize with and benefit from the efforts of others.

This book attempts to create that same safe atmosphere for you—a place where you can discover LifeKeys that will help you orchestrate your life in ways that lead to a sense of purpose or indi-vidual calling.

Think about how Webster's defines orchestrate. It means "to arrange or combine so as to achieve a maximum effect." Orchestra-tion means "harmonious organization."[2] Wouldn't it be refreshing to feel that you have put together all the pieces of you in a harmo-nious way?

But life isn't as safe as a school orchestra, is it?

Perhaps you are one of the lucky ones who found a good fit in life, settling somehow into a good place. You feel effective. You find meaning in your activities. If that describes you, we hope that LifeKeys will provide a structured method to help you continue to make fulfilling choices.

Many more people, however, struggle to find any place where they feel as though they fit. Perhaps you never have had a chance to explore what kind of "instrument" you might play. Perhaps your

[2]Webster's New Collegiate Dictionary (Springfield, Mass.: G. & C. Merriam Company, 1977), 807.

life was orchestrated for you long ago by a parent or someone else who thought they knew what suited you best. It was as if they purchased an expensive, nonreturnable instrument without your input, leaving you no choice. Or perhaps your orchestration was somewhat haphazard—you are where you are more by accident than by design.

Maybe your parents thought your special interests were a waste of time. Or teachers or counselors discouraged you from trying anything new. Or you felt left out, as if you were destined for the drudgery of run-of-the-mill duty for the rest of your days.

There *is* a place for you in the orchestra of life. This book and the thoughts behind it came about because people all around us are asking: *Where is my part? What is my purpose? How can I find meaning and yet give of myself to others?* Each *LifeKey* we will explore together adds to understanding who you are, why you're here, and what you do best. Viewing your various *LifeKeys* as a whole lets you begin to orchestrate a fulfilling life—not merely for personal ends, but to bring harmony to you *and* your world as you use everything that God has built into you.

In the ever-popular *What Color Is Your Parachute*, Richard N. Bolles describes the concept of your unique mission in life:

(a.) To exercise that Talent which you particularly came to Earth to use—your greatest gift which you most delight to use

(b.) in the place(s) or setting(s) which God has caused to appeal to you the most

(c.) and for those purposes which God most needs to have done in the world.[3]

LifeKeys guides you through the process of finding that unique mission God had in mind when you were created. We first help you find your greatest gift—as Bolles describes above (a.)—in the chapters on life gifts and spiritual gifts. Next, the chapters on personality types and passions help you recognize the places or settings that God has caused to appeal to you the most, as described in (b.). Finally, the chapters on values and life choices can aid your process of discovering the purposes for which God most desires your help, as described in (c.).

---

[3]Richard N. Bolles, *What Color Is Your Parachute?* (Berkeley, Calif.: Ten Speed Press, 1996), 449.

As you read, keep in mind that you are searching for your personal *LifeKeys*—the gifts that *you* take delight in using and the places that appeal to *you* the most, in accordance with how God has uniquely designed *you*. Without such an exploration, you may miss a life that harmonizes with God's plan for you.

What Keeps Us From Discovering Our LifeKeys?

As we used *LifeKeys* throughout the world, we found that the majority of our participants—and these were people from *all* walks of life—struggled with our underlying premise that they were gifted by God! The doubts came from various sources. Some had been tossed from their current track by a downsizing company or a changing industry. Some were approaching the second half of their lives with a vague lack of purpose. For many, though, the doubts came from deeper sources.

Some assumed that their gifts were insignificant. We heard people say, "My talents are absolutely unimpressive. My only option is to be content to sit and listen, right?" Assuming that only the world-class talents of virtuosos are valuable can be a major stumbling block. Our culture tends to celebrate certain gifts at exceptional levels. If you're not a millionaire, or successful in business or government leadership, athletics, acting, or public speaking, it is easy to underrate or shortchange yourself.

Certainly some gifts are easier to recognize than others. When a three-year-old can sit down at the piano and play by ear a song she's heard just once, people take notice. When an athlete takes the Olympic gold, people take notice. When someone makes millions of dollars, people take notice. However, even if your gifts are less recognizable, they are indeed as worthy as the gifts to which the world pays attention. Consider the person who has a special knack for encouraging others to try again, or the friend with a gentle, calming influence during a crisis, or the young adult who can easily turn chaos into an organized filing system. Given the biases of our society, these individuals may not be recognized as the gifted people they are.

However, if you compare yourself to earthly standards, you miss one of the most amazing messages God has for you: You were created in a way that reflects God!

Then God said, "Let us make humankind in our image, according to our likeness" (Genesis 1:26 NRSV).

If you view your gifts as insignificant, remember that somewhere inside of you is the *image of God*. God considers your soul a fitting home and wants you to think of yourself in that way as well. Your Creator has granted you the necessary resources to reflect back to the world all the love with which you were made.

This book is meant to encourage you to take a fresh look at the part you were meant to play. Your part is unique to you—your life gifts, spiritual gifts, personality, values, and passions. You have been given a special place in the orchestra of life. As one little boy put it, "I know I'm worth something, because God don't make no junk." The same holds true for you: You resemble God.

Some assumed they were missing the "right" gift. Do you mourn along with Dorothy's friends in the Land of Oz because you lack "a brain . . . a heart . . . the nerve"? Many are convinced that they are of little value because they don't have the "right" gift. By fixating on that one "right" gift, they often miss noticing the multiple gifts they *do* have.

This focus can make otherwise talented people feel inadequate. One woman belittled herself, saying, "All I do is cook meals for the sick and pray." In truth, her prayer and visitation ministry was a vital part of her church's spiritual life and a significant help to those in need.

> For you created my inmost being; you knit me together in my mother's womb. I praise you because I am fearfully and wonderfully made; your works are wonderful, I know that full well. My frame was not hidden from you when I was made in the secret place. (Psalm 139:13–15)

Remember, God gave you everything you need—the truly right gifts chosen just for you. What may be lacking is confidence in *your knowledge* of what God can do through you.

Some people claimed that their gifts don't mesh the way they should. Do you feel like a violinist with drumsticks instead of a bow? If you feel mismatched, consider taking a different perspective. For example, a swimmer could time each lap of a twenty-lap race perfectly for each segment of the race but wasn't tall enough to beat the competition. She wondered why God had given her an uncanny talent for distance swimming without also giving her the body type she needed to be a champion. Frustrated, she turned to coaching, where her natural gifts for stroke mechanics and race strategies, along with her passion for the sport itself, brought meaning to her and success to her teams.

Others felt as if they had practiced the wrong instruments. You may wonder how your training matches with who you are *now*. A fifty-two-year-old dentist told us, "An eighteen-year-old who didn't know what he was doing (me!) chose my career." However, your experiences may someday be used in ways you can't yet imagine. For example, Dr. Paul Brand, a renowned surgeon, could not understand why God had allowed him to spend four years in architectural engineering school, delaying his entry into medical school. Years later when he worked as a doctor with lepers, he realized that God had plans for those engineering skills. His surgical expertise allowed him to pioneer techniques for repairing hands damaged by leprosy. He also designed tools with special features to safeguard the insensitive hands of lepers, allowing them to find useful employment. The tools could only have been designed by someone who understood both engineering principles and the medical needs of those with leprosy. His engineering training was just what God had in mind!

Some wondered why they felt drawn to certain areas but lacked the gifts they believed were required. If this describes you, consider that within each arena there are many roles to play. For example, one woman taught Sunday school quite skillfully for five years. Despite her success, she felt completely drained after each class, as if she were teaching out of determination instead of a gift for teaching. After much prayer, she decided to channel her love and passion for children into an administrative role, providing teacher workshops, organizing classroom supplies, and making other resources available. This new role allowed her to use her gifts and continue to serve out of her passion for children. Gone was the feeling of being drained. Along came a sense of enthusiasm. In her realignment, she influenced not only a single class of children but every child in the church.

Some doubt there is any part for them to play. If you can't believe that God has a use for you, humor us for a moment. Perhaps you haven't given yourself the time to discover your *LifeKeys*. Or your life hasn't taken you to settings where you could stumble upon them. If that sounds like you, consider that you might be like a fidgety drummer, awaiting your opportunity to shine.

Back in school, kids who wanted to be drummers needed imagination. While the other orchestra members got to play real instruments from the start, first-year drummers began their lessons on practice pads—blocks of wood with a rubber circle glued on top.

Pads have two advantages for the director: they're quiet, and students are forced to work on technique, not noisemaking. Pads have two disadvantages for the students: they're quiet, and students are forced to work on technique, not noisemaking.

But for the drummers who persisted, the big day finally came when they graduated to the real instruments. They took charge of the snare drum, the cymbals, the marimba, the bass drum, maybe even a whole drum set. Exalting in the crashes and cadences their nimble sticking now produced, they filled the school cafeteria with rhythm and music!

If you have never played the instrument God designed for you, a rich experience awaits. However, before you can receive and enjoy that feeling, you need to discover your niche—the niche that God promises is there for us:

> For we are God's workmanship, created in Christ Jesus to do good works, which God prepared in advance for us to do. (Ephesians 2:10)

But you want a different assignment? You can't read the notes or follow the score? Please believe us—perhaps you haven't yet heard the music. Or your time has not yet come.

Now, What About You?

Do you see yourself in any of our stories about others who questioned their gifts? Can you only picture yourself as a "swimmer," unable to envision taking your place as a coach or referee or trainer? Or is it difficult to see yourself as a "teacher," able to switch to administration of an educational endeavor? Or do you struggle with understanding how some of your skills or past experiences could possibly mesh with what you can do now?

Of even greater concern, have you given up on yourself? Have you taken whatever comes along? Do you doubt that God has a plan for you—that there is a Creator who truly cares about you and your search for meaning? We and those who have worked through these materials know with certainty that God cares, that there is a connection between who you are and what God has in mind for you. It may take effort to find that connection, but the effort is worth it both for yourself and for others in your life.

And God *passionately* desires that you find that connection. Keith Miller and Bruce Larson put it this way:

> All that we are meant to be! God's dream for each of us is so vastly greater than the largest dream we have for ourselves. But what is his dream for us? I believe he has given us clues to what that dream is. And the longings and yearnings buried in each of us often provide those clues. It is like being on a cosmic treasure hunt. Follow one clue and it will lead you to another . . . and then to another . . . until you find the treasure himself. For to find God and his ultimate will for us is to find ourselves. This is the discovery for which all of creation stands on tiptoe—to see God's sons and daughters coming into their own.[4]

Join us through the pages of this book and allow yourself to uncover your gifts, personality, values, and passions—your *Life-Keys*—that instrument God meant you to be. Place before yourself the wonderful truth that somewhere deep inside of you is a person designed by God. There can be no path more fulfilling than the one that uses your unique gifts as God intended.

Prayer

Lord, I may be confused about choices I face. I may have given up on who I am, but I want to open my heart to understanding my LifeKeys. Show me that discovering how You created me can guide me to a more fulfilling life. Protect me from being sidetracked by my doubts or past failures. Instead, let me grasp the ways in which I am fearfully and wonderfully made by You. Amen.

---

[4]Keith Miller and Bruce Larson, *The Passionate People* (Waco, Tex.: Word Books, 1979), 14.

For Journal or Discussion

Note: Whether you are reading LifeKeys *alone or in a small group, we suggest that you record your thoughts in a separate notebook or journal.*

At this point you might also wish to review the four LifeKeys *Applications (Volunteer and Service Opportunities, page 255; First Career Direction, page 263; Midlife Transitions, page 269; Retirement Planning, page 277). You can use the additional questions and exercises they include as you read each chapter of this book.*

1. How did you get on your current path? Your parents' wishes? By accident? A "sensible" decision?

2. What goal do you have for yourself as you read *LifeKeys*? Better self-awareness? New, more meaningful volunteer activities? A first job? A career change? Retirement? Consider how you want to use these pages and set some goals about what you wish to gain.

3. Take a hard look at your image of God. Loving creator? Disciplinarian? Earnest counselor? Fearful judge? At a deep level, your image of God influences how you view yourself. Ponder the following Bible verses:
   a. Psalm 46:1
   b. Jeremiah 31:3
   c. John 15:9–11
   d. Matthew 10:30
   e. Psalm 103:12

LifeKey #2

Doing what comes naturally is part of God's plan.

CHAPTER 2

LIFE GIFTS—DOING WHAT COMES NATURALLY

... God has already revealed His will to us concerning our vocation and Mission, by causing it to be "written in our members." We are to begin deciphering our unique Mission by studying our talents and skills, and more particularly which ones (or One) we most rejoice to use.[1]

—Richard N. Bolles

Can You Really Be Anything?

"You can be anything you want to be if you just work hard enough." Have you heard that line? In many ways it may be true, but there are some limitations. For example, could you tour as a concert pianist? Not if your hands aren't big enough to stretch for the chords of some of the great concertos. Could you play trumpet with a famous jazz trio? Not unless your embouchure (mouth position) is naturally suited to it, no matter how much you practice. Obviously, only a few of us could ever perform with the Metropolitan Opera—or even sing the National Anthem before a televised ball game. There are some things we cannot do, no matter how hard we work at them.

There are other things that simply do not capture our interests, whether we could learn to do them well or not. For example, Jane

---

[1] Richard N. Bolles, *How to Find Your Mission in Life* (Berkeley, Calif.: Ten Speed Press, 1991), 43.

will never become a tree surgeon—too many tools and too few people. Sandra has no plans to go into tax accounting—too much detail and not enough variety for her. David would resist being an air traffic controller—too much focused attention.

But the things we are interested in and that we do well—what a different story! These are a *LifeKey* to the way God has gifted us.

- Jane can look back to childhood and see overstuffed bookshelves. She often asked her teachers to let her write stories to show what she had learned and chose to major in English in college—it is no surprise that she is a writer.
- David was president of every school he attended, and even managed to get his fraternity row to organize a Christmas pageant for a local children's home—it is no surprise that he turned his leadership skills toward helping others through ministry.
- Sandra began teaching Sunday school when she was only a bit older than the children she taught. She raised money to travel as a YMCA youth delegate to Europe—it is no surprise that her consulting business focuses on training, teaching, and helping others to understand themselves.

The three of us can see how our talents, combined with our interests—and certain conditions in our past (family, academic, financial)—molded us into what we do occupationally today. Yet some people assume that they simply "fell into" their life's work. To test this, think of things you could *never* "fall into." Jane couldn't fall into computer programming, David hasn't the slightest desire to be a dentist, and Sandra will never operate heavy machinery. If you find your natural bent, your inclination, what we will call your *life gifts*, then you can find the things that you enjoy and will most likely do well.

Does God Really Give Life Gifts?

Each of us has life gifts, given by God, to fit perfectly within our overall design. Proverbs 22:6 points out our design:

> Train children in the right way, and when old, they will not stray. (NRSV)

Perhaps in the past you have heard this verse as a guarantee—teach your children God's ways and even if they rebel for a while, eventually they will come back to the fold.

But there is another, perhaps more *accurate*, meaning. There is a *right* way we *should* go, and it is different for each of us. *The Amplified Bible* expands "the right way" as "in keeping with his or her individual gift or bent." According to *Webster's*, a bent is (1) a strong inclination or interest; (2) a special inclination or capacity: talent.[2] We are describing that bent as your *life gifts*.

Bible stories show that God intended for us to have different life gifts for many different purposes. The building of the first tabernacle is a good example. As the Israelites began their forty-year wandering in the wilderness after being led out of Egypt, God commanded them to build a tabernacle, or sanctuary. The structure was mobile, yet a beautiful and symbolic place where God would dwell among them.

God not only gave very exacting instructions about the building design, but also revealed the specific people who had the life gifts to do various parts of the work. (The Bible here is using the word *skill* in the manner in which we have defined life gifts—God-given talents.)

> Then Moses told the people of Israel ... "The Lord has filled Bezalel with the Spirit of God, giving him great wisdom, ability, and expertise in all kinds of crafts. He is a master craftsman, expert in working with gold, silver, and bronze. He is skilled in engraving and mounting gemstones and in carving wood. He is a master at every craft. And the Lord has given both him and Oholiab ... the ability to teach their skills to others. The Lord has given them special skills as engravers, designers, embroiderers in blue, purple, and scarlet thread on fine linen cloth, and weavers. They excel as craftsmen and as designers.
>
> "The Lord has gifted Bezalel, Oholiab, and the other skilled craftsmen with wisdom and ability to perform any task involved in building the sanctuary. Let them construct and furnish the Tabernacle, just as the Lord has commanded" (Exodus 35:30–36:1 NLT).

Again, this story relates how the artisans were given life gifts to carry out God's purposes. These workers also used their life gifts in

---

[2] *Webster's New Collegiate Dictionary*, 103.

other arenas, even for their livelihood, but God's people needed their skills for this moment. The next three chapters of Exodus relate that the beauty and intricacy of the tabernacle inspired the Israelites to give abundantly to the project; Moses finally had to ask them to stop giving because the project was over-funded! The life gifts of the artisans provided blessings to the entire nation.

Why Determine Your Life Gifts?

Knowing your life gifts, whether they show themselves in forms of communication, problem-solving, or time management, can help you focus your energy on the areas that God intended for you. This knowledge can keep you from a lot of frustration! A root source of satisfaction in life is doing what comes naturally—using your own unique blend of life gifts. None of us wants to struggle and strain in an attempt to succeed as a concert pianist if God designed us to build houses or to teach or to run a business.

Life gifts are much more than proficiencies gathered along the way. Instead, they're a special blend of interests and talents that make up your unique design. Things that seem so easy for you that you assume anyone could do them may, in fact, be your life gifts. For example, are you a problem-solver? All of us at one time had to learn basic algebra, but only some of us have a life gift for mathematical problem-solving that allows us to apply those algebraic principles years later. Or, are you able to create things? While in school, most of us were required to make things like a model dragster car or sew a pillowcase. However, today only a few of us are interested in building furniture or cars or designing and sewing our own clothing.

Perhaps your life gifts fit well with your current career or situation. If so, use this chapter for personal confirmation. But because of our cultural idea that anyone can succeed at anything if they try hard enough, some of us try to squeeze ourselves into positions that fit our life gifts no better than a drum can play the melody of a song. Success is far easier when your efforts are in harmony with the life gifts God chose especially for you. God *designed* people to have diverse talents and abilities for different purposes.

Are Life Gifts Easy to Identify?

Some people identify their life gifts easily. One geologist could trace her career interests back to the rock collection she started as a preschooler. A top sales representative always outsold his friends in the annual "candy for campers" sales. Other people, though, find it more difficult to name their life gifts, often because of three main reasons:

- *The influence of our families may have kept us from exploring the unique gifts God chose for us.* Understandably, we often absorb our parents' interests, values, and sometimes passions. Separating parental interests from our own interests can be difficult. When we don't do this, we are often propelled into jobs, volunteer organizations, or situations that may or may not be a good fit for our unique pattern of life gifts.

- *We may downplay or even bury life gifts out of fear of appearing proud.* People often discount their contributions. They remark, "I made so many mistakes!" when they have just completed a dynamic and nearly perfect marketing presentation. Or they may say, "Oh, it was just luck, I guess," when their life gifts have allowed them to successfully coordinate a large social gathering. Perhaps a clue to your life gifts is to consider what you are doing when you feel most lucky! Using our life gifts may or may not push us into the spotlight, but think of how our Creator must feel if we never use the tools, the interests, the life gifts we were given.

- *We might select occupations or tasks based on a distorted self-concept.* This misperception of who we are often leads to inappropriate choices or unrealistic ambitions. Whether we're pursuing choices that others made for us or choices that seemed practical or realistic, if our ambitions don't line up with our God-given life gifts, we often experience fatigue or feelings of inadequacy. It takes more energy to do what *doesn't* come naturally. Further, discouragement comes easily because no matter how hard we try, we will most likely be surrounded by people who are doing what *does* come naturally for them—who may be producing at a higher level with seemingly less effort.

What If I'm Good at Something, but Don't Really Enjoy It?

Feeling discouraged frequently happens when we mistakenly identify and confuse a skill or competency (learned through experience, training, or education) with a life gift. A good way to think of this is to consider what fruits are yielded through piano lessons. Think of all the children who progress to the easier sonatas and even master a favorite jazz rag. Multitudes of them still find practicing an effort-filled chore. Compare that to the teenager who loves to play the accompaniment for the school choir—or the musician who enjoys playing carol after carol for harried department store shoppers during the Christmas season. Surely their life gifts enhance any skills they've developed!

The difference between skills and life gifts becomes easily clouded as we choose careers because of the specialized training (i.e., skills development) we receive—and the fact that most of us focus on doing the best job that we can. Carla, a friend of ours, spent her freshman year of college carefully evaluating the job market, finally choosing medical technology because of the growing opportunities and probable job security. A good student, she applied herself diligently to each class and landed a choice laboratory position before graduation. It wasn't until her children and husband were competing with the medical lab for a limited resource—her energy!—that she realized how little interest her medical technology work held for her. She didn't seem to have the knack or the enthusiasm that some of her colleagues had for intuitively designing research studies or improving diagnostic methods.

Did Carla change careers? Not right away, for she fell into the common trap of thinking that working harder would make things better. Only after much soul-searching did Carla realize that her early success was tied to all of the administrative tasks assigned to her when she first joined the lab. These went by the wayside, replaced with pure lab work, when she was promoted. This new self-knowledge allowed her to select a second career—in hospital management—that matched her life gifts.

Can you see the pattern?

- Practical considerations led to Carla's career choice.
- Diligence led to scholastic and early career success.
- Early success led to enhanced responsibilities.
- Life changes led to less energy and enthusiasm for her work.
- Evaluation of the original choice through the framework of life gifts helped her identify the mismatch and possible better choices.

You may know someone or may *be* someone who through a similar fate find yourself in a career or situation where you struggle with your assigned responsibilities or other people's expectations for you. Once, however, you identify your true bent—your life gifts—you may be able to spend more of your time using your life gifts by:

- readjusting your work environment;
- delegating;
- developing a specific skill that will lessen your stress; or
- changing to a new job environment or adding a new volunteer activity.

If you decide that the only solution is a major change, you can decrease your anxiety by first discovering your *LifeKeys* and then acting on that information.

If These Are My Gifts, What Next?

Carla's discovery that she was operating outside her life gifts came through three factors:

- the stress of a growing family (for others it could be major changes in health, aging, a traumatic event, or even boredom);
- a shift in job responsibilities so that she was using her life gifts less and less;
- a feeling of burnout.

There is a huge difference between consciously putting yourself in a place where you *know* you will struggle to fit in versus anticipating that you will fit in and instead feeling like the only oboe on a team of harpists. (It's one thing to struggle at a summer job—like detasseling corn or filing papers for weeks on end—that you took for the money and no other reason. It's quite another to choose a career, work hard, and not understand why you are so frustrated.)

Frequently, understanding your life gifts can help you better position yourself. One man whose work involved facilitating seminars found himself growing more and more frustrated. He felt inadequate teaching large groups, since he found it difficult to discern whether he was reaching each person. He finally realized that one of his favorite life gifts was counseling individuals one-on-one. Eventually he changed to a more fulfilling career as a therapist.

Another individual inherited a family business that her father had headed. After several years of struggling with sluggish sales, she realized that persuasion was not one of her life gifts. Hiring a sales and marketing manager allowed her to better use her managerial life gifts by concentrating on manufacturing, human resources, and strategic planning.

In each of these cases, the people were able to concentrate their efforts on what they naturally did well by turning over to others the areas where they lacked life gifts. Or, by seeking new opportunities where they could put their life gifts to use.

Does Everyone Really Have Life Gifts?

Is it difficult for you to believe that you have any life gifts? Maybe bruises from past failures or the impossible standards you or others set for you leave you afraid to try anything new. A lack of self-esteem may mean that you struggle to convince yourself that you even have life gifts or that they are worth using.

If these doubts reflect your current inner conflict, you are in good company. The Bible is full of people who didn't understand their life gifts until in some way God gave them new insights. The apostle Peter, busy with his fishing boat, had no idea that his speeches could rouse others to action. Mary, the sister of Martha, had no idea that her ability to give all her attention to Jesus' words was something that others struggled to do. Martha had no idea that she was loved whether she worked in the kitchen or not. If you find yourself saying, "But I don't . . ." or "Not me . . ." trust as you explore your life gifts that perhaps your path up to this point has detoured past what comes to you naturally. Keep going—we maintain that there *will* be things that interest you. Those are clues to how God has gifted you, to the way you should go.

A Framework for Finding Your Special Life Gifts

Let's take a fresh look at the things you do that energize you—where your life gifts are—that natural bent. For more than seventy-five years many people have found answers through theoretical work on career choices, particularly that of John Holland. The theory postulates that people's interests can be categorized into six areas of preference—that is, six areas where people tend to cluster as they look for fulfillment through using their life gifts. Holland labeled these six areas as Realistic [R], Investigative [I], Artistic [A], Social [S], Enterprising [E], and Conventional [C]. People who have similar interests or life gifts tend to enjoy similar work, co-workers, and work environments. Their life gifts often derive from these interests. Doesn't that make sense—that we gravitate toward work that we like and do well? These interest areas, then, can help us find our life gifts.

Holland pictured the relationship between these areas by diagramming them as a hexagon:

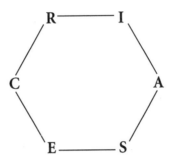

In Holland's hexagon, Realistics have more in common with Investigatives and Conventionals, which neighbor Realistics on the hexagon, than they do with Socials, which are farthest away on the hexagon and have the most dissimilar interests.

Typically, people find that their interests, when prioritized, reflect this similarity. Some people feel that just one interest area describes them well. Most of us are actually a blend of two and sometimes three of the six areas. Their interest areas lie next to each other on the hexagon model. Sometimes, however, an atypical pattern occurs—that is, when someone has interests in opposite areas such as Realistic and Social. While this pattern is normal, it is less common.

Choose Your Areas, Find Your Life Gifts

What follows is a brief description of each of the six areas, indicating common interests, characteristics, and life gifts of each group. Refer to the hexagon chart on pages 70–71 to keep track of the areas that interest you most. To find your life gifts, work through the following process:[3]

- Read through *all* the descriptions first, ignoring for now the charts that contain the life gifts.
- Using the descriptions, identify those (at least one but no more than three), that describe you best, abbreviating them by their first letters. Jane, for example, is an SAI, Sandra an ASE, and David an EIS. If you are unsure, look back through the cartoons shown for the interest areas and sort them into your order of priority—which roles would you hope for in a theater or musical production? Write your own interest area letters below:

_____   _____   _____

- Beginning with the *first* interest area you wrote in the blanks above, fill out the life gifts charts. The second life gifts chart you complete will be the one for the second interest area you wrote in the blanks above. Then continue through the interest areas in their order of priority for you. We ask you *not* to start with the Realistic area (unless that is your first interest area) because we want you to discover quickly how gifted you are—and you'll find more gifts in your chosen interest areas.
- Most people do not have all the life gifts listed in their interest areas. Your chosen interest themes, though, are good places to start the search for your natural bent.
- Remember to consider the life gifts outside your interest areas. Jane, for example, is SAI, but has the Conventional life gift of managing time and priorities. David is EIS, but has the Realistic life gift of taking physical risks. Sandra is ASE, but has the Investigative gift of synthesizing research.
- There is a difference between being attracted to an area and being truly interested in that area. For example, many children may say they want to play soccer, but few are out there every day after school practicing their ball-handling skills. As you work through the life gifts charts, *concentrate on whether those life gifts motivate you to action.*

---

[3]If you want to dig deeper, the *Strong Interest Inventory*® (Consulting Psychologists Press, Mountain View, Calif.) is a widely available instrument that can help you identify your interest patterns. If you wish to take the *Strong*, which matches your interest patterns with those of people in diverse occupations, contact your local community college or the publisher at 800–624–1765.

- Sum up your life gifts by highlighting the ones on which you rate highly for both ease and enjoyment on the hexagon chart (pages 70–71). *Highlight no more than ten as your* top *life gifts.* Some people identify twenty or thirty, which won't provide enough focus. If you find yourself having only two or three, work through the suggestions at the end of this chapter.
- Record your top ten life gifts in My *LifeKeys* Notations, pages 286–287, a place where you can summarize your discoveries as you work through each chapter.

The Realistic Type—"Let's Roll Up Our Sleeves and Get It Done!"

Would you describe yourself as

- good at fixing or repairing things;
- practical, matter-of-fact;
- reliable, steady in a crisis;
- modest, adept at avoiding attention;
- a seeker of physical risks;
- outdoorsy, athletic, mechanical, hands-on?

These are just a few of the phrases that describe people with Realistic life gifts. Few Realistics choose to spend time at major social events—and they may also resist being behind a desk! Many prefer working alone or with one or two carefully chosen friends rather than on large teams.

Realistic children can typically be found building superhighways in the sandbox, climbing trees, or perhaps training their dog. One boy was fascinated by anything on wheels from the age of two; his parents let him celebrate one birthday with a visit to a truck dealership. Vocationally, he's a fitness director, but he also joined the Army Reserve, where he could drive jeeps and equipment vans every other weekend.

School can be frustrating for Realistics if no practical applications are made for what they are learning. They prefer hands-on experiments, concrete problems to solve, and maybe an extra period of physical education or industrial arts. Without these elements or a teacher who helps them understand future uses of what they are learning, they may long to be elsewhere—especially outside.

In their spare time, Realistics enjoy the out-of-doors, even if they tackle maintenance tasks just to get out in the fresh air. Many own recreational vehicles, sporting goods, and whatever tools they might need to get a job done.

Typical careers for Realistics include manufacturing, agriculture, engineering, construction, law enforcement, the military, piloting, teaching industrial arts, and other paths that let them

- use large and fine motor skills to produce tangible results;
- allow for pragmatic approaches to problems;
- focus on things rather than on people, ideas, or data;
- provide safety and order.

Typical volunteer activities include providing transportation, maintenance work, leading outdoor activities, repairing furniture or machinery, helping with event set-up, and other tangible tasks.

Realistic Life Gifts

Life Gifts	How have I used this? Dreamed about using this?	Was it enjoyable? (0=terrible; 10=great)	Was it natural? (0=no; 10=yes)	✓ if life gift
Mechanical aptitude—Understand and apply the principles of mechanics/physics				
Operating heavy equipment, driving, piloting—includes construction equipment as well as transportation vehicles				
Manual dexterity—skill and ease at using one's hands or fine tools				
Building mechanical/ structural devices—design and/or assemble materials as well as execute repairs				
Physical coordination—using multiple muscle movements to a single end, such as needed in athletics, skilled trades, etc.				
Organizing supplies or implements—identify methods that lead to ease of retrieval and maintenance				
Taking physical risks—attracted to activities or occupations with elements of physical danger				
Emotional stability, reliability— react impersonally to situations and thereby stay on course				

The Investigative Type—"Let's Figure This Out!"

Would you describe yourself as

- independent and self-motivated;
- original and creative;
- scholarly and intellectual;
- absorbed by your own interests—work seems like play;
- motivated to find out how and why;
- curious, rational, introspective, perhaps reserved?

These are just a few of the phrases that describe people with Investigative life gifts. As the name implies, they want to find out all they can, not settling for simple answers.

Investigative children have their nose in a book, in a library, or in the great outdoors where they can observe phenomena for themselves. Most are never satisfied with only *asking* why; they observe, experiment, and analyze until they figure it out. They may be attracted to complicated games such as chess or to amassing and classifying a collection of fossils or butterflies. One woman spent her adolescence with her eyes on the sky, studying astronomy. She built her own telescope from a kit, spent much of her allowance on books on the subject, and belonged to a stargazing society. To no one's surprise, as an adult she chose a career in scientific research.

Investigatives tend to be independent, choosing their own paths. They may seem reserved around others because of their preoccupation with understanding the subjects that interest them.

In school, Investigatives generally have special interests in scientific and mathematical topics and enjoy researching and gathering information. They persevere in solving problems, are adept at collecting and studying data, and prefer to design their own work. Many pursue higher education because of a love of knowledge for its own sake. Most Investigatives like working with ideas rather than working with people. This doesn't mean they dislike others but simply that they would rather discover a cure for cancer than work directly with cancer patients, for example.

In their spare time, Investigatives choose complex activities such as skiing, mountain climbing, spelunking, or sailing, where technology and skill play a major role. If they are interested in computers, they know the ins and outs of new hardware devices and how to optimize systems performance. For Investigatives, work and play are one and the same.

Typical careers for Investigatives include the sciences, medicine, higher education, strategic planning, market research, systems analysis, teaching science, pharmacology, and other paths that let them

- work independently;
- research, theorize, solve complex problems;
- continue to learn;
- concentrate on ideas rather than people or things.

Typical volunteer activities include setting strategies, collecting or organizing data, researching background information, using computer skills, producing long-range plans, and other intellectual tasks.

Investigative Life Gifts

Life Gifts	How have I used this? Dreamed about using this?	Was it enjoyable? (0=terrible; 10=great)	Was it natural? (0=no; 10=yes)	✓ if life gift
Inventing—imagine or produce something, especially in technical, scientific, or theoretical realms				
Researching—investigate or experiment to get knowledge, examine theories, or find new applications of current knowledge				
Conceptualizing—originate and develop abstract ideas or theories				
Working independently—work well without guidance or input from others				
Solving complex problems—find solutions to difficult situations or unique issues, usually through logic, analysis, or knowledge base				
Computer aptitude—computer skills or systems and software design and development				
Synthesizing information—organize or combine information from different sources so that it is easily understood				
Theorizing—articulate explanations, find connections, or project future trends				

The Artistic Type—"Let's Create!"

Would you describe yourself as

- non-conformist, concerned with self-expression;
- unstructured, flexible;
- original, free-spirited, creative, or imaginative;
- having an aesthetic flair;
- motivated by bursts of inspiration;
- artistically or musically talented?

These are just a few of the phrases that describe people with Artistic life gifts. Few Artistics want to follow set instructions or pursue careers that involve bureaucracy or routine. They seek their own unique paths.

Artistic children often display gifted imaginations (although adults may refer to this pastime as daydreaming) and create new and novel things, stories, ideas, or ways of being. Depending on their artistic bent, they tend to seek out opportunities to express their gifts at an early age. They may also have a love for visiting art museums or attending cultural events, concerts, or theatrical performances. One musician remembers that as a child he grasped any opportunity to perform. He enjoyed being a camp counselor more for the chances to play his guitar than for the work he did with the children.

At school, Artistics do best when allowed to "color outside the lines." They prefer to add their own touch to assignments and feel stifled if required to stick to specifications. Additionally, many Artistics have a natural verbal/linguistic bent that allows them to easily express themselves in writing or speaking. When the subject matter or teacher allows for creativity, they tend to do well in school.

In their spare time, Artistics often pursue leisure activities that mirror their life gifts. They especially enjoy listening to, seeing, or appreciating their own artistic gifts, or those of others. Writing, photography, interior design, dance, music, or acting, are just a few of the specific life gifts they might pursue.

Typical careers for Artistics include environments such as music studios, museums, libraries, galleries, law firms, interior design or advertising firms as well as positions such as broadcasting or reporting. Note that not all of the Artistic interests involve "artists." Attorneys, research librarians, and many other paths have a creative bent that let Artistics

- work independently or with one or two others;
- be creative, using their particular life gifts;
- find avenues for self-expression;
- seek variety and change with little structure.

Typical volunteer activities include sharing drama, musical, or artistic talents; taking part in one-time creative efforts; making decorations; handling graphic design tasks; or publicity. Those with writing, musical, or artistic life gifts *may* struggle with making a living wage using those talents and therefore *might* choose to use them avocationally or in volunteer work.

Artistic Life Gifts

Life Gifts	How have I used this? Dreamed about using this?	Was it enjoyable? (0=terrible; 10=great)	Was it natural? (0=no; 10=yes)	✓ if life gift
Acting—project emotions or character by performing roles, either formally in theater settings or informally				
Writing, reporting, technical writing—communicate clearly through written words, including reports, letters, and publications				
Verbal/linguistics skills—adept at studying or learning languages, using and comprehending spoken words				
Musical expression—compose music or perform musically, with voice, body, or instruments				
Creative problem solving—find novel or unusual solutions to problems or issues, especially in artistic or interpersonal areas				
Sculpting/photography/graphic arts/painting—creative expression through artistic mediums				
Creative design through use of space—work with spatial concepts, as in interior design or architecture				
Creative expression through color—coordinate colors and patterns, as in clothing design, decorating, etc.				

The Social Type—"Let's Work on This Together!"

Would you describe yourself as being

- friendly and cheerful;
- kind and generous;
- ready to listen, tactful;
- cooperative and supportive;
- people-oriented;
- interested in the well-being of others?

These are just a few of the phrases that describe people with Social life gifts. Most Socials would rather work in a group than alone and are interested in the development of others. (Compare this with our description of Realistics to appreciate the diversity of these interest areas.)

Social children are often well-liked because they tend to be accepting of others and have natural people skills. They may become involved in social concerns at an early age. Sandra remembers trying to garner support at her church to start a shelter for stray animals. Jane spent a summer working with her friends to organize bake sales and talent shows, raising money for a children's charity foundation. Many Social children become heavily involved in religious organizations, connecting with the people- and service-oriented atmosphere.

Most Socials view school positively because of the many opportunities to develop friendships there. They learn best when they can work cooperatively and share with others what they have learned. They usually prefer the humanities or social sciences to more scientific subjects.

In their spare time, many Socials choose to coach, teach, offer hospitality to others, or do volunteer work. Because Socials focus so heavily on the needs of people, which can be draining, they sometimes choose Realistic activities for their leisure time to avoid burnout.

Typical careers for Socials include teaching, social work, physical therapy, nursing, counseling, religious professions, recreation, customer service, and other paths that let them

- be of service to others;
- resolve problems through cooperation;
- focus on people rather than data or things;
- develop and maintain relationships.

Typical volunteer activities include working with community service organizations, planning social events, child care, leading small groups, and counseling or tutoring.

Social Life Gifts

Life Gifts	How have I used this? Dreamed about using this?	Was it enjoyable? (0=terrible; 10=great)	Was it natural? (0=no; 10=yes)	✓ if life gift
Teaching—instruct, demonstrate, train, or guide others in learning information or concepts				
Listening and facilitating—encourage others to volunteer information and discuss issues, either one-on-one or in groups				
Understanding or counseling others—give appropriate advice and guidance tailored to the needs of others				
Conversing/informing—offer hospitality, talk and listen informally about daily events, issues, or personal concerns				
Being of service—consider and act to aid the welfare of others				
Evaluating people's character—discern the motives and values of other people				
Being empathetic and tactful—aware of the feelings of others, able to adjust one's own behavior and respond accordingly				
Working with others—establish harmonious working relationships based on trust and synergy				

The Enterprising Type—"Let's Get Going!"

Would you describe yourself as

- a natural-born leader;
- optimistic and self-confident;
- at ease with taking risks;
- competitive and ambitious;
- influential, perhaps seeking status and possessions to influence others;
- persuasive and witty?

These are just a few of the phrases that describe people with Enterprising life gifts. They often gravitate toward leadership positions. They enjoy promoting and selling products and people, themselves included.

Enterprising children fill their time with money-making activities, student leadership positions, and other hints of persuasive savvy to come. In college, David convinced his father to let him have the smaller trees from the family tree farm to sell on campus. He and his partners sold enough dorm-room-sized Christmas trees to treat themselves to a great lobster dinner. Enterprising types want to enjoy the fruits of their labor and may work hard to attain certain status symbols so that others are aware of their industry and see them as influential.

In school, Enterprising types may pursue leadership roles or spend time figuring out how to work around the system. One Enterprising type persuaded his social studies teacher to count his run for class president as his independent project for the term. While they can be excellent students, they tend to dislike long academic pursuits or scientific efforts.

In their spare time, Enterprising types may pursue political activities or leadership in community organizations. They enjoy attending important sporting events, traveling to key destinations, and entertaining. Participating in sports like tennis or golf has the added benefit of frequenting prestigious clubs or social organizations where they can network.

Typical careers for Enterprisers include entrepreneurial pursuits, sales or marketing, elected government positions, brokerage (real estate, travel), financial planning, television production, management, or lobbying. They enjoy settings where they can

- set monetary or advancement goals for themselves;
- interact with "movers and shakers";
- lead endeavors—their own and those of others;
- have a chance to shine and be rewarded.

Typical volunteer activities include fund-raising, leadership roles, recruiting others, giving speeches, and promoting events or outreaches.

Enterprising Life Gifts

Life Gifts	How have I used this? Dreamed about using this?	Was it enjoyable? (0=terrible; 10=great)	Was it natural? (0=no; 10=yes)	✓ if life gift
Public speaking—communicate clearly and with comfort in front of a live audience				
Selling and persuading—advocate the acceptance by others of products, services, ideas, values, or points of view				
Networking and building coalitions—connect people and resources to enhance personal or organizational effectiveness				
Leading—influence others to work together and direct people's efforts toward common missions or goals				
Managing—plan, organize, delegate, and direct projects and resources to attain goals				
Negotiating—aid others in listening to diverse opinions or demands so as to reach agreement or compromise				
Taking action—respond decisively in emergency or stressful situations				
Being adventurous—take above-average financial and interpersonal risks; entrepreneurship				

The Conventional Type—"Let's Be Dependable!"

Would you describe yourself as

- practical, methodical, efficient, and orderly;
- responsible and conscientious;
- contained and content;
- careful with things;
- at ease and accurate with details;
- comfortable with structure and routine?

These are just a few of the phrases that describe people with Conventional life gifts. They are the ones who frequently keep things running smoothly for everyone else. Conventionals are a blessing for those who can't keep track of important papers, let alone track the details necessary to carry off a big meeting or event.

Conventional children often enjoy structured activities such as scouting and youth organizations, school or community-sponsored leagues, and games with prescribed rules. They frequently have the cleanest room in the family and take good care of their belongings. One woman still has every piece of her *cardboard* Barbie dollhouse and car from 1959, all pieces in mint condition. She played with it constantly but carefully, putting each piece away in the same manner at the close of each play session. Her meticulous habits help identify her Conventional life gifts.

School subjects that require mastery of set rules are often favorites for Conventional children. They tend to like arithmetic and spelling, where they can easily chart their progress in learning required material. They may dislike school subjects that require heavy use of theory, intuition, or creativity, preferring topics that have practical uses or concrete answers.

In their spare time, many Conventionals choose to vacation in familiar places such as a family cabin or seaside resort where they can renew old acquaintances and seek rest in customary surroundings. They may enjoy hobbies such as collecting (stamps, figurines), building detailed models (railroads, dollhouses), playing structured games, and home repairs or decorating.

Typical careers for Conventionals include accounting, office management, information processing, nursing home administration, production management, banking, business education, small business ownership, and other paths that let them

- enjoy structure, schedules, and routines;
- be rewarded for careful handling of data and details;
- work methodically on clear responsibilities;
- focus on pragmatic tasks and causes.

Typical volunteer activities include working with established organizations such as churches or the Red Cross, organizing supplies and equipment, performing office tasks, establishing procedures, and accounting or auditing.

Conventional Life Gifts

Life Gifts	How have I used this? Dreamed about using this?	Was it enjoyable? (0=terrible; 10=great)	Was it natural? (0=no; 10=yes)	✓ if life gift
Organizing—arrange records, finances, offices, production lines, homes, etc., in a structured manner				
Appraising/evaluating—accurately estimate the value or significance of investments, antiques, real estate, business opportunities, etc.				
Attending to detail—aware of the small elements that make up the whole, as in printed words, administrative tasks, or the environment				
Managing time, setting priorities—arrange activities and schedules so that deadlines, appointments, and goals are consistently met				
Calculating and mathematical skills—adept at working with numbers and figures; add, subtract, multiply, divide				
Systematizing—classify information or things for ease of use				
Persevering—follow-through, thoroughness, and patience when handling responsibilities				
Stewardship—conservative handling of money, data, things, and people				

Making Your Life Gifts Your Own

As you worked your way through the life gifts pages, you might have said, "Yes! These are my life gifts. That's why that project went so well . . ." Or you might be less sure and will need to process what you have learned. You probably already use some of your life gifts nearly every day. And there may be other life gifts you have never recognized. You may have been on time in every project you have ever undertaken, for example, and not realized that such organization is a natural bent—one of your life gifts.

If you are unsure about some of your life gifts, here are some suggestions:

- Ask friends, co-workers, or others close to you about your use of a particular life gift. Encourage them to give you specific examples.
- Observe others using the life gifts you have identified for yourself. Ask yourself whether this is something you could do and would love to do.
- Volunteer for a task that will allow you to use a life gift you are questioning. If possible, ask someone you can trust to give you honest feedback on your performance.
- Brainstorm about how you might use each life gift, both in your current life and in the future. For example, a retiree might use a life gift for selling to raise funds for a project, recruit volunteers, or gather support for a new program. A student might use a teaching life gift as a volunteer with children or as an assistant coach. An at-home parent might use a life gift for listening to facilitate family discussions, work out school site council issues, or be a part of a church's caregiving ministry. Each life gift can be used in a variety of settings, whether at work, home, church, or for leisure pursuits.
- Think about what you might do if you could choose your own job or take extra time for a hobby. Are there any clues to your life gifts?

Working With Your Life Gifts—Writing a Sentence

Discovering your life gifts, a part of you since birth, is an exciting process for many people, but you may be asking, "Where do I go from here?" Use the following exercise to link your life gifts into a sentence or series of phrases that will help you remember not only what your life gifts are, but how they often work together.

David wrote out his life gift list as follows after working through the life gifts charts (the letters in parentheses show the first letter of the interest area for that gift):

1. Taking interpersonal risks (E)
2. Researching, investigating (I)
3. Synthesizing (I)
4. Acting (A)
5. Listening and facilitating (S)
6. Teaching (S)
7. Public speaking (E)
8. Selling and persuading (E)
9. Leadership (E)
10. Being of service (S)

While a list is helpful, linking these life gifts in a sentence helps David's natural bent come alive in a dramatic way:

I first research and investigate in order to synthesize information. I then use the information to teach, train, promote, persuade, speak, or act so that I might be of service to people, especially in areas of interpersonal risk.

To construct his sentence, David asked himself the following questions:

- Which life gifts do I use most often? Which are central to who I am? (For David, these were all communication gifts: teach, train, promote, persuade, speak, act.)
- Which gifts are normally used first, if applicable, before the other gifts are used? (David tends to use his Investigative gifts first, in support of the others.)
- Which gifts are normally used after the others?
- What motivates me to use my gifts? (For David, the motivation is being of service or encouraging others to take risks.)

One way to begin to answer the above questions is to look at something concrete.[4] Choose three projects/events/tasks that you willingly took part in and enjoyed. These can be from your personal, work, or volunteer roles. Examples might be:

---

[4]This exercise is included on page 12 of the *LifeKeys Discovery Workbook*.

- a social function or family reunion;
- projects you became involved with because of your hobbies, such as building with Habitat for Humanity;
- a one-time service opportunity or ongoing volunteer role;
- your favorite task at work.

Then think about the following questions. You might even make a grid that shows your answers for each of the three projects or tasks you listed above:

- Why did you work on the project? What motivated you or what made it seem like an attractive option?
- What did you hope would happen as a result of your involvement, both for you personally and for others?
- What were the results or products? For example, because of your involvement, did things go more smoothly? Were people influenced? Was an event more fun or meaningful? Did you ward off problems or discover new approaches?
- Were there gifts you used to prepare to make your main contribution? For example, Jane often uses her *listening* and *conversing* life gifts to gather information before she *writes*, which is one of her more central life gifts.
- Try to distinguish between those life gifts you used to prepare for the result or product and those you used during "the moment"—when the event happened or the "product" was made or the interaction took place.

Now look for themes in what you have written. Are there any similarities in your motivations? In what you hope to accomplish? In the gifts you choose to use at different times? Use those themes to construct your own life gifts sentence. To show other examples, here are Jane and Sandra's sentences:

Jane: *I am drawn to things that need to change and use my life gifts of researching, listening, conversing, facilitating, synthesizing, writing, and teaching to creatively solve problems in service to others.*

Sandra: *Personal and spiritual growth for myself and others motivates me. I listen, facilitate, gather, and synthesize information to create a knowledge base from which I can teach, write, coach, and advocate in order to spark insights for myself and others.*

Work with your list of life gifts and see if you can construct a similar statement that links them together into a coherent picture.

Don't worry about using every gift or about having sentences that flow easily. The point here is to create phrases or sentences that help you remember your life gifts and provide guidance in choosing how you might use them.

Prayer

Dear God, It is beyond my understanding that because of Your love for each one of us, You took the effort to gift us individually with our own natural bent, life gifts, the way we should go. Help me enjoy the process of finding my life gifts. Guard me from comparing mine to those of others. Reassure me that You have made me this way for Your purposes. In that confidence I can rejoice. Amen.

For Journal or Discussion

1. Reflect back on your childhood dreams and interests. Is there anything you would like to recapture? Consider watching the movie *The Kid*, where a man is confronted by his childhood dreams as he turns forty.

2. People who don't like their gifts, or think that they only have one or two life gifts, often have the ones our society doesn't celebrate—listening, attending to detail, or working independently, are a few examples. If this describes you, sit down with someone you trust who has worked with you. Ask them about where you contribute. What do people ask you to do? Then relate the answers to the life gifts. Which gifts are you using? Why are your gifts important?

3. Consider the role you might play in the following scenario:
   The church's fiftieth anniversary [or a community event] is coming up and a huge celebration is planned. With which part of the celebration would you like to be involved? (Decorations, program planning, refreshments, publicity, finances, child care, entertainment, set-up, etc.) Which life gifts would you be using?

4. Which is one of your favorite life gifts? When did you first become aware that this was one of your life gifts? How have you developed it? How are you currently using it?

HEXAGON OF INTEREST AREAS WITH ASSOCIATED LIFE GIFTS

Realistic

Mechanical aptitude
Operating heavy equipment,
    driving, piloting
Manual dexterity
Building mechanical/structural devices
Physical coordination (athletics, etc.)
Organizing supplies or implements
Taking physical risks
Emotional stability, reliability

R

Conventional

Organizing
Appraising/evaluating
Attending to detail
Managing time, setting priorities
Calculating and mathematical skills
Systematizing
Persevering
Stewardship

C

Enterprising

Public speaking
Selling/persuading
Networking and building
    coalitions
Leading
Managing
Negotiating
Taking action
Being adventurous

E

Investigative

Inventing
Researching
Conceptualizing
Working independently
Solving complex problems
Computer aptitude
Synthesizing information
Theorizing

I

Artistic

Acting
Writing, reporting,
    technical writing
Verbal/linguistics skills
Musical expression
Creative problem solving
Sculpting/photography/graphic
    arts/painting
Creative design through use of
    space
Creative expression through
    color

A

S

Social

Teaching
Listening and facilitating
Understanding or counseling others
Conversing/informing
Being of service
Evaluating people's character
Being empathetic and tactful
Working with others

LifeKey #3

There are no second fiddles in God's orchestra.

CHAPTER 3

SPIRITUAL GIFTS—GOD'S SPECIAL INSTRUMENTS

Like good stewards of the manifold grace of God, serve one another with whatever gift each of you has received.[1]

If the theme song from *The Twilight Zone* comes to mind at the mention of spiritual gifts, please don't tune out quite yet! Spiritual gifts are simply another *LifeKey*, the special instruments God gives for the unique tasks of the church. Life gifts meet the needs of other arenas, but spiritual gifts help us carry out a special task: bringing people to God. Given human nature, this is not a simple job; it is a job that cannot be completed without God's help.

Spiritual gifts cover an incredible array of possibilities for being God's hands here on earth. At one end of the spectrum are gifts that are easy to understand and recognize. For example, people with the spiritual gift of *helps* accomplish practical, behind-the-scenes tasks that further God's work. We may not even think of their work as very spiritual until we realize three things:

- Not everyone has this spiritual gift. Think of times you've been in meetings where just one or two people notice that a door needs to be closed or a light switch flipped or more chairs set up. People with the gift of *helps* notice these things.
- People with the gift of *helps* understand at a deep level that their work connects them spiritually with the people they serve or the ministry that is taking place. For them, using their gift is like praying.

[1]1 Peter 4:10 NRSV

- The work of other, more visible (*not* more important) gifts would be stymied without the gift of *helps*. Think of a worship service without bulletins, sound systems, lighting, and so on. People with this gift are as essential as those who teach or preach or lead.

At the other end of the spectrum are some very visible gifts that the Bible specifically mentions in 1 Corinthians 12:28: *healing, miracles,* and *speaking in tongues.* These cause a lot of controversy, often because they are misunderstood in this day and age or are so rare that few of us are familiar with their sound or purpose.

Why might God use such gifts? Think of our Creator for a moment as an orchestra conductor before a new audience in a strange hall, an audience that doesn't know how much they are loved. God wants to get that audience's attention, so this time the orchestra includes a synthesizer, or electric guitars, or an unfamiliar folk instrument. These aren't used very often in the orchestra (can you imagine a bagpipe in Beethoven's Fifth Symphony?) but when God asks them to play a part, these special instruments, the spiritual gifts, can have an effect that is beautiful, stunning, eye-opening, even staggering to those who hear or experience them.

Some of the spiritual gifts, like some of these more unusual instruments, take some getting used to. Others are so powerful that they must be used sparingly. We need to understand these instruments, the spiritual gifts, to appreciate where and why God calls us to use them.

In this chapter, we'll first explore what spiritual gifts *are* and then help you identify which gifts you have. Knowing your spiritual gifts helps you understand the roles God wants you to play.

What Is a Spiritual Gift?

Let's leave that unusual orchestra behind for a moment and come back to it after we understand the more conventional instruments used in God's church. Paul tells us: "Now to each one the manifestation [revelation, unveiling, evidence, demonstration] of the Spirit is given for the common good" (1 Corinthians 12:7, our amplification). Spiritual gifts, then, are *evidence* or a *demonstration* that God's Holy Spirit is working in us, enabling us to do things we could not otherwise do.

Identifying our spiritual gifts can help steer us to the right places to give and serve. Did you ever volunteer for a ministry or task only to find that your willingness was a major mistake? That happened to Jane and her husband, Brian. Having worked with teens in the past, they agreed to chaperone a Christian rock concert. Four hours later they found themselves with severe headaches and a nagging feeling that they had aged way beyond their years. They had little energy left for leading the encounter groups for those teens that chose to stay after the music ended. Afterward, Jane and Brian agreed that they lacked the spiritual gifts of *encouragement* and *evangelism* to work with youth in this way! After this experience they stuck to their spiritual gift of *teaching*.

One retiree willingly assumed the missions coordinator post that her friend had previously held. Not only did she feel overwhelmed once she saw how well organized her friend had been, but the tasks weren't fulfilling for her—they called for gifts of *administration* rather than the tangible acts of *mercy* that she did so well.

What conductor would lead an orchestra the way the church approaches so many recruitment efforts, or the way we choose our own places? Hmmm, the drums did such a great job keeping the beat last week—let's give them the melody for *The Blue Danube*. And the strings? Well, the bows would make great drumsticks. The cellos can be the timpani and the . . .

None of us would lead an orchestra that way, yet too often we behave in this manner, asking people to serve or volunteering ourselves without finding out what each of us does best. God has a better plan. God is a giver of gifts, gifts meant to build us up for ministry to the world.

The early church continually saw spiritual gifts in action, but they were often confused about how to use the gifts. In writing to the church at Corinth, where the gifts were causing harsh disagreements, Paul explained:

> There are different kinds of gifts, but the same Spirit. There are different kinds of service, but the same Lord. There are different kinds of working, but the same God works all of them in all [people].
>
> Now to each one the manifestation of the Spirit is given for the common good. To one there is given through the Spirit the message of *wisdom*, to another the message of *knowledge* by means of the same Spirit, to another *faith* by the same Spirit,

to another gifts of *healing* by that one Spirit, to another *miraculous powers*, to another *prophecy*, to another *distinguishing between spirits*, to another speaking in different kinds of *tongues*, and to still another the *interpretation of tongues*. All these are the work of one and the same Spirit. (1 Corinthians 12:4–11, *emphasis ours*)

Paul makes three important points in this passage:

- The Holy Spirit gives gifts to all who want to carry out the work of God.
- Spiritual gifts are distributed according to God's will, not because of some effort on our part.
- In the body of Christ, each of us has something to contribute.

Let's look at these one by one.

Gifted for God's Work

Each of us receives different gifts so that the body of Christ has what it needs to spread God's message of love. Note what this simple point really means.

First, we all have gifts. Many Christians are either unaware of their spiritual gifts, have left them dormant for a long time, or doubt if they exist at all. Picture a Christmas tree on January 15, with all of the presents still under it, still wrapped. That's how many people treat their spiritual gifts—they don't know what they are because they haven't unwrapped them and tried them out. Biblically, there is no doubt that we all have spiritual gifts and that each person and gift is important. "Now here is what I am trying to say: All of you together are the one body of Christ, and each one of you is a separate and necessary part of it."[2]

Second, the gifts are given for the common good, not for the benefit of the individual who receives them. We are simply stewards of the gifts we are given.

Gifts Are Given, Not Earned

LifeKeys came out of our experiences in teaching about spiritual gifts. At first, participants often concluded that they'd received

[2] 1 Corinthians 12:27 TLB

inconsequential gifts compared to the people around them. We heard people say things like "God must not value me (or trust me) very much if these are the only gifts I have." Paul strongly refutes this:

> The eye cannot say to the hand, "I don't need you!" And the head cannot say to the feet, "I don't need you!" On the contrary, those parts of the body that seem to be weaker are indispensable, and the parts that we think are less honorable we treat with special honor. And the parts that are unpresent-able are treated with special modesty, while our presentable parts need no special treatment. But God has combined the members of the body and has given greater honor to the parts that lacked it, so that there should be no division in the body, but that its parts should have equal concern for each other. If one part suffers, every part suffers with it; if one part is hon-ored, every part rejoices with it. (1 Corinthians 12:21–26)

In other words, the gifts we have are in no way a mark of maturity or of how much God loves us. The gifts you have are the ones God wants you to have. If you doubt this, think about the apostle Paul. In the early church, God gifted Paul to spread the Gospel to the Gentiles, to the amazement of many whom Paul had persecuted. Paul was one of the greatest evangelists and teachers in the history of the church, yet in human eyes he probably deserved *no* gifts, given his early animosity toward Christians.

Further, Christian maturity is shown not by spiritual gifts but by the fruit of the Spirit, such as love, peace, and patience. Think about how often you've seen incredibly gifted Christians act imma-turely. The familiar start to 1 Corinthians 13, "If I could speak all the languages of earth and of angels, but didn't love others, I would only be a noisy gong or a clanging cymbal" (vv. 1–2 NLT), points out the dissonance that occurs from using spiritual gifts unaccom-panied by the love and joy that maturity brings.

Gifts Are for Service

God gave us our gifts for one reason: to put them to use. If for some reason we choose not to use the gifts God gave us, some part of God's work may be left undone. Remember the words of Paul in Ephesians 2:10: "For we are God's workmanship, created in Christ

Jesus to do good works, which God prepared in advance for us to do." For each of us, our unique contributions count. Picture yourself as a vital element in God's plan for the church, for that is what you are: a special mix of spiritual gifts and life gifts that God has chosen uniquely for you.

Spiritual gifts, understood within the context of these principles, can allow all believers to achieve their highest goals, seeing God's will done on earth as it is in heaven.

Aren't Spiritual Gifts Just for Leaders?

Another common reaction of believers is to assume that a person with several of the more public spiritual gifts, such as *leadership* and *teaching*, can manage things just fine alone. Frequently these gifts are viewed as more important because they are so visible:

> If the whole body were an eye, how would you hear? Or if your whole body were an ear, how would you smell anything?
> But our bodies have many parts, and God has put each part just where he wants it. How strange a body it would be if it had only one part! Yes, there are many parts, but only one body. (1 Corinthians 12:17–20 NLT)

Thinking that leaders can do it all has two problems. First, when leaders think they have to do everything, the results are often less than satisfactory. Perhaps a visionary ministry led by someone with the gift of *apostleship* falters because of inherent disorganization; someone with the gift of *administration* may have helped bring order to the chaos. Maybe an *evangelism* outreach fails because people don't connect with others who could help them grow in faith; someone with the gift of *shepherding* might have found places for them to connect. Maybe an education class falls short of its goal because the materials weren't ready for the *teacher*; someone with the gift of *helps* could have solved the problem. God makes it clear every day how much we need each other.

Second, an unexamined belief that a minister can do everything means that the leader isn't allowed to discover which gifts he or she really has. Think of all the gifts that ministers can be called on to use: *teaching, administration, leading, shepherding, mercy, knowledge, wisdom, helps, giving, encouragement. . . .* Let's be honest: Most leaders lack at least some of these! We can force them to do it all, a pathway to exhaustion and defeat by the endless needs of the congregation. Or we can let them use the gifts God has given them and step forward with our own gifts to fulfill the roles God meant for us to play.

A church that understands the spiritual gifts of its people can move forward as a group of mutually *interdependent,* mutually *accepting,* mutually *supportive,* and mutually *synergistic* people serving together, carrying out the work of Christ.

Supernatural vs. Sensational—What's the Difference?

You may not have realized that you are already using spiritual gifts. While all of the gifts are *supernatural,* coming through the Holy Spirit and enabling us to do more than we could do on our own, not all of them are *sensational,* that is, enough out of the ordinary that we are astounded by how they operate. For example, two retirees saw nothing unusual about the way they had surveyed the trade skills of senior citizens in their congregation and organized a system so that plumbers, painters, electricians, and others could be called on for maintenance projects at the church and the ministries they supported. They didn't connect their efforts with their gifts of *leadership* and *administration* until others pointed out that no one else had known how to make this system happen.

Would you place their abilities in the same category as someone who commanded a wheelchair-bound person to rise and walk—enabling a visible *healing* to take place? The latter is more *sensational,* but the spiritual gifts of healing, leadership, and administration are all *supernaturally* given by God so that people can carry out those good works prepared in advance for them to do.

If you want to be a part of God's plan and feel the "specialness" that is yours alone, believe that you have been given spiritual gifts, find out what they are, develop them as best you can, and put them to use!

What Is the Difference Between Life Gifts and Spiritual Gifts?

There is definite overlap between life gifts and spiritual gifts, but life gifts have many applications while spiritual gifts are given to carry out God's purposes. Consider teaching, which is both a life gift and a spiritual gift. As a spiritual gift, God tunes *teaching* to a different pitch: conveying spiritual truth as opposed to conveying other truths, such as mathematical theories.

Frequently, but not always, life gifts and spiritual gifts are related. Some, but not all, Christians with a life gift for public speaking use that life gift through the spiritual gift of *evangelism*. The same is true with the spiritual gift of *teaching*. Some, but not all, people with a life gift for teaching will find that they have a spiritual gift for *teaching* that allows them to help others understand our faith.

This principle holds true in reverse as well. A spiritual gift may or may not be active as a life gift. Think of pastors with the spiritual gift of *leadership*. How many of them would enjoy a similar role in business or government? Some, but certainly not all. *Evangelists* may be gifted in persuading others to consider Christianity, but may not be gifted in selling anything else.

Even so, a good way to start to discern your spiritual gifts is to look at your life gifts. If you previously listed teaching or persuading or organizing as life gifts, consider the spiritual gifts of *teaching* or *evangelism* or *administration*. If you aren't sure, volunteer for several tasks. Which ones come easiest to you? Which give you and those you serve the most satisfaction? Remember, volunteer organizations generally have easy requirements for previous experience.

Are Our Spiritual Gifts Fully Developed When We Receive Them?

Another trap is thinking that God gives us our gifts fully ready to use, no assembly required. However, David and Jane will tell you that their spiritual gift of *teaching* developed over time. They have practiced specific skills, learned from other teachers, and pray for guidance in what they write and say. Sandra and others with the spiritual gift of *leadership* will point to improvements in their communication skills, better planning processes, or other acquired management skills. Those with the gift of *mercy* may relate how special training in counseling or grief support has enabled them to expand their use of this spiritual gift.

Additionally, some are given a fuller measure of a gift than others. Only a few *evangelists* who can fill stadiums are necessary, but

God needs an infinite number of *evangelists* to share the Gospel with others one at a time.

All three of us can tell stories of how we've improved in using our gifts and how our opinions of which ones we have has changed over time. Here's a partial list of the ones we see in ourselves and each other:

Jane: teaching, administration, knowledge, faith

David: teaching, shepherding, evangelism, apostleship

Sandra: counseling/encouragement, teaching, leadership, and giving.

If you are serious about discovering your gifts—especially if the idea of spiritual gifts is new to you or you have limited volunteer experience—try to picture yourself using each gift as we describe them. Try to ignore any ideas about which ones are "best" for you or "better" to have and concentrate on those that God has in mind for you or that you feel you've been given.

Do All Spiritual Gifts Operate in the Church Today?

Many Christians are so opposed to the gifts of *healing* and *speaking in tongues* that they tend to ignore *all* spiritual gifts. Yet denying the existence of these particular spiritual gifts leaves us without explanations for many documented events involving *healing* and *speaking in tongues* that exist today.

The spiritual gift descriptions included in this chapter give more details about each of the gifts, but the personal experience of one Christian may lend perspective. In the early 1960s, John Sherrill, longtime editor of *Guideposts* magazine, set out to do an objective story on the modern-day use of the gift of *tongues*. The more he heard, the deeper his confusion. A friend finally pointed out how he was concentrating on the wrong thing. *Tongues* were an obstacle to Sherrill, blocking him from seeing the workings of the Holy Spirit. His friend likened it to the way a garish red entrance door could detract from the beauty of a Gothic cathedral:

> Tongues, John, are like that door. As long as you stand outside your attention is going to be riveted there and you're not going to be able to see anything else. Once you go through, however, you are surrounded by the thousand wonders of light and sound and form that the architect intended. You look around and that door isn't even red on the inside. It's there. It's

to be used. But it has taken its proper place in the design of the whole church.

That's what I'd hope for you, John. I think it's time for you to walk through that door. If you really want to discover what the Pentecostal experience[3] is all about, don't concentrate on tongues, but step through the door and meet the Holy Spirit.[4]

Don't let yourself be distracted from the true nature of spiritual gifts. Don't worry that God might lead you into an experience you are not ready to handle. If you stay open to ideas and beliefs that challenge you, God can work through you to bring new understanding. In discovering your gifts and finding ways to use them to do God's work, let the same Holy Spirit, who has led countless others, also be your guide.

Prayer

Dear God, I believe that You have given spiritual gifts to those of us who seek to carry out Your purposes. Now walk with me as I learn more about each of these gifts and which ones You have given me. Don't let anything distract me, but allow me to "step through the door" and see how I can use them for Your glory. Amen.

Using the Spiritual Gift Descriptions

We have described each spiritual gift with true stories of the gift in action, mostly from people we know well. The three of us have seen each of these spiritual gifts at work within our congregation. Most likely, you will see them within your community of faith as well.

The gifts are grouped into *four categories*, which we developed based on the different purposes the gifts seem to serve. In addition, people often find that they have more than one gift within certain categories; the gifts are sometimes related to each other. The categories are:

- **Gifts of the Heart:** Helps, Hospitality, Mercy, Faith, and Giving. These gifts involve direct opportunity for service to individuals, for being God's hands on earth.

---

[3]Meaning, experiencing the Holy Spirit personally.
[4]John Sherrill, *They Speak With Other Tongues* (New York: McGraw Hill, 1964), 114.

- **Gifts of Proclamation**: Evangelism, Teaching, Discernment, Knowledge, Prophecy, and Wisdom.
  These gifts involve conveying God's truths or revelations to others.
- **Gifts of Action**: Leadership, Administration, Shepherding, Encouragement/Counseling, and Apostleship.
  These gifts involve moving individuals or organizations toward accomplishing what God wants done.
- **Gifts of Inspiration**: Healing, Miracles, Speaking in Tongues, and Interpretation of Tongues.
  These gifts make us aware of God's power in our lives or provide new energy for the work of God's kingdom.

While these categories aren't found in the Bible, we find that they help people compare similar spiritual gifts and more easily discover which ones they have.

As you go through the descriptions, we offer the following hints:

- Be open. For many people, their spiritual gifts are already present, but they have not yet "unwrapped" them. For this reason, our stories illustrate the gifts as people who have just discovered them might use them rather than how they might be used by someone who has known about and used that gift for years.
- Look at the above categories of spiritual gifts. Start by reading the stories for the ones that sound most appealing to you or are the most like the life gifts you have identified for yourself. *Then read through the rest of the stories.* As you read each story, consider these questions: Do you see yourself in it? Does it remind you of someone you know? If so, jot down your thoughts about the gift.
- Read through the common characteristics of a person with that gift and mark the ones you might share. If this subject or Christian service is new to you, please be kind to yourself! Even if some of the descriptions name things you have never done, please think about them. Do they sound interesting to you? Would you consider trying some of the things mentioned? Can you picture yourself using a particular spiritual gift because it is similar to one of your life gifts? And remember, while the spiritual gifts identified in this manner may not be your actual

ones, it does give you a way to start. It suggests places to experiment in volunteer service.

- If you are undecided about a spiritual gift, look up the Bible references. Record any new insights you find in these sources.
- Check through the suggestions for developing a spiritual gift. Do any of these sound like a match for you? If so, you might wish to visit with someone in formal or informal leadership at your church about the places available to use each gift—and to ask whether they see this gift operating within you. In what place or volunteer role would you be most comfortable?

After reviewing a spiritual gift, turn to page 130 and record your results for that gift according to the instructions.

And remember, remain open to each spiritual gift so that you can find that spot that God designed you for in the body of Christ.

For Journal or Discussion

1. After completing the exercises above, reread the suggestions for developing your spiritual gifts. Choose one to work on. What will you do? With whom might you speak? Remember that most people need mentoring to fully develop a gift.

2. What fears or joys do you have regarding your gifts? Do you feel trapped in any way or afraid of how others might view you if you use a certain gift?

3. If you are weary of using a gift or don't feel as if it is a valuable one, be honest. What is robbing you of the joy of using that gift? Is it more of a skill than a spiritual gift? Is it time to change settings?

4. Take a risk—acknowledge with others the gifts that you have.

5. Once you've read through the spiritual gift descriptions, use the following story to explore further how you might use your spiritual gifts. Read the following scenario silently or aloud. Then use the questions that follow the story for discussion or reflection.

   Leah and Rob Hunter are members of a local church. Their two daughters are five and two years old. They're expecting their third child in three months.

Leah just learned that to prevent early delivery, she'll be hospitalized for the next four to eight weeks, with total bed rest and intravenous drugs prescribed. These drugs, while effective in preventing a good percentage of premature births, could damage Leah's internal organs. Her previous pregnancy ended in a stillborn child, and she is extremely anxious over the health of this baby.

Rob's job requires sporadic travel. In addition, he has sole responsibility for his elderly grandmother, now in a nursing home.

If the baby is delivered successfully, Leah and her newborn will face a lengthy recovery period.

- As you listened to the story, did you think of specific needs this family would have? Which one or two of these needs might you feel motivated to act on?
- Share your responses as a group. How do the various responses reflect your differing spiritual gifts? Your life gifts?
- You might wish to list everyone's responses. Did anyone have an idea that no one else thought of? How do your answers reflect the biblical image of the body of Christ?

Spiritual Gift Descriptions

Below are stories, suggestions for development, and questions to help you determine which of the spiritual gifts God has given you. You may wish to first read the section that seems most like you, or to read them in order.

GIFTS OF THE HEART

Helps, Hospitality, Mercy, Faith, and Giving

These gifts involve direct opportunity for service to individuals, for being God's hands on earth.

Helps

The ability to work alongside others, attaching spiritual value to the accomplishment of practical, often behind-the-scenes, tasks

Bible reference: "And in the church God has appointed . . . those able to help others" (1 Corinthians 12:28).

Chandra frequently spoke at women's luncheons and so was expecting the usual church-basement atmosphere for her presentation. But when she walked into the fellowship hall of this small church, it glistened with a festive atmosphere that almost took her breath away. She examined the "starlit" ceiling more closely; the stunning effect was masterfully created with simple black paper, small lights, and a bit of cheesecloth. In the far corner, two people were up on ladders, taping the last few decorations into place.

Chandra walked over to the man and woman to introduce herself. She said, "I don't think I've ever spoken in such a beautiful room. How did you dream up such lovely decorations?"

"They weren't *my* idea," Tom answered. "All I did was show up about an hour ago and make myself available."

"But Tom," commented Ellen, the woman on the other ladder,

86

"when you show up, things start getting done! The decorations may have been my idea, but we'd be eating this dinner on paper placemats under fluorescent lights without your assistance!"

"I just help with what needs to be done."

"That's an interesting way to put it," said Chandra. "You know, God uses the word *helper* to describe Eve in the book of Genesis. The only other times it is used are once to describe King David and *sixteen times* to describe *God* as the source of strong, powerful help. I don't know why I have a gift for teaching and you have a gift for helping, but this wouldn't be much of an event if either one of us were missing. Helping is much more important than most people think."

Ellen spoke again. "I've always known that to be true. You know, I love helping with the costuming for our annual children's program, but don't ask me to lead the rehearsals. And I love helping with fund-raising for our missions team. I believe so strongly in what they are doing, but I don't think I'd make a very good missionary. It feels right, though, to be a part of their work in a different way."

Tom added, "To me, it doesn't matter what I do. I can celebrate the ways that God operates through whatever team I'm on, whatever role I play, however I help."

Do you have the spiritual gift of helps?

_____ I tend to notice and assist with practical tasks that need to be done.

_____ As I do routine tasks, I feel a spiritual link to the ministries or people I serve.

_____ I would rather take on set responsibilities than be involved in leadership.

_____ I prefer to work behind the scenes and often avoid public recognition for what I do.

_____ I receive satisfaction through quietly serving others.

_____ I enjoy working on odd jobs, often seeing a need and tending to it without being asked.

Suggestions for developing your spiritual gift of helps

1. Remember that the gift of helps furthers God's purposes. Reflect on how events, outreach efforts, and practical ministries such as

meal delivery would suffer without people with the gift of helps. How do you contribute to God's work?

2. Talk with people who share your passions or interests but have different gifts, and discover where you can help them. Leaders, evangelists, teachers, and shepherds all need help.

3. Not everyone sees what needs to be done. When working with others, speak up about what has to happen.

Biblical example

Distribution of food in the early church (Acts 6:1–7).

Hospitality

The ability to provide a warm welcome for people that demonstrates God's love by providing food, shelter, or fellowship.

> *Bible reference:* Be hospitable to one another without complaining. Like good stewards of the manifold grace of God, serve one another with whatever gift each of you has received. (1 Peter 4:9–10 NRSV)

Take yourself back to the 1970s, when most people still dressed up for church, even when attending a committee meeting. For a certain suburban congregation, the attire of many teenagers in the very active youth group had become an issue. With a worried expression, the minister told the teen leaders, "You wouldn't believe the number of phone calls I get from members of the congregation who assume that clothes reveal a person's attitude toward worship! I know we should welcome the teens no matter what they are wearing, but this issue is splitting the congregation. Either they stop wearing jeans or they stop coming."

Ben, one of the youth leaders, leaned over to talk to his wife, Trish. Nodding, she spoke up, "There are things happening with the teens that are more important than what they wear. I understand your dilemma, but we have a different solution. We'll meet at our house. They can come in chains and leather, as far as I'm concerned, so long as they want to grow in their faith."

The others looked at Ben and Trish in surprise. Attendance at the Sunday teen Bible study averaged seventy-five students, several guitars, and a lot of food. In their house? Ben added, "They can come Wednesday nights, too. *We* will welcome them until the church agrees on how to do the same."

And welcome them they did. The teen leaders arrived a bit early to help push back furniture, pop popcorn, and pour beverages. The young people were astounded at the warmth of the hospitality shown to them. When one boy asked why they did it, Ben replied, "No matter who we are entertaining, we like to challenge ourselves—can we make our guests as welcome as we would want Jesus to feel if He were our visitor today?"

Trish added, "We found long ago that our attitude matters the most. If we hustle and bustle to serve the finest hors d'oeuvres, our guests may feel our anxiety and be uncomfortable. Better to serve takeout chicken by a lighted fire and enjoy the conversation, if that's what helps us relax and enjoy our guests."

Ben continued, "Everyone deserves the feeling that they are important to others. That's why we wanted to have all of you gather here. For our part, we have the privilege of seeing you learn and grow spiritually. What other reward do we need?"

Ben and Trish hosted the teens for a little over two years. In that time, the congregation grew to recognize the powerful impact that this ministry had on the young people. Eventually the meetings returned to the church building. Years later, though, Ben and Trish continue to receive letters and calls from those teens, thanking them for the role the couple played in their faith journeys. What other reward did they need?

Do you have the spiritual gift of hospitality?

_____ I am comfortable around strangers and care deeply about how they are welcomed.

_____ I enjoy providing a safe environment for those who are in need.

_____ I feel fulfilled when I can open my home to others for food and fellowship.

_____ I can easily concentrate on whether guests feel welcome rather than on whether my house is in order or the food is extraordinary.

_____ I like to create appealing, appropriate environments for people.

_____ I view new relationships as opportunities to pass on God's love.

Suggestions for developing your spiritual gift of hospitality

1. Step out in faith! If your dining room is cramped or your budget doesn't allow for shrimp, know that card tables, hot dishes, and potlucks are blessings to others. As you try different ways of entertaining, be aware of how you approach the events. You can pick and choose how you demonstrate hospitality. Not everyone with this gift needs to host crowds.
2. Study the importance of true simplicity and how it can set you free to concentrate on the people you are serving rather than on the preparations and details of showing hospitality.
3. Find out who works with visitors or congregational care at your church. Partner with those people. Make it a point every week to meet someone new. Realize that almost every ministry in the church needs to offer a welcoming atmosphere.

Biblical example

Lydia opens her home (Acts 16:13–15).

Mercy

The ability to perceive the suffering of others and comfort and minister effectively with empathy.

> *Bible reference:* We have different gifts, according to the grace given us ... if it is showing mercy, let [us] do it cheerfully. (Romans 12:6, 8b)

Steve knew he needed an extra helping of prayer before his morning's scheduled visit. *God, You know I have no answers for this young family. We have prayed so hard for their little boy to be healed, and we struggle so with his pain. Please let me show Your love to them today and give us Your peace. Amen.*

Through years of experience, Steve knew that God would help him come alongside others during times of grief and loss. He had long since given up searching for the "right" things to say, instead concentrating on prayer to help him show God's love in some way. But this visit he knew would be especially tough. The doctors held little hope that young Alex's cancer could be brought under control, and the boy's mother had called Steve, who had been a frequent visitor, to let him know that Alex was having a bad day.

Not quite knowing why, Steve tucked a couple of squirt guns in his pocket. When he arrived, Alex was lying down as he had been all morning. Steve started to sit down beside him, then instead handed him one of the little pistols. "Do you want to have a water fight?"

Alex sat up, his eyes alight for the first time in days. "Do you have two of those? Let's go outside!"

Out they went onto the deck, squirting each other, watering the flowers, and ambushing insects. The morning flew by as Alex reveled in the gift Steve had brought—not only the toys, but the relief of forgetting for a few fun hours that he was so sick.

What seemed like a simple gesture opened the door to heartache for Steve. The joyful play with Alex increased his love for the little boy, heightening his grief when Alex eventually died. But Steve's gift of mercy allowed Alex to experience love and joy during his short stay on earth. As it is with many gifts, the impact can be subtle and complex. Steve's gift of mercy clearly helped him minister in ways that were beyond what he could do on his own.

Do you have the spiritual gift of mercy?

_____ I notice when people are hurt, displaced, or rejected, and I want to reach out to them in their suffering.

_____ I enjoy finding ways to show others how much God loves them.

_____ I can frequently see how to help people who are in need of comforting.

_____ I can easily gain the confidence of those in need.

_____ I tend to see each person as a life that matters to God and reach out to people who are avoided by others.

_____ I enjoy conveying the grace of God to those who feel guilt or shame.

Suggestions for developing your spiritual gift of mercy

1. Ask to be mentored by those who have the gift of mercy. Go with them to pray and minister to those in need. Pray for God to show you how to be tender and merciful. In many situations, there are no right things to say or do. Memorize Scripture verses that might bring comfort.

2. Using the gift of mercy can be physically and emotionally draining. Therefore, beware of overextending yourself. Realize that

you may need the help of people with other gifts such as those of administration, counseling, or encouragement as you work with those in need.

3. Setting boundaries is important for those who have the gift of mercy. Work to help people function on their own and become once again independent. Remember, it is *not* merciful to allow people to become too dependent on your help.

Biblical example

Jesus and the woman of Samaria (John 4:1–30).

Faith

The ability to recognize what God wants accomplished as well as to sustain a stalwart belief that God will see it done despite what others perceive as barriers.

> *Bible reference:* Now to each one the manifestation of the Spirit is given for the common good . . . to another faith by the same spirit. (1 Corinthians 12:7, 9)

Sixteen, seventeen, eighteen robes with holes or split seams. . . . This was not a matter of vanity, unrealistic expectations, or dissatisfaction. This was a matter of necessity. Nyssa knew that if the choir robes went through the wash one more time, the holes in those eighteen robes would be visible from the back of the church balcony.

Some people probably thought choir robes were too formal, but other members of Nyssa's church might quit the choir if they had to sit up front with their clothes on display week after week. Robes equalized the wardrobes of the haves and the have-nots in their urban neighborhood. There wasn't enough money to purchase new robes of any quality, nor did she have the ability or time to make new ones. Then a thought came to her—a ministry she had heard of. . . .

She dialed the number. "Yes, is Félice there? I read an article about the way you help churches sew their own choir robes. Could you explain your program to me?"

Félice was glad to share what she did. "Well, several years ago I happened upon a style of needlework that adapts well to assembly-line sewing and created robes for my church that many others admired. Only a few of the steps required more than basic sewing skills. I enjoyed showing others how to do it, but thought, *Why not turn this into my own little ministry?*

"You provide a sewing team that cuts out the garments and stitches the basic seams. Then I smock the tops and finish the corners before turning the hem work and hooks back to you. I just ask that you also make sets for two other churches that are in need. So far, I've helped over fifty churches—a few groups couldn't stop at three sets but kept going!"

Nyssa thought quickly. There weren't many women in her congregation with idle time on their hands, but the idea of passing on their gift might be enough of an incentive. "We'll do it. Would you tell us about your work in person?"

Félice went on to explain the number of work hours it would take to make forty robes for themselves, then eighty more. After the phone call, Nyssa added it up, divided it, adjusted it for coffee breaks, and started to pray, "Lord, change my mind quickly if we don't really need choir robes, for once Félice places the fabric order, there's no backing out.

"But if this is right for us, help me find the right prayer partners, the right hands . . . and a couple of serger machines for all of those long seams!"

The choir director thought Nyssa was crazy—hundreds of volunteer hours were needed. Her friends agreed to help, but told Nyssa, "We few are going to be sewing for years to meet our obligations—it will be too hard to find others to help!" However, one friend recalled another project that Nyssa had put her shoulder to, and said, "If she says we can do this, maybe we can."

Nyssa called two women in the congregation who made their living as tailors and was delighted to find that they had been eyeing the old robes with thoughts of action as well. With these experienced garment makers at the helm, they had no trouble finding people to commit to starting three or more robes apiece.

Not only that, but Project Robed in Majesty turned into a time of spiritual renewal for those who participated. Gathering weekly in a back room of the church where they were able to spread their supplies, they chose to listen to tapes and readings, discussing the content as they worked.

When the choir at last was clad in the new robes, Nyssa tried to sidestep the role her faith had played, but perhaps her example inspired those around her to step out in faith when it was their turn to trust and act.

Do you have the spiritual gift of faith?

_____ I firmly believe God is active in our lives.

_____ Sometimes I sense that God is orchestrating a project or idea. I find it easy to support it when others have doubts.

_____ I believe deeply in the power of prayer and am aware of God's presence in my life.

_____ I am able to believe that God is faithful, even in the face of seemingly insurmountable difficulties.

_____ People often tell me I am an incurable optimist.

_____ My personal experiences help me believe in the power of faith.

Suggestions for developing your spiritual gift of faith

1. Pray with those who have the gift of faith. Talk through your life circumstances with them to see where God has been at work.
2. Study the lives of those with the gift of faith such as George Müller, a nineteenth-century Christian. Müller is best known for the orphanages he founded and headed and his commitment to depend only on prayer for financial support. A summary of his life can be found in the Appendix of Andrew Murray's _Teach Me to Pray_ (Bethany House Publishers, 2002).
3. Practice trusting the Lord with small things. As your faith and insight increase, look to God for help in larger arenas where God is at work.

Biblical example

The centurion who asked for help knowing Jesus would provide it (Matthew 8:5–10).

Giving

The ability to give of material wealth freely and with joy to further the work of God.

Bible reference: We have different gifts, according to the grace given us ... if it is contributing to the needs of others, let

[them] give generously. (Romans 12:6, 8)

The question of replacing the old electric organ with a pipe organ had never been raised before, but the company that had serviced it for years declared that the old organ was irreparable. As Lee, the head of the worship committee, looked over the estimated replacement costs, she thought to herself, *Why not a pipe organ now? The new sanctuary is designed to hold one, and the estimates are still on file.*

As she looked at the significant amount of money a pipe organ would cost, a plan began to form in her mind. She thought of people in the congregation who agreed with her that while great music was perhaps not required by God, it definitely helped many members deepen their worship experience. She decided that her vacation savings could start off the fund-raising drive—she'd willingly make do with a week of fun here in town, knowing that her "vacation" was spent on the organ!

With the blessing of the church staff, over the next week she met with eight couples, outlining the possibility of a new pipe organ. "I don't want to bring this before the congregation unless the idea is well-supported. I hope to find a few individuals who are willing and able to donate enough money to give the organ fund a substantial start. If the rest of our members see that the goal is attainable, perhaps they will want to make contributions they can afford."

Several of the couples decided that they wanted to support the project—provided their names remained anonymous. Three families agreed to give additional matching grants if others in the congregation donated larger sums.

By the time Lee was ready to tell the congregation of the plans for a new organ, about half the needed money had been pledged. She urged, "Pray about whether this is a project you should support. I know that some may say an organ benefits our congregation in a selfish way. We don't want this to detract from the other causes and missions we support. Yet music can enhance our own spiritual lives. We aren't going for the fanciest organ available, but believe that we are being wise stewards of what we have."

The church posted a thermometer chart so the incoming pledges could be recorded. One family made a large pledge—for their financial situation—by agreeing to make their own pizza on

Fridays rather than order takeout. A men's prayer group volunteered to do some extensive repair work for the church on condition that the savings be donated to the organ fund. The youth group decided to change their annual ski trip destination to a closer resort, giving the savings to the fund.

Soon Lee reported to the congregation that more than 90 percent of the needed money was pledged. "We will have a new organ, but let's stick to our plan of not borrowing funds. This is a spiritual adventure of sorts, and we'll have to wait for the last page to discover the ending."

In the end Lee received a note from one of the families she had contacted initially. *"We knew that God wanted us to contribute to the organ fund, but we waited to see what others could do without us. This check should cover the remainder needed—and may our church continue to raise funds in this way."*

Do you have the spiritual gift of giving?

_____ I often give generously and joyfully.

_____ I am resourceful in finding ways to free up my resources to benefit others.

_____ I feel a special connection to the ministries and projects I support financially.

_____ I'd rather give anonymously for the most part, unless my example might inspire others to be generous.

_____ I tend to manage my own money well, often basing financial decisions on what will be made available for giving.

_____ I feel comfortable and have success with approaching others to give of their resources.

Suggestions for developing your spiritual gift of giving

1. Study the Bible's teachings on money and possessions.

2. Network with others who have developed systems for knowing when, where, and how much to give. Research the ministries that interest you in order to discern whether your resources are used in the way you intended.

3. Sometimes giving can become a source of conflict. If those with whom you make financial decisions do not have the gift of giving, involve them in your decision-making process as much as possible. Be sensitive to their needs for financial security. If pos-

sible, pray together about giving opportunities and/or look for other ways to give.

Biblical example

The early church in Jerusalem (Acts 4:32–35).

GIFTS OF PROCLAMATION

Evangelism, Teaching, Discernment, Knowledge, Prophecy, and Wisdom

These gifts involve conveying God's truths or revelations to others.

Evangelism

The ability to spread the good news of Jesus Christ in ways that inspire others to learn more about our faith.

Bible reference: But to each one of us grace has been given as Christ apportioned it. . . . It was he who gave some to be . . . evangelists. (Ephesians 4:7, 11)

Sarah listened carefully to her friend Beth's description of the painful end to yet another romantic relationship. Beth complained, "Why do I always end up on the hurting side of love?"

Sarah and Beth had known each other all through their school years. While Sarah had never kept her church membership a secret, she seldom had opportunities to discuss her faith at school or with her friends. Now as she and Beth talked about Beth's need for approval and the void left when her father moved out, Sarah felt a need to take the conversation to a deeper level. "You know, Beth, this romantic void in your life is really just a symptom of the bigger void in your spiritual life. The more I learn of how Jesus loves us, the less I am hurt by what happens in my relationships."

Beth looked at her, startled, and said, "No, you're wrong. I don't feel a void like that."

Sarah wisely went back to her listening mode, but just a few days later, Beth asked her what she meant about Jesus' love. Sarah told her the story of Jesus in her own words, explaining the differences it made in her own life. Beth asked one or two questions and then changed the subject to the upcoming weekend's events.

A few weeks later Beth called, asking if Sarah would meet with some friends of hers. Together they challenged Sarah with every spiritual question in the book: If God is so good, why is there pain? What about people who have never heard about the Gospel? Is the Bible for real? And so on. Sarah carefully and enthusiastically answered each question as fully as she could, knowing that their interest showed a thirst for faith. She had always been interested in these same themes and had prayerfully sought out answers in the past few years. However, Beth was still not open to Sarah's message.

Three months later Beth called Sarah and excitedly told her about a seminar on Christianity she had attended. After talking with the speaker at length, Beth had joined a Bible study. Beth finished, "Thanks so much for your listening ear and for your patience."

Do you have the spiritual gift of evangelism?

_____ I get excited about sharing the Gospel with others.

_____ I enjoy studying the questions that challenge Christianity.

_____ I frequently think about people who do not have a faith commitment, wishing they could understand how my faith helps me.

_____ I look for ways that might help others understand the difference Christianity can make in their lives.

_____ I can see how people's needs can be met through faith in Christ.

_____ I can comfortably talk about my Christian faith with others in a way that makes them comfortable as well.

Suggestions for developing your spiritual gift of evangelism

1. Basic to using the gift of evangelism in any setting is a clear understanding of the Christian faith and the ability (which may come only through practice) to convey Jesus' message in your own style. Talk with others who have this gift about methods they use. There are also many books on this subject.

2. Study the areas that block people from accepting the Christian message by studying apologetics—the defense of the Christian

faith. Become well-informed about how to respond to their questions. There are many workshops and books about apologetics.

3. Seek out a person on your church staff who either has this gift or can direct you to someone who does so that you can network with him or her.

Biblical example

Philip's obedience in ministering to the Ethiopian eunuch (Acts 8:26–38).

Teaching

The ability to understand and communicate God's truths to others effectively—in ways that lead to applications in their lives.

> *Bible reference:* We have gifts that differ according to the grace given to us ... the teacher, in teaching ... (Romans 12:6–7 NRSV)

Over their usual cup of coffee after the evening Bible study, Phil asked his friends, "What did you think of the lesson tonight? Did you follow it all?"

Karen said, "Grant is such a nice guy, and I'm grateful that he agreed to teach all month, but the study guide is a lifesaver, given the way his teaching jumps around."

"I found myself wondering how the class would go if he stuck to just a couple of points and maybe let us take on some of the questions in small groups," Phil mused. "The whole passage could be better applied to our lives, too. It reminded me of a news story I read today." And Phil went on to describe the connections he saw.

Rachel broke in, "You should teach the class."

Phil shook his head. "I'm too new to all of this, so new that I feel foolish criticizing Grant after all the work he puts into those lessons. When I listen to him, though, I find myself thinking of other ways to get the message across."

Ted spoke up. "Why don't you give it a try, Phil? Pick a lesson and share it with us. We'll be kind to you! And we'll give Grant a call. Besides, he told me he'd enjoy a breather."

Phil went to the library to prepare and surrounded himself with books on the next week's topic. When he finally paused to look at his watch, he couldn't believe that two hours had passed; he had been so engrossed in the subject. He was eager to share what he had learned, but was still unsure of the approach to take. What would really drive the message home? Suddenly he thought of a clip from a movie he had seen a few months before. "If I use that as an introduction, then let them talk about the characters with whom they can identify, it will lead right to my main point," he decided.

At the next meeting, watching his friends become as excited over the material as he was, he realized that something more than the hours he had studied had enlivened his teaching. When Rachel said that not even her minister could do any better, Phil replied, "You know, I really enjoyed teaching this lesson. I felt like something took hold of my thoughts and inspired me. I'm not sure it'll happen again."

"Try next week," kidded Ben, "and we'll let you know. From what I heard tonight, I'll be signing up for the rest of the year, if you'll teach."

That was the start of Phil's teaching ministry. As his own biblical knowledge and experience grew, he came to recognize the role that God played in inspiring his thoughts, providing his energy, and guiding the atmospheres that surround his teaching.

Do you have the spiritual gift of teaching?

_____ I want to make God's truths relevant to life in ways that help people grow and develop.

_____ I like gathering information, especially with the goal of effectively communicating it to others.

_____ I often easily envision how to present spiritual concepts in ways that people find useful.

_____ I love to study the Bible. I receive new insights fairly easily.

_____ When I listen to other teachers, I often think of alternative ways to present the materials.

_____ When I communicate what I have learned, others are motivated to learn more about the Bible and their faith in God.

Suggestions for developing your spiritual gift of teaching

1. For depth and impact, those with this spiritual gift may need to strengthen their skills in the areas of discernment and wisdom.
2. Keep learning! Study teaching methods by taking classes or

observing your favorite teachers. Also continue to study the Bible.

3. Create a system for keeping examples, stories, humor, images, quotations, etc., that will enliven your teaching and bring the message to your listeners.

Biblical example

Peter and John's testimony and teaching (Acts 3:11–4:4).

Discernment

The ability to recognize what is of God and what is not of God.

Bible reference: Now to each one the manifestation of the Spirit is given for the common good ... to another distinguishing between spirits. (1 Corinthians 12:7, 10)

"What a great evening!" Ann said as she got into the car. "I expected a typical, boring fund-raiser, but Melissa's stories? My heart melted as she told of the struggles the one woman went through to get her diploma—and her description of helping her choose clothes for her first job interview? I think we should double our contribution. They are doing such a good work."

Norm glanced over at his wife, one eyebrow raised. "You were touched? All she did was toot her own horn. I'm not sure I trust her motives, or everything she said."

"You're kidding, aren't you?" Ann said. When Norm shook his head, Ann snapped, "Why shouldn't she toot her own horn—the ministry's tripled in size since she became its director. She's the best thing that ever happened to this women's shelter. You saw people writing out checks tonight—funds are pouring in from new sources all the time."

"I'm sorry, honey, but there's something about her that sets my teeth on edge. I honestly wonder if things are going as well as she says." He stared ahead, silent as they drove home.

The next morning Ann pointed to an article in the newspaper about Melissa. "Look," she said, "here's another affirmation of Melissa's work. She was just named Community Leader of the Year. And here's a quote from the foundation's board chair about her tireless dedication to changing the lives of the women they help."

Norm grimaced. "I saw her having lunch the other day with several business people. Melissa was dressed to the nines and obviously aware of being in the spotlight. She's after prestige, I swear."

"Norm, you're being too cynical. She obviously has to network, hobnob with the powerful, to fund her work. That's what running a foundation is all about."

"Well, maybe you're right," he sighed, "but please, let's not hand her any more of our money. I'd rather just give what we did in the past." Ann reluctantly agreed.

Several months later at an open house at the shelter, Melissa was conspicuously absent. In her place, the board chair spoke. "While our purpose tonight is unveiling our remodeled facilities and celebrating the new ways we can help those we serve, we need to also inform you of something not so pleasant. In reviewing the financial records for this project, we discovered several discrepancies in bank deposits and bills. When our auditors sat down with Melissa to review the errors, she admitted to embezzling tens of thousands of dollars. I promised to read her resignation letter to you."

Gasps echoed around the room at the announcement. Ann caught her husband's expression. While his brows furrowed in anger, he nodded his head as if not surprised. "How did you know?" she whispered.

"She never seemed genuine to me," he replied. "I even prayed about whether I should agree with you to give more money, but everything in me still said no."

Do you have the gift of discernment?

_____ I can generally rely on my first impressions of people and whether their motives or character are authentic. I tend to "know" where a person is coming from.

_____ I sometimes sense when something like a book or presentation will bring people closer to God—or cause them to be hurt or pushed away.

_____ In many situations I find my gut reacting to the circumstance or atmosphere I am experiencing, whether good or bad.

_____ My mind tends to pick up on whether books or speakers are in line with God's truths. Contradictions stand out to me.

_____ I can distinguish sources of energy and motivations in people, whether from the Holy Spirit or others.

_____ I can tell if someone is operating from Jesus' commandment to love one another or if they are putting themselves before God.

Suggestions for developing your gift of discernment

1. Consider enrolling in an in-depth Bible study to strengthen your knowledge and understanding.
2. To test your discernments, work with others who have this gift. Review church curriculum, participate in book studies, or work through difficult personal issues.
3. Of paramount importance for those with the gift of discernment is understanding the biblical difference between judging to condemn and judging in a merciful and compassionate way. Some people with this gift find a need to refrain from confrontations until they have grown in Christian maturity. Using discernment in difficult situations requires love, patience, kindness, and understanding.

Biblical example

Peter's response to Simon the sorcerer (Acts 8:18–24).

Knowledge

The ability to understand, organize, and effectively use information, from natural sources or the Holy Spirit, for the advancement of God's purposes.

> *Bible reference:* Now to each one the manifestation of the Spirit is given for the common good. To one there is given ... the message of knowledge by means of the same Spirit. (1 Corinthians 12:7–8)

At a missions committee meeting, the general consensus was this: "We have to find a project close to home that will fire the imaginations of the congregation. Most of our members can't afford to travel or take a week off of work, but many say they want to be involved in a hands-on outreach." When Vicki volunteered to check into some possibilities, no one on the committee expected the kind of report she gave the next week.

"As we discussed last time," Vicki began, "we want a project that's within an hour's drive of here and where multiple talents are needed—not just a building project, for example, but one where people from our church are also needed for educational efforts, child care, meal preparation, or some such combination, so that all family members can participate.

"I called several other churches and foundations in the area and identified seven alternatives." Vicki handed out charts that showed each project's goals and needs, the ideal number of volunteers, cost to the church, location, and almost anything else they needed to know.

One of the committee members asked, "Which project do you believe would be best?"

Vicki said earnestly, "I didn't really think about it—I just wanted you to have all the information necessary for us to make a good decision. Are there any questions?"

With the information so well gathered and presented, the members adjourned, agreeing to pray about the alternatives before their next time together.

The committee leader began the next meeting by asking for input on Vicki's seven alternatives. Bill spoke first. "While all of the choices have merit, I found myself drawn to the second. As I prayed about this outreach, I saw an image of the teens from our church building a bridge with the teens at this crisis center. If this is the project we choose, my impression is that our youth would be the main connection through which the rest of us are able to serve."

"A lot of teens *are* at that center all the time," Vicki added. "Your insight seems right on target, Bill."

Note that while Vicki's gift of knowledge operated in a *typical* way here, Bill's gift of knowledge operated in a *sensational* way— Vicki's report had mentioned nothing about the teens. Both gifts of knowledge guided the committee's decision.

Do you have the spiritual gift of knowledge?

_____ It is easy for me to gather and analyze information for projects, ministries, or other causes that serve God's purposes.

_____ I enjoy studying the Bible and other books to gain insights and background for God's Word.

_____ I can organize information well to pass on to others.

_____ I seem to understand how God acts in our lives.

_____ At times I find myself knowing information about a situation that has not been told to me by anyone else.

_____ I have insights about how things come together for God's purposes.

Suggestions for developing your spiritual gift of knowledge

1. Consider enrolling in an in-depth Bible study. Knowledge of Scripture will enhance your understanding of efforts you undertake.
2. List the areas in which you already have a vast knowledge base and other areas where you have a passion to learn more. Talk to leaders at your church about where your gift of knowledge can be used.
3. If you find yourself having hunches or inspirations that seem to be giving you information, write them down or talk it out. This will allow you to ponder later what the information might mean. Test your hunches against Scripture.

Biblical example

Jesus and the temple tax (Matthew 17:24–27).

Note:

Understanding the difference between gifts of *knowledge, prophecy,* and *wisdom* can often be confusing. To clarify:

> *Knowledge* is generally factual information about people or a situation that can be useful and insightful for making decisions.
>
> *Prophecy* generally means declaring from a godly perspective what is right or wrong in a given circumstance, perhaps indicating the future consequences of continuing on the present path.
>
> *Wisdom* is generally a *clarifying* insight that cuts to the core of a paradox or conflict, identifying the solution or exposing the deeper dynamics of an issue.

Prophecy

The ability to proclaim God's truths in a way relevant to current situations and to envision how God would will things to change.

Bible reference: But to each one of us grace has been given as

Christ apportioned it.... It was he who gave some to be ... prophets. (Ephesians 4:7, 11)

For the past six months D'Andre and Jasmine had worked together on a planning team for a new worship service for young adults at their church. D'Andre, a minister, led the team. Jasmine signed up to help because she'd worked with similar worship formats at another church. "Besides," she'd told D'Andre, "with two small children at home, I need to be a plain committee member right now!"

The planning team members had visited services at several different churches. One afternoon as D'Andre and Jasmine walked toward the chapel of their own church, D'Andre explained, "This group has been meeting a couple times a month for quite a while now. We're from different churches—pretty traditional ones. We gather here for a little more spirited worship. Nothing over-the-top, but you'll see a lot more hands in the air as well as shouts of 'Amen' or 'Thank you' as Harold prays."

Jasmine nodded. "And this Harold's in charge?"

D'Andre laughed. "Harold would say that God's in charge. I've known him for years, and the more I hear him speak, the more I think he's a prophet."

"A prophet? To me, prophets are 'Woe to you' and fire and brimstone," Jasmine replied.

D'Andre slowly shook his head, "Harold's thoughts are more like needed, caring messages straight from God. You'll see ..."

When they entered the chapel, seven or eight people had already arrived. D'Andre waved to a dark-haired, smiling man who was placing Bibles around a circle of chairs. "Harold, this is Jasmine," he called.

Harold walked over briskly and gave Jasmine a firm handshake. "D'Andre's told me all about your great ideas for worship. You're definitely serving where God wants you."

Then Harold's face grew thoughtful. "Prayer. Your prayer life ... I can see your ideas and gifts blossoming into wider and wider fields of ministry when your own prayer life blossoms into maturity, bearing more fruit."

Jasmine stared at him, then nodded slowly. "I used to journal my prayers every day. But being the mother of an infant and a toddler, well, a week can pass without my prayer life being more than, 'God, grant me sleep!' You're right; I need to grow in how I pray."

After the service, D'Andre and Jasmine discussed various books and workshops on prayer that she might explore. Jasmine reflected, "Harold was absolutely right about my prayer life. How could I have forgotten how much I need to pray? And the image he used of praying in order to bear fruit definitely motivates me to make room for prayer. God's got my attention now!"

"Harold's done the same for me before," D'Andre replied, "giving me just the right message to call me back to where God wants me to be."

Do you have the spiritual gift of prophecy?

_____ I often spot the differences between cultural trends and what we are called to do as people of faith.

_____ I tend to see or think of images that convey God's truth.

_____ To me, repentance, change, and challenge are a healthy part of our spiritual life. I am very aware of the future consequences of choosing one path over another.

_____ When necessary, I am able to confront people with the truth of a situation.

_____ It saddens me when others ignore or take lightly life's problems.

_____ Often I can interpret God's truths in situations where that truth is encouraging—or even where that truth is unpopular or difficult for listeners to accept.

Suggestions for developing your spiritual gift of prophecy

1. Spend time improving your understanding of biblical standards, the roles and messages of biblical prophets, and the difference between biblical absolutes and relative standards (to avoid, for example, proclaiming that just because the Bible gives instructions for how to treat slaves, it is okay to own slaves—a justification relied on for centuries).

2. Sometimes believers with the gift of prophecy have difficulty in leadership roles because of a tendency to use the gift judgmentally. If this is the case for you, make sure you network with people with the spiritual gifts of discernment, encouragement, and wisdom so that you will have a way to test your prophetic revelations.

3. If you receive hunches, visions, or images, record them in a notebook. How are you led to interpret them? Be aware that the receiving of a prophecy from God and being called to deliver it are two different events. Ask God when, how, and to whom the prophecy is to be given.

Biblical example

John's conveying his vision and words of Jesus (Revelation 2).

Wisdom

The ability to understand and apply biblical and spiritual knowledge to complex, paradoxical, or other difficult situations.

> *Bible reference:* Now to each one the manifestation of the Spirit is given for the common good. To one there is given through the Spirit the message of wisdom. (1 Corinthians 12:7–8)

For the umpteenth time in two years, church leadership gathered to ponder the topic of location: Should they stay at their urban location despite the lack of room for expansion, or should they relocate? Each time new issues surfaced. Each time committees reported more information. Everyone by now knew the alternatives:

- Stay put and pour several hundred thousand dollars into repairs and renovation of the century-old building.
- Purchase a nearby storefront location that could house some of their activities.
- Rebuild in a developing suburban area where they'd have plenty of space for expansion.

As usual, attendees raised concerns, unanswered questions, and fears about each of the alternatives. They took a straw vote; none of the choices garnered strong support. The church leadership was not only divided but overwhelmed and confused by the choices at hand. The meeting's atmosphere grew even grimmer as the finance committee reported on best-case, worst-case scenarios.

Finally Corinne, a long-standing member, took the floor. "It just occurred to me that we have gathered information and discussed the alternatives for *two years,* and most of us are no closer to a decision than we were at the start of the process. I think we have a different, much more crucial, problem to solve—that of our faith. Do we believe that God is with us?

"There are going to be problems and stresses whatever choice we make. The real issue is whether we're ready to take a step in faith and lead this congregation toward its future."

After a silence, one of the committee members said thoughtfully, "That *is* the issue. I've been so afraid of making the 'wrong' choice that I haven't been open to any of the options." Others nodded in agreement. The discussion gradually turned to a celebration of the ways in which God had guided their thriving congregation in the past.

Corinne's words clarified for church leadership that their true obstacle was being willing to move ahead. The location deadlock was finally over. By the end of the next meeting the church leadership fleshed out their strategy for moving their church toward its future.

Do you have the spiritual gift of wisdom?

_____ It is easy for me to make practical applications of the truths found in the Bible, thinking through different courses of action and determining the best one.

_____ People often come to me for advice about personal and spiritual matters.

_____ I am known for my depth of understanding and insights into complex problems.

_____ I am often able to find a profoundly simple solution in the midst of a difficult situation.

_____ I have resolved paradoxes by cutting through to the essence of an issue.

_____ I help others see God's way in the midst of conflicting viewpoints.

Suggestions for developing your spiritual gift of wisdom

1. James says, "The wisdom that comes from heaven is first of all pure; then peace-loving, considerate, submissive, full of mercy and good fruit, impartial and sincere" (James 3:17). You can deepen your understanding of this type of wisdom through study of how to apply the teachings of the Bible to life. Wisdom often improves with spiritual maturity. Nurturing your own

spiritual growth can add to your gift of wisdom.

2. Work to continually expose yourself to people and ideas so that you are aware of cultural trends, attitudes, and conflicts. Consider pursuing this with a small group whose members will challenge your thinking.

3. Practice stepping out and trusting some of the gut-level intuitions you have. Then test your solutions with others.

Biblical example

Peter, Paul, and James at the Council of Jerusalem (Acts 15:5–19).

GIFTS OF ACTION

Leadership, Administration, Shepherding, Encouragement/Counseling, and Apostleship

These gifts involve moving individuals or the church toward accomplishing what God wants done.

Leadership

The ability to motivate, coordinate, and direct the efforts of others in doing God's work.

> *Bible reference:* God has given us different gifts for doing certain things well. . . . If God has given you leadership ability, take the responsibility seriously. (Romans 12:6, 8 NLT)

A true leader knows when a task is too great for one person to handle, but true leaders don't get people to work *for* them. They get people to work together *with* them toward a common goal. Excellence in leadership happens when that person convinces two or three others to work on the same common goal. They surround themselves with dedicated, knowledgeable people who perform their tasks in a consistently superior, coordinated manner.

For Joel, leadership happened when his young daughter asked, "Daddy, I want to do something really special with you—can we go camping again?" Given that it was wintertime in Minnesota, Joel thought long and hard before replying, "Let me see what I can do."

Joel called a few of the other fathers in his men's prayer group, "What if we held a camp-in at church—a fun time to be with our kids, play games, and have snacks. We could really have some great 'quality' time in the midst of the Minnesota deep freeze."

His friends willingly joined in the planning, keeping the details simple so that everyone could have a good time. During the camp-in, Joel saw delight on so many faces that he wondered, "What if I could get fathers this excited about parenting more of the time? So many of the dads I know did not have good role models in their own fathers—times were different then."

In the weeks that followed, Joel contacted some friends whom he thought might share his passion for becoming better fathers. Together they met with two of their ministers who were also young fathers. "Could the next men's retreat focus on fatherhood?" Joel began. "We've got a lot of ideas and are willing to do the bulk of the organizing." The ministers promised their support.

The retreat came together as Joel had hoped. He and thirty other men laughed and prayed together, confided in each other about the difficulties of parenting, and listened intently to speakers. On the second night, Joel stood to speak. "I've heard many of you say that this experience has opened your eyes to how much you have to learn about being the kind of father God intended you to be. I know that's been true for me! Who would like to continue meeting so that we can work on these ideas together?"

About a dozen men signed up at the retreat, but as they talked to their friends about what they had learned, more fathers in the church became interested. Joel recruited two of the retreat participants to co-lead with him in planning the direction of the group.

That spring, on Father's Day, Joel announced a new small group ministry—Down-to-Earth Fathering—to the congregation. "We'll meet once a week before work for fellowship, teaching, and a chance to share our struggles as earthly fathers trying to live up to the example set by our God in heaven. Of course, none of us can be perfect, but we can be more intentional. We can change the less healthy patterns of how we parent for better ones in order to touch the lives of our children."

The group grew quickly to more than thirty men at each meeting. Joel encouraged others to take on various organizational and teaching roles. One father remarked, "I am so grateful that I've discovered more joy in being a father. Because of your efforts with this ministry, I've had a chance to be a kid again—and it's even better than the first time, because my dad *never* did these kinds of things with me."

Do you have the spiritual gift of leadership?

_____ I can motivate others and get people to work together toward a common goal.

_____ I have enough confidence in my vision of what could be done to give direction to others.

_____ I frequently accept responsibility in group settings where leadership is required.

_____ People under my leadership sense that they are headed in a good direction.

_____ When necessary, I can make unpopular decisions and work through any conflicts that follow.

_____ I can see in advance what people can achieve and know what needs to be done to make it happen.

Suggestions for developing your spiritual gift of leadership

1. The Bible has much to say about the servant role of a leader. Study the passages of Scripture that describe God's perspectives on power, submission, and accountability. A good topical Bible helps in this.

2. Analyze the methods of those you consider great leaders in the eyes of God.

3. Leaders need the support of other visionaries as a check and balance that they are following God's path. Many find it helpful to join a small group for prayer, study, and accountability so that they have a base for discernment. Seek out people with the gifts of wisdom, knowledge, faith, administration, discernment, and perhaps prophecy, to partner with you.

Biblical example

Moses' successor, Joshua (Joshua 1:1–9).

Administration

The ability to organize information, events, or materials to work efficiently for the body of Christ.

Bible reference: And in the church God has appointed . . . those with gifts of administration. (1 Corinthians 12:28)

"That sounds like a great project, but there just aren't enough staff resources to cover it right now," was the message that came back to Jeff from the church. Jeff wanted his congregation to sponsor the rebuilding of the playground across the street from their inner city sister church—and he wanted to see it done before school resumed in just five weeks. While the playground had long been in need of repairs, six days earlier vandals had destroyed most of the useable equipment. The insurance settlement would cover only the cost of materials, not the cleanup and labor needed to make the kind of playground the kids deserved.

As Jeff considered the church staff's reluctance, he thought, *Why should the staff take time away from their other responsibilities? I think I can organize this myself.*

The church staff agreed that Jeff could publicize the playground rebuilding needs in the newsletter and recruit members through the church's usual methods. Jeff methodically listed his needs:

- a plan for the playground
- coordination of the purchase of all materials, both for equipment and landscaping
- a counterpart to himself at their sister church so that they could provide volunteers as well
- a liaison to ensure that all safety and equal access standards were met
- volunteers to act as supervisors for the job, preferably two or three so that one could always be present during construction
- volunteer workers
- someone to schedule volunteers
- someone to coordinate delivery of refreshments for workers

Jeff was not a contractor but had helped construct the playground at his children's school. He quickly contacted the leaders of that project to get the names and numbers of people who could make this project happen in the short time they had. He got a friend to photograph the ruined playground and displayed the photos on church bulletin boards to build support for the project. He found a supplier to help them design the playground including only materials that were on hand so that construction would not be delayed by special orders. Jeff called the head of the teachers' association at the school, and she in turn organized many of the teachers to volunteer.

Jeff never pounded a nail or lifted a board on the playground project—not because he wanted to keep his hands clean, but because the administrative details kept his hands full. He sent out reminder notices, contacted equipment renters, delivered food, and dropped off volunteers. He focused the spotlight on the volunteers, emphasizing what people can do when they mobilize for a task that is bigger than anyone could do alone. He saw himself as an administrator, not a leader. "The project led itself once people recognized the need. I didn't inspire or motivate, I just kept the machinery well-oiled," he said when a friend tried to praise his leadership skills.

The gift of *administration* often acts this way. A person with a life gift such as time and priorities, finances, or organization simply comes alongside an effort and adds the ingredients needed to carry out what God wants done.

Do you have the spiritual gift of administration?

_____ I like to organize facts, people, or events.

_____ When I am working on a project or effort, it is easy for me to see the necessary steps in the process to solve potential problems.

_____ I tend to be frustrated when I see disorganization.

_____ I enjoy learning about management issues and how organizations function effectively.

_____ I can easily manage schedules, finances, or supplies.

_____ I am generally careful and thorough in handling details.

Suggestions for developing your spiritual gift of administration

1. Observe how others with this gift organize events, outreaches, offices, or other tasks in which you have an interest. Consider where you would be most comfortable helping with a similar event.

2. Develop skills that can improve your efficiency, such as computer applications, accounting, strategic planning, or oral or written communication.

3. If you are unsure whether this is one of your gifts, start by taking administrative responsibility for a small project.

Biblical example

Joseph during the famine in Egypt (Genesis 41:33–57).

Pastoring/Shepherding

The ability to guide and care for others as they experience spiritual growth.

> *Bible reference:* But to each one of us grace has been given as Christ apportioned it. . . . It was he who gave some to be . . . pastors. (Ephesians 4:7, 11)

As the service ended and people began to greet one another, Nick looked around the sanctuary. Sure enough, Bob Rodriguez was once again trying to get his wife out the door as soon as possible, even as she tried to visit with a friend. And there was Lou Stafford, staring at his feet, acting like he'd rather be anywhere else. Nick spotted a couple of other men he knew who didn't seem to be finding "kindred spirits," people to whom they could relate and with whom they could grow spiritually.

Nick often seemed to sense a person's spiritual needs. As he made his way over to Lou, he recalled his own first Sundays at this church, feeling as if he was the only one who couldn't find the Scripture passage for the morning's lesson. "Hi, Lou," he began. "I saw you here last week, but you disappeared so fast that I couldn't get over to talk to you. Found anyone you know?"

Lou, glad to see a friendly face, brightened and replied, "Well, Cheryl met these ladies at the women's Bible study and says this feels like home already. Not that it matters much to me where we go."

Nick smiled. "Seems like most churches make it easier for the women to connect with each other than the men, doesn't it? You know, for a long time I've wanted to get together with some other men from here that are close to retirement. I'm down by your office every Tuesday. What would you think of lunching together, along with perhaps Bob Rodriguez and some others. This wouldn't be anything formal, just a chance to meet with other men who are looking ahead to life after work."

"I'm pretty busy," Lou began, "but we could at least meet once for lunch. How about next week? I see Bob all the time, so I'll check with him."

Over the next few days Nick managed to find three other men to join them for lunch, provided it was "not really a religious discussion." Nick carefully planned the first meeting so that no one would feel threatened. He asked everyone to commit to keeping job-related conversation to a minimum. "Let's save this time together to talk about the next chapters of our lives."

The first meeting proved to be a refreshing change of pace for all of them, and they agreed to continue meeting bi-weekly for the rest of the spring. A month or so later, they began reading together a secular book on values. Soon their discussions took a deeper turn.

After one of the meetings, Lou asked Nick if the two of them could talk a bit longer. "Nick, does this church thing really help you live out this stuff?" Nick took the time to tell Lou how his faith had helped him.

Lou said, "Bob and I have both been thinking of attending the new members' class. These lunches have helped us feel more welcome at church. They've given us more familiar faces—and to be honest, I've realized that I'm not the only one struggling with how to make retirement meaningful. Thanks for including me."

Nick said, "It's funny, but I think sometimes God shows me how to band people together. I know I grow more when I meet with the same people for a long period of time, so I enjoy providing these opportunities. If you ever want to help me start another group, give me a call."

"I just might. Thanks."

Do you have the spiritual gift of shepherding?

_____ I enjoy encouraging others to develop in their faith.

_____ As I work to help others I tend to think in terms of groups, teams, and task forces rather than individual personalities.

_____ I can often assess where a person is spiritually; I try to create or look for places where they can connect to enable them to take the next step.

_____ I have compassion for those who seem to be getting off track. I long to see them come back to the fold.

_____ I would enjoy nurturing and caring for a group of people over a period of time.

116

_____ I like to see people form long-term, in-depth spiritual relationships.

Suggestions for developing your spiritual gift of shepherding

1. Learn about small group ministry and consider taking small group leadership training.[5] Be careful to have your own shepherd, perhaps someone with related gifts such as encouragement or teaching, to help you guard against fatigue or imbalance in your personal life.
2. Study how Jesus shepherded His disciples—one of the most diverse small groups ever assembled.
3. Consider working in the recruitment and placement side of the church. Become active in assisting people to connect with or relate to others.

Biblical example

Jesus and His disciples (the Gospels).

Encouragement/Counseling

The ability to effectively listen to people, comforting and assisting them in moving toward psychological and relational wholeness.

Bible reference: God has given us different gifts for doing certain things well.... If your gift is to encourage others, be encouraging. (Romans 12:6, 8 NLT)

Kendra exclaimed, "Whew!" as she set her tray at the last empty spot at the table. "Just in time for an upbeat lunch hour."

"What do you mean?" asked Jamal.

"If *you're* here, Jamal, everyone is cheerful," Kendra said as she reached for a napkin. "We forget all our cares and talk about subjects that are above the grapevine or office politics."

"Jamal, I'll never forget my first months here," added Paul. "I was so intimidated by all of the talented advertising experts that I nearly gave up. You encouraged me to draft my brochure idea, which brought in some of my prime accounts. I never would have tried it if you hadn't bugged me about it; I didn't think I could

---

[5]*Growing People Through Small Groups* by David Stark and Betty Veldman Wieland (Bethany House, 2004) is an excellent resource for small group ministries.

design marketing materials, and look at me now—a group manager!"

"Ditto for me," broke in Kendra. "The rest of you probably don't know that Jamal asked me to do new employee training when I was really just a new employee myself. Remember, Jamal? You saw me demonstrate the new phones to two of my colleagues who had missed the demo session. You told my manager that anyone who could help others understand that voicemail system could teach company procedures—and I love the work I do in training now."

"And you encouraged me to write up my ideas for the annual meeting after I vented my frustration to you about the planning session," added Tanya. "They didn't use all of them, of course, but they asked me to head the customer relations committee."

Jamal smiled at his friends around the table. "It's a God thing for me, really. A bad day is any day that I'm stuck at my desk with no chance to listen to your ideas or frustrations and help you dream about what you *could* be doing."

"Well, I move that we figure out how to get you out of your office a bit more," said Paul. "Your job description should carry the title of Official Sounding Board. I feel that all of my ideas are safe with you; you listen to what I have to say and give credit for the merits of the idea before making suggestions. We all gain through your encouragement."

Do you have the gift of encouragement/counseling?

_____ People tell me that I am a good listener and approach me with dreams and concerns.

_____ I often see attributes or gifts in others that they are slow to recognize for themselves.

_____ I am usually aware of the emotional state of people around me, whether they are content or whether something is bothering them.

_____ In stressful situations, I often find myself able to give perspective on what is positive in a way that others find helpful.

_____ I tend to have more faith in people than they have in themselves.

_____ I sympathize easily with others and am tolerant of their shortcomings, yet I enjoy helping people mature in their faith.

Suggestions for developing your spiritual gift of encouragement/counseling

1. Consider your other spiritual gifts to discover how they best work with the spiritual gift of encouragement/counseling. Teachers or shepherds may work best with groups. Some people with the spiritual gift of mercy might seek areas of service that allow one-on-one interactions.
2. Consider training for one-on-one counseling or lay ministries that emphasize listening to others and walking beside them in times of crisis.
3. If you have this spiritual gift, remember that it is easy to become overloaded with the demands of others. Make sure you have your own encouragers to give you strength as you pursue your encourager/counselor role.

Biblical example

Barnabas encouraging those at Antioch (Acts 11:22–24).

Apostleship

The ability to minister transculturally, starting new churches or ministries that touch multiple churches.

> *Bible reference:* But to each one of us grace has been given as Christ apportioned it. . . . It was he who gave some to be apostles. (Ephesians 4:7, 11)

Ed and Linda Garrick started looking for short-term mission opportunities after hearing how much their children had gained from church youth group service trips. As Ed put it, "Why should the kids have all the fun?"

Volunteering with several local organizations had given the Garricks a taste of working with different ethnic backgrounds. They jumped at the chance to join a construction crew in a developing country. After they returned, they corresponded with the people they'd met, found more volunteers to go the next year, headed a crew the third year, and couldn't wait to go for a fourth year. Once was not enough!

Reflecting back over what they had experienced, Ed said, "The first year I went with my *own* mission—if other teams built one house in a week, why, we could build two! I borrowed a generator and a block cutter to speed us along. Fortunately, I met with the project director *before* I mentioned my plans to anyone else!

"She told me, 'If we build two houses this week, we'll fail at our *real* mission, which is building community. We use *their* tools so we understand the challenges they face. We want to get to know them and their needs.' As she talked of the transient, despair-filled lives of the townspeople who lived in cardboard houses, I began to understand the true nature of our mission.

"We *are* really building a community, not just homes, so that these people can put down roots instead of being drawn to the big cities where subsistence jobs and horrid living conditions await. Now that the project has built almost two hundred houses, the people themselves have built a church! They've started a store! Those whose houses are already finished can't wait to help build one for their neighbors."

Linda added, "But if they have a choice between finishing a house or sitting down to an extra meal with us, they'll choose the meal every time. They place a much higher value on relationships than we do. We fit in best when we leave our watches behind and focus on friendships rather than tasks. Right now, we can only stay there a few weeks at a time, but we continually feel *connected*."

Ed spoke earnestly about spotting new needs and meeting them. "My son joined us last year. He pointed out the children dodging cars in the road to play soccer. So this year we are helping them build a children's center and playing field. Because they know we'll be back, they've grown to trust us *and* they are willing to join with us."

Linda nodded. "The town is now a magnet for people who want a more stable home. As they settle, they can't help but learn of the active role that Christ plays in the lives of their new neighbors. As we carry bricks and linger over meals, we know that it is really God at work building their community. We just get to be God's hands."

Do you have the spiritual gift of apostleship?

_____ I am excited about working in multiple church settings and diverse religious communities.

_____ I am interested in how the Gospel can be brought to those who have never heard it.

_____ I am attracted to new ministries, churches, or settings at home or abroad where a whole new approach to evangelism or service is needed.

_____ Presenting the Gospel to a different culture or in a different language sounds fulfilling.

_____ The idea of living in or visiting different places excites me.

_____ I have often envisioned myself as a missionary.

Suggestions for developing your spiritual gift of apostleship

1. Begin by taking advantage of the many short-term mission opportunities available today. See if you can thrive in a different culture, local or far away, and minister effectively in that setting.
2. Seek out and interview missionaries or those who have started new ministries. Talk to them about what they consider essential to the success of their efforts. Read biographies of famous missionaries.
3. Consider working with a ministry that works to bring new methods, services, or ideas to many churches or other cultures.

Biblical example

Paul taking the Gospel to Athens (Acts 17:16–34).

GIFTS OF INSPIRATION

Healing, Miracles, Speaking in Tongues, and Interpretation of Tongues

These gifts make us aware of God's power in our lives or provide new energy for the work of God's kingdom.

Healing

The ability to call on God for the curing of illness and the restoration of health in a supernatural way.

Bible reference: Now to each one the manifestation of the Spirit is given for the common good . . . to another gifts of healing by that one Spirit. (1 Corinthians 12:7, 9)

In *Light in My Darkest Night,*[6] Catherine Marshall tells of her personal struggle with the death of her infant granddaughter despite the fervent prayers and efforts of many Christians, including sixteen friends who joined her family for a four-day prayer retreat. One of these friends, Jamie Buckingham, related how during a prayer session for the baby, he suddenly remembered a letter from a friend who asked for prayers for a little girl who was dying of cystic fibrosis. Jamie realized that the little girl was in the very same hospital. He found her room and stepped into a crazed scene as two nurses worked to restore the child's breathing. He asked if he could pray for her:

> "Lord, heal this child in Jesus' name," I prayed. It was brief. Just a few sentences, then I withdrew my hand and was gone. It was not until after I returned to my home in Melbourne, Florida, more than a week later that I got the news. . . . A miracle had happened, [my friend] reported. Remember the little girl with cystic fibrosis who had been dying in the Boston hospital? Well, she has just been released, allowed to go home. The doctors said they must have made a mistake. It wasn't cystic fibrosis after all—because that's incurable. And the child is fine now. Healed completely.

This is the enigma of the gift of healing in the church today: Though both were blanketed in prayer, the Marshall baby died and the other young girl lived. Jamie Buckingham might have denied having the gift of healing, witnessing few miracles and many deaths.

Some say that the gift was more prevalent during apostolic times to strengthen faith, but the same questions arose then. Paul clearly had the gift, as he showed during his stay on Malta:

> There was an estate nearby that belonged to Publius, the chief official of the island. He welcomed us to his home and for three days entertained us hospitably. His father was sick in bed, suffering from fever and dysentery. Paul went in to see him and, after prayer, placed his hands on him and healed him. When this had happened, the rest of the sick on the island came and were cured. (Acts 28:7–9)

---

[6]Catherine Marshall, *Light in My Darkest Night* (Old Tappan, N.J.: Fleming H. Revell Company, 1989).

Yet we read in Philippians 2:25–27 that Paul's close friend Epaphroditus was very sick and nearly died. Trophimus, another friend of Paul's, had to be left behind at Miletus because of illness (2 Timothy 4:20). Apparently Paul could not heal all those who were very ill, and clearly the gift of healing does not function at all times.

The New Testament contains little direct instruction about healing. While Jesus models a vibrant healing ministry for us, much is left as a mystery. Healing is best understood as just one more way we might experience God's love. When healing is elevated above the other spiritual gifts, God's love can get lost in the distraction. Those who are not healed may feel that God disapproves of them. A healing ministry can remain authentic by staying biblical, focusing on God as the healer rather than on those who are doing the praying.

People with the gift of healing are without exception good listeners. They listen to God, following inner leadings on when to speak, when to stay silent, and how to pray. They listen to the sick, discerning the root causes of illness, whether physical, emotional, relational, or spiritual. Occasionally the sick have heard too many healing prayers; they just want to talk to a friend.

Those with the gift of healing operate out of compassion and view using this gift as an act of humble obedience to God. Rather than seeing healing prayer as something to aspire to, they see it as a normal part of the Christian life. They pray with confidence, believing that God is present and that prayer can overcome any evil influence hindering a person. They also pray honestly, making sure that those they pray for understand that not all are healed and that the whys and wherefores are truly a mystery.

Do you have the spiritual gift of healing?

_____ I am naturally drawn to those who are sick either in spirit or in body.

_____ Sometimes God seems to work through me to bring physical, spiritual, relational, or emotional healing to others.

_____ I am aware of God's presence and listen for God's guidance on how to pray in each situation where healing is desired.

_____ Often I can sense whether a person's problems are physical or emotional in origin.

_____ When petitions for healing are spoken, I find myself wanting to pray.

Suggestions for developing your spiritual gift of healing

1. Seek out people who are already operating in this gift. Observe their methods. If possible, meet regularly for prayer and support.
2. As a source of encouragement for yourself, journal or record the places where you see God at work in healing ministries, through your own prayers or those of others.
3. Remember not to be discouraged if people aren't healed the first time you pray. Sometimes multiple prayers result in healing; sometimes God has another agenda.

Miracles

The ability to call on God to do supernatural acts that glorify God.

> *Bible reference:* Now to each one the manifestation of the Spirit is given for the common good. To one there is given through the Spirit . . . miraculous powers. (1 Corinthians 12:7–8, 10)

By definition, a miracle is an act or event that is contrary to natural laws, exhibiting God's power over disease, evil, nature, matter, or life itself. In the Bible, miracles often help people see who God is and open the way for faith. The book of Acts is filled with accounts of miracles that gave authority to the testimony of the apostles as they spread the Gospel. We see no ill effects from a snake bite (Acts 28:1–6), people being raised from the dead (Acts 9:36–42), and more.

Do miracles still happen? What appears as a miracle to some will be explained as coincidence by others. However, some people's lives are filled with so many of these "coincidences" that the term *miracle* begins to be appropriate.

Corrie ten Boom was imprisoned in a Nazi concentration camp for her work in hiding Jewish people.[7] Both she and her sister Betsie were in their mid-fifties at the time of their arrest, not at all prepared to withstand the horrors of prison life. In defiance of their circumstances they used every opportunity to help others and share their faith.

Bibles were forbidden. Corrie hid hers inside her thin cotton

[7]Corrie ten Boom, with John and Elisabeth Sherrill, *The Hiding Place* (Old Tappan, N.J.: Chosen Books, 1971).

dress as the guards searched them during their arrival at Ravens-bruck. The woman in front of her was frisked three times; Betsie and everyone behind her were searched thoroughly. Corrie was never touched. Her Bible was used for study and worship services in the barracks. So many of the prisoners wanted to participate that they held two gatherings each day.

Then there was the matter of the vitamins. Corrie managed to smuggle in a small sample-size bottle of vitamins for Betsie, who was ill. Betsie refused to hoard it for herself, sharing the precious drops with two dozen other women every day. Even with so many partaking, every time Corrie tipped the bottle another drop appeared. Then one day a friendly guard slipped them a sack full of vitamins, enough for all. Ever practical, Corrie decided that before they touched the new supply, they would finish the bottled drops first. She was unable to coax even one more drop from the bottle. It was completely empty!

After her release, Corrie founded a ministry to ex-prisoners and war victims, including the Nazis who had caused so many to suffer. In 1959, she returned to Ravensbruck to honor her sister and the other 96,000 women who had died there. Only then did she learn that her release was the result of a clerical "error." Just a few days after she was freed, all of the women her age had been sent to the gas chamber.

While some would dismiss these incidences as coincidences, events like these characterized Corrie's life. In the midst of circumstances as trying as those faced by the early church, Corrie prayed and saw her prayers answered in mysterious ways time after time.

People with this gift recognize that their prayers are sometimes answered in ways that defy explanation. Many also have a strong gift of faith and therefore wait confidently for God to act. They are convinced of their own powerlessness apart from God. Rather than specify how God should act to deliver them or others from a situation or what kind of miracle God should perform, those with the spiritual gift of miracles simply pray, as did Corrie and her sister.

Today miracles still seem to occur where faith is most needed, authenticating the Gospel in the same way the miracles performed by the apostles did in the early church. Some people believe, though, that when we focus too much on visible miracles we neglect the many inner healings, courageous efforts, and conversions that are brought about by prayer. Jesus pointed to this when

He healed the lame man lowered through the roof: "Which is easier: to say to the paralytic, 'Your sins are forgiven,' or to say, 'Get up, take your mat and walk'? But that you may know that the Son of Man has authority on earth to forgive sins. . . ." He said to the paralytic, "I tell you, get up, take your mat and go home" (Mark 2:9–11). Jesus used the external miracle to authenticate the internal miracle—the kind of miracle that can last an eternity.

Do you have the spiritual gift of miracles?

_____ I find myself praying for things that are obviously beyond the natural capacity of people.

_____ I seek for God to be glorified however my prayers are answered.

_____ I have witnessed God perform supernatural acts when I have prayed for intervention.

_____ I have seen others accept the Christian faith through these displays of the impossible being accomplished.

_____ I have faith that miracles happen even today.

_____ Often I see God at work when others only see coincidences.

Suggestions for developing your spiritual gift of miracles

1. If you believe that miracles is one of your spiritual gifts, become involved in a small group of mature Christians who can hold you accountable as you minister to others.

2. Study the role of miracles in the Bible. Understand God's purposes in allowing miracles to occur.

3. Keep a journal of prayer requests and how they are answered. While moving mountains may be difficult, those who record prayer in this way often see a pattern of God at work.

Speaking in Tongues and Interpretation of Tongues

The ability to speak in a language, known or unknown to others, supernaturally, or to interpret such languages.

> _Bible reference:_ Now to each one the manifestation of the Spirit is given for the common good . . . to another speaking in different kinds of tongues, and to still another the interpretation of tongues. (1 Corinthians 12:7, 10)

When the day of Pentecost had come, they were all together

in one place. And suddenly from heaven there came a sound like the rush of a violent wind, and it filled the entire house where they were sitting. Divided tongues, as of fire, appeared among them, and a tongue rested on each of them. All of them were filled with the Holy Spirit and began to speak in other languages, as the Spirit gave them ability.

Now there were devout Jews from every nation under heaven living in Jerusalem. And at this sound the crowd gathered and was bewildered, because each one heard them speaking in the native language of each. Amazed and astonished, they asked, "Are not all these who are speaking Galileans? And how is it that we hear, each of us, in our own native language? Parthians, Medes, Elamites, and residents of Mesopotamia, Judea and Cappadocia, Pontus and Asia, Phrygia and Pamphylia, Egypt and the parts of Libya belonging to Cyrene, and visitors from Rome, both Jews and proselytes, Cretans and Arabs—in our own languages we hear them speaking about God's deeds of power." All were amazed and perplexed, saying to one another, "What does this mean?" But others sneered and said, "They are filled with new wine" (Acts 2:1–13 NRSV).

Two thousand years later, the general reaction to the gift of tongues has not changed very much. It was as divisive a subject then as it is now. Paul devotes the entire fourteenth chapter of 1 Corinthians to the subject of the proper role of tongues in the church. In contrast, Paul gives little or no explanation of the other spiritual gifts in the rest of his writings.

Many believe that God uses the gift of tongues to circumvent our rational minds. Experientially, many people receive personal prayer languages, sometimes referred to as praying in tongues. In his book *How to Be Pentecostal Without Speaking in Tongues*, Tony Campolo describes the difference:

> *Speaking* in tongues occurs when an individual becomes a "mouthpiece for God" and has a special message from God for the church. The "words" that such a person utters are in an "unknown language." The apostle Paul contends that when someone is exercising this gift, someone should be on hand who has the gift of interpretation (1 Corinthians 12:10). Otherwise, says Paul, all that we have on our hands are some vain babblings. . . .
>
> *Praying* in tongues is quite another thing. Sometimes the feelings and yearnings of a Christian are so intense and so

profound that the ordinary words of human languages cannot express them. There are occasions when what is happening in the mind is so awesome that there are no words in the common vocabulary that can convey its meaning. According to Pentecostals, it is in such times that the individual can become surrendered to God and let the Holy Spirit prompt in him or her prayers and praise in sounds that make no sense to anyone who may be listening. These sounds are not meant to be interpreted because they are not a message from God. Instead these "words" are "groanings" of the heart of the Christian. (Romans 8:26)[8]

The gift of tongues is definitely present in the church today in some form; the important factor is ensuring that it is kept in perspective. Contrary to what some argue, the gift of tongues is not the only sign of "baptism in the Holy Spirit." Paul says, "I thank God that I speak in tongues more than all of you. But in the church I would rather speak five intelligible words to instruct others than ten thousand words in a tongue" (1 Corinthians 14:18–19). Further, many spiritual giants such as John Wesley, George Müller, and Dwight L. Moody never spoke in tongues. If you have the gift of tongues, use it for the benefit of others and your own spiritual life. If you do not have it, understand that God does not command us to speak in tongues. The presence of the Holy Spirit is the important thing.

There is also the separate gift of interpretation of tongues. As someone speaks in a spiritual tongue, people with the gift of interpretation of tongues can often understand what is being said. Many times they understand only the first few words and need to begin interpreting aloud before the rest of the message is revealed to them. As with the spiritual gifts of prophecy, teaching, and wisdom, we are called to test the spirit of what has been said and interpreted before acknowledging it to be true.

Do you have the spiritual gift of tongues?

_____ I have prayed in words or language(s) I have never before heard.

_____ Sometimes in prayer, my love for God feels so strong that I have difficulty expressing myself in words.

[8]Tony Campolo, *How to Be Pentecostal Without Speaking in Tongues* (Word Publishing, 1991), 32.

_____ I have been inspired or have inspired others to step out in faith through the use of personal prayer languages.

_____ I find during worship that my tongue wants to express itself in syllables I do not understand.

Suggestions for developing your spiritual gift of tongues

1. Be aware of our modern bias toward the concrete, material world and its denial of those things we cannot see or explain. During prayer time, pray aloud. Allow yourself to be open to this manifestation of the Holy Spirit; allow the tongues to express your feelings.
2. Find a prayer group or fellowship where you may freely express yourself through this gift.
3. Talk to leaders in your Christian fellowship about how they might be open to this expression of faith. Pray for interpreters to be identified.

Do you have the spiritual gift of the interpretation of tongues?

_____ I can interpret the words of others who have spoken in languages ("tongues"), even though I have never before heard the languages.

_____ I understand how messages given through the use of tongues serve to glorify God and our faith.

_____ When somebody speaks in tongues, I sense the Holy Spirit giving me the ability to interpret or speak.

Suggestions for developing your gift of interpretation of tongues

1. Place yourself in atmospheres where the gift of tongues is used (a prayer group, worship services, or conference settings, for example).
2. If you believe you have been given the first part of a message, step out in faith and begin to speak that interpretation aloud. Trust God to give you the rest of the meaning as you speak.
3. Ask those around you to give you feedback about the accuracy of your interpretations from their perspective.

Drawing Conclusions About Your Spiritual Gifts

Based on reading the spiritual gift descriptions and reading the common characteristics of people with each gift, rate whether you have each spiritual gift as follows:

5. This is definitely one of my spiritual gifts.
4. This is probably one of my spiritual gifts.
3. I am unsure—I need to learn more about this gift or experiment with ways to use this gift to find out if I have it.
2. This is probably not one of my spiritual gifts.
1. This is definitely not one of my spiritual gifts.

Gifts of the Heart

_____ Helps
_____ Hospitality
_____ Mercy
_____ Faith
_____ Giving

Gifts of Proclamation

_____ Evangelism
_____ Teaching
_____ Discernment
_____ Knowledge
_____ Prophecy
_____ Wisdom

Gifts of Action

_____ Leadership
_____ Administration
_____ Shepherding
_____ Encouragement/
Counseling
_____ Apostleship

Gifts of Inspiration

_____ Healing
_____ Miracles
_____ Tongues
_____ Interpretation of
Tongues

Regardless of the scores you gave them, highlight your top three to five spiritual gifts and record them in "My _LifeKeys_ Notations," on pages 286–287.

LifeKey #4

If you know yourself, you can find your God-given place.

CHAPTER 4

PERSONALITY TYPES—MELODIES FOR LIFE

It is not too much to hope that wider and deeper understanding of the gifts of diversity may eventually reduce the misuse and nonuse of those gifts. It should lessen the waste of potential, the loss of opportunity.[1]

—Isabel Briggs Myers

Picture yourself as a violinist. Do thoughts of symphonies, concert halls, formal dress, and chamber music appeal to you? Now picture yourself as a fiddler. Are you excited by thoughts of barn dances, jeans, and toe-tapping fun? Most people are more attracted to either the violin or the fiddle, yet *they are the same instrument.* We simply call it by a different name when it is used in different places. Fiddles aren't played at concert halls and violins aren't played at country western halls. And those who choose to play the violin or the fiddle are attracted to markedly different atmospheres!

Fiddlers and violinists not only play different kinds of music, but interact differently with their audiences, follow different dress codes, and practice in different ways. A few musicians play both "violin" and "fiddle," but most choose one or the other.

God gives us certain preferences, causing certain places or settings to appeal to us, including the places where we work, play, serve, and worship. Much of what appeals to us is related to our personality type. While there are dozens of books on personality type and its various applications, from corporate team building to

[1]Isabel Briggs Myers with Peter B. Myers, *Gifts Differing: Understanding Personality Type* (Mountain View, Calif.: Davies-Black Publishing, 1995).

marriage counseling—some even written by us—here, in these comparatively few pages, we use the concepts of type as a tool for finding the places or atmospheres that appeal to you.

Your personality type is really your essential nature, a framework for describing your strengths and preferences for gaining energy, gathering information, making decisions, and approaching life. Each type is equally valid and valuable—just like violins and fiddles—but each approaches life in a way that differs from other types.

Imagine it this way: You've always been a fiddler, but some significant person in your life convinces you to try the violin. So there you are, donning a tuxedo for the first time in your life. You have to follow the director exactly. No playing faster just to see how the dancers handle it. No last-minute changes in the program for audience requests. And no talking or singing allowed while you play! You might think that sounds great—you like order, harmony, and working with others. But you also might wonder if playing your violin in a concert hall produces "real" music. Its precision preempts your style. You could just put on a recording and go home.

Neither kind of music is better or worse, just different. In the same way, no personality type is better or worse, just different in its approach to living. Most of us grew up with siblings or are the parent of more than one child; we've experienced the widespread differences in behavior even within a single family.

These differences are natural, God-given aspects of personality. Being who you are—the person God intended you to be—is of paramount importance. No one else has been crafted quite like you. Besides that, the differences make life interesting. Can you imagine what the world would be like if everyone were just like you—your gifts and your shortcomings magnified by the billions?

The Concept of Preferences

To help you understand your unique, God-given personality, we will be using a theoretical construct based on Jungian psychology and popularized through the Myers-Briggs Type Indicator tool (MBTI®). Carl Jung, the son of a minister, was intensely interested in spiritual matters. A sign over the doorway of his home read, "Seek or not, God is there." He saw personality type as a tool through which we can better understand ourselves and therefore deepen that spiritual part of us. Many religious denominations use Jungian theory to help people explore who they are personally and spiritually.

Jung theorized that a person's behavior is far from random. When he carefully observed others, patterns emerged that point to inherent preferences. To better grasp this concept of preferences, think about your *preferred* hand for writing. Try signing your name in the space below with your preferred hand, right or left:

_____

Writing with your preferred hand is easy, natural, and comfortable. Now do the same with your non-preferred hand:

_____

Note how long it took and how the quality of the output differed. Writing with your non-preferred hand is awkward, unnatural, and slow. With enough practice, you can improve the output of your less preferred hand, yet most people still gravitate toward the *preferred hand.*

Similarly, we have personality preferences. We can use any of the preferences, but we *prefer* the ones that are more natural. As we describe each of the eight preferences, you can keep track of those that seem to best describe you. The preferences are commonly referred to by the following names and letters:

Extraversion (E) or Introversion (I)   How we gain energy

Sensing (S) or Intuition (N)[2]   How we take in information

Thinking (T) or Feeling (F)   How we make decisions

Judging (J) or Perceiving (P)   How we approach life

---

[2]N is used for Intuition, since I already stands for Introversion.

These eight preferences mix and match for sixteen distinct personality types that can be identified by their four-letter codes. Every one of the sixteen personality types has its own strengths and contributions to make to society, the work we do, and the atmospheres where we choose to live and work.

If you choose tasks, work settings, or occupations that are not a good fit for your personality, you may often feel tired and discouraged—like a fiddler trapped in a tux! It's more wearing on you to use your less-preferred processes, much like what you experienced when writing with your non-preferred hand. You feel discouraged by the fact that even your greater efforts can't match the quality you produce when you use *preferred* processes. Not only that, but if you choose to work in a setting that uses your less-preferred processes, you will no doubt be surrounded by people who are using their preferred processes and love what they do. This can make you feel even more inept or out of place.

So let's learn about the preferences, find the type that best describes you, and apply that information to identifying the settings God causes to appeal to you the most.

How We Are Energized—Extraversion or Introversion

Sandra: During my graduate studies, I was offered a plum internship—great company with a good chance of permanent work, excellent pay, an impressive office with a nice view, and responsibilities in line with my life gifts and my passion for being of service to others. However, my interactions with people were mostly via computer and telephone, not face-to-face. In fact, there were only three other people nearby, each in an office fortress similar to mine. When I answered the phone, my voice echoed down the corridor, *Hello, hello, hello, hello....* Without actual contact with people, I felt unmotivated, lonely, and isolated—as if I were swimming in pea soup! Give me an interactive, stimulating workspace any day. Otherwise, I lose my energy.

When I complained to my co-worker in the next office, she said with surprise, "You're kidding! This is the best situation I've ever had. Lots of peace and quiet, someone answering the phones and guarding against interruptions so I don't lose my train of thought.... I love it here. This spot energizes me!"

People are *energized* in one of two ways, through Extraversion or Introversion. Those with a preference for Extraversion enjoy action, interaction, and activity. While not all Extraverts want to be the life of the party, they are still energized by the people and things around them.

Extraverts tend to function best in settings where they can work as a part of a group or team and where the results are tangible. They are often generalists who possess a breadth of knowledge about many subjects. They process their thoughts by talking out loud, receiving input from others, and then modifying their ideas based on those interactions.

In contrast, people with a preference for Introversion are energized by their inner world of thoughts and ideas. While as many Introverts jog or bike as Extraverts, they are more likely to be in their own inner world, drawing their energy from contemplation instead of from the activity itself. They like quiet, enjoy their own company, and seek privacy.

Introverts tend to prefer settings where they can work alone or one-on-one. Often the fruit of their labor is more conceptual, with a narrower, specialized focus. Their knowledge may run deep in a few selected areas or topics. They prefer to process their thoughts silently, sharing them only when they are well formulated or, preferably, finalized.

As an Extravert, Sandra struggled with her solitary setting; her

Introverted co-worker found it ideally suited to her. Some of you may clearly identify with Sandra; others with her co-worker.

Keep in mind that Extraversion and Introversion are not about sociability—they relate, in this context, to the concept of energy, not shyness or other social qualities.

As you look through the following lists, think about the word or phrase in each row that most appeals to you (you may wish to check the ones you choose and add up the marks in each column):

Settings That Appeal to Extraversion

☐ Lots going on, active
☐ Interruptions are stimulating, fun
☐ Outgoing, communicative atmosphere
☐ Group or team approach
☐ Discussion for processing ideas
☐ Busy, energetic places
☐ Thoughts and feelings shared readily
☐ Experimentation, then reflection
☐ Focus on the outer world
☐ Emphasis on people and things

Settings That Appeal to Introversion

☐ One thing going on, reflective
☐ Interruptions are distracting, annoying
☐ Reserved, protective atmosphere
☐ Solo or partnership approach
☐ Introspection for processing ideas
☐ Quiet, contemplative places
☐ Thoughts and feelings guarded until ready to share
☐ Reflection, then experimentation
☐ Focus on the inner world
☐ Emphasis on thoughts and ideas

If you are unsure whether Extraverted or Introverted atmospheres are most appealing to you, place yourself in the story about Sandra's quiet, isolated office space. Do you share Sandra's opinion (E) or are you more like her co-worker (I)?

Circle which setting appeals to you if other factors were equal:

E (Extraversion)   I (Introversion)

What Gets Your Attention?–Sensing or Intuition

Jane: Fresh out of college, I worked as a bank examiner. A good bank examiner follows procedures, is detail-oriented, and seldom makes errors of fact. The *best* examiners repeat tried-and-true processes in the same way at each bank. Good job, high visibility, great place to start a career. However ... I kept asking, "Why are we doing things this way? What if we tried another procedure? Couldn't we computerize this part so I can avoid making mistakes?" I often annoyed my co-workers with my "hunches" that a bank was doing something wrong, but struggled to provide the step-by-step proof the other examiners needed to understand the accuracy of my hunches. I felt like a troublemaker, even though I was just trying to make things better by finding ways to improve the process. Fortunately, I soon moved to a special projects group where we were *supposed* to look at things differently.

Another examiner couldn't understand my choice. "Why would anyone leave?" he asked. "Once you know the ropes, you know *exactly* what's expected of you, and the more you do it, the more efficient you become. I enjoy the certainty the job gives me. It's a good job for me." And it was for him, but not for me.

There are two ways of perceiving, or *gathering information.* People with a preference for *Sensing* pay attention to the information gathered through their five senses. Sounds, sights, textures, and details constitute their domain. They are generally good at identifying *what is.* They like to work with people or real things that clearly represent factual reality. Career success is perceived to be a progression from entry level through to mastery (i.e., bank examiner trainee, assistant examiner, examiner, senior examiner, and so on).

In contrast, those with a preference for *Intuition* pay attention to *what could be*—their hunches, analogies, or connections with other knowledge. It's almost as though they rely on their sixth sense more than the other five. Intuitives like places and settings where the emphasis is on new developments and finding possibilities. They define career success as the ability to make career changes as needed (i.e., from bank examiner to research specialist to bank controller to consultant).

As an Intuitive, Jane struggled to be a good examiner but excelled when new ideas were required. Her co-worker's preference for Sensing meant that working with the tried and true while improving upon what *already* worked was the road to satisfaction.

As you look through the following lists, consider which setting would be most appealing to you. Check your choices:

Settings That Appeal to Sensing	Settings That Appeal to Intuition
☐ Practical, commonsense focus	☐ Innovative, insightful focus
☐ Accuracy required	☐ Creativity required
☐ Past experience valued	☐ Inspiration valued
☐ Methodical approaches used	☐ Novel approaches used
☐ Current reality emphasis	☐ Future possibilities emphasis
☐ Rewards for following procedures	☐ Rewards for finding a better way
☐ Improving the real world	☐ Designing the ideal world
☐ Practical application of learning is key	☐ Theoretical understanding of learning is key
☐ Command of details, procedures is honored	☐ Agility, making connections, and hunches are honored
☐ Predictable routines	☐ Variety, unpredictability

If you are unsure whether you prefer Sensing or Intuitive work settings, think back to the story of Jane and her co-worker. Do you naturally notice and pay attention to things as they are (S), or are you more likely to pay attention to seeing the possibilities (N)? Sensing types might say, "A rose is a rose is a rose." Intuitive types might say, "A rose ... that makes me think of my high school prom."

Circle which settings fit you best:

S (Sensing)   N (Intuition)

When Faced With a Decision—Thinking or Feeling

David: With a father who is a geologist, botanist, and ornithologist, my family valued scientific thinking and logical analysis of issues. No hike in the mountains was complete until every plant had been identified down to the genus and species. What could be more natural than for me to head for graduate school in horticulture and agronomy? I had lofty dreams of using my knowledge to fight world hunger.

I soon found myself the comic relief in an immunology lab amidst a group of logical, objective colleagues. My behavior was probably an instinctive attempt to cope with the analytical procedures I had to follow all day long. When a new professor announced that the next round of lab work would be the most rigorous yet, I found myself wondering not how I would pass, but how others in the class were *feeling* about the assignments. Did they fear for their grade-point averages? Would any of them have time to come to the evening Bible study I taught?

The last straw for my scientific career came as I classified weeds in a farm field. Bent over in the hot sun for hours, scribbling numbers in my notebook, alone and very lonely, I made an instant decision that helping people through the Bible studies I taught suited me *much more* than fighting hunger through the logical, detached grid work of science. I almost shouted, "Eureka!"

As I cleaned out my locker, my lab partner remarked, "How can you give this up? We've made such progress on these plant diseases." His *mind* was set on scientific progress, but my *heart* was in a different place—how to directly help people.

Although we are often taught otherwise, there are truly two valid, *rational ways of making decisions.* People with a preference for *Thinking* like to work in settings where decisions are based on logic, consistency, and fairness. Once they have objectively analyzed the situation, they are ready to proceed. Generally, while Thinkers are interested in building relationships with co-workers, they are *more* interested in the tasks to be completed. The career of a Thinker often includes objective criteria, goals, or milestones focused on attaining academic degrees or other credentials, product improvements, new competencies, etc.

In contrast, people with a preference for *Feeling* include values or priorities in their decision-making process. Typically, their values have to do with the needs of the people involved. The Feeler's process is still rational, although not logical. Feelers often consider their business relationships as important as the work they do. Feelers are most at home in settings where they can focus on best outcomes for people and work in concert with their own personal values. The careers of Feelers need to provide meaning or purpose—they may even turn down promotions if the new responsibilities remove them too far from the people and projects they care about.

David's life was enriched by his scientific studies (and you should hear him preach using gerbera daisy analogies!), but as a Feeler he prefers meeting people's needs rather than finding objective truth.

In the context of personality type, Feeling does not mean *emotional.* It is a larger concept related to decision making. *Feelers can be just as intellectual as Thinkers; Thinkers can hold caring values just like Feelers.* However, their priorities and decision-making styles differ. As you read through the following lists, think about the way decisions are approached in settings that honor Thinking and Feeling. Which setting sounds most appealing to you?

Settings That Appeal to Thinking

- [ ] Emphasis is on logic, analysis

- [ ] Ideas for data and things
- [ ] Decisions made fairly but firmly—few exceptions

- [ ] Business first—orientation toward task
- [ ] Recognition desired for meeting or exceeding task requirements
- [ ] Analyze—find the flaw
- [ ] Objective—decisions made with the head
- [ ] Skepticism and controversy enrich productivity
- [ ] Drive for competency
- [ ] Reasons—clear rules and principles

Settings That Appeal to Feeling

- [ ] Emphasis is on harmony, diplomacy
- [ ] Ideas for people
- [ ] Decisions made empathetically—considering the circumstances

- [ ] Camaraderie first—orientation toward people
- [ ] Praise desired for personal effort as tasks unfold
- [ ] Sympathize—find the positive
- [ ] Subjective—decisions made with the heart
- [ ] Acceptance and sympathy enrich productivity
- [ ] Drive for relationship-building
- [ ] Values—discerning what is important to each person involved

If you are unsure whether Thinking or Feeling atmospheres are most appealing to you, place yourself in David's story. Are you more likely to make decisions based on objective truths (T), as do scientists and attorneys, for example? Or, are you more likely to work toward the most tactful and agreeable outcome for those involved (F), as do counselors and people-oriented professionals? Are you more excited by the research process (T) or by outcomes for people (F)? With whom do you most identify?

Circle which atmosphere best describes the way you approach decisions:

T (Thinking)   F (Feeling)

Do You Plan Your Moves or Go With the Flow?–Judging or Perceiving

We like being a team—working together on LifeKeys. *However, we have slightly different approaches . . .*

Jane, who comes to meetings with a separate file of materials for each chapter, says, "Hey, if we're going to finish this book of eight chapters in four months, let's nail down the structure by this Tuesday. Then we can meet twice a week and finish a chapter every two weeks, okay?"

Sandra and David, who come to meetings with loose papers and heads full of ideas, say, "If we're going to write a book, let's start with a chapter and stay with it until we hit a block or get bored, then move on to another chapter. In fact, let's work on several chapters at the same time up to the *very* deadline and then put it all together. Sounds like a plan to us."

"Yikes," says Jane, "and the worst of it is I know that your ideas tend to get better *the closer we get to the deadline*. But then I have to make all of those changes on *my* computer. . . ."

Yes, there are two *approaches to life*. Those with a preference for *Judging* (J) like to plan their work and work their plan. (Any guesses as to which one of us has a preference for Judging?) Providing organization and structure to any endeavor is truly a calling for Jane and other Judging types. While not all Judging types organize for the fun of it, they are attracted to places where there is a *reason* for order. Examples might be tax offices (where filing systems are crucial since penalties are substantial) and operating rooms (where people can be harmed by disarray). They tend to believe that work should come first so that they can then be free to play. A great meeting, Judging types might say, is a planned meeting.

By comparison, those with a preference for *Perceiving* (P) find that planning can get in the way of living life to the fullest. Perceivers seek to be open and spontaneous as they adapt to what comes their way, and they enjoy environments that call for flexibility. Examples are journalism (where the best reporters are open to late-breaking developments) and building renovation or repair (where no one is certain what the job will entail). Most Perceivers, like David and Sandra, like play to be a part of their work—they try to make life *and* work more fun. Meetings that are best, say Perceivers, are those that deal with whatever is needed to get the job done.

Remember that *Judging in this context does not mean being judgmental, but wanting to come to closure (judgments) on things. Similarly, Perceiving does not imply being more perceptive, but the enjoyment of searching for more options (the act of perceiving information).*

As you read through the following lists, think about the settings you like and the way you approach life. Check the phrases that describe the atmospheres in which you do your best work:

Settings That Appeal to Judging

- ☐ Organized and efficient

- ☐ Emphasis on planning projects and events
- ☐ Planning ahead is key to reducing stress
- ☐ Settled and decided

- ☐ Work before play
- ☐ Much is accomplished through regular, steady effort

Settings That Appeal to Perceiving

- ☐ Flexible, allowing for multiple tasks
- ☐ Emphasis on allowing projects and events to unfold
- ☐ Allowing for contingencies is key to reducing stress
- ☐ Open to late-breaking information
- ☐ Work and play coexist
- ☐ Much is accomplished through last-minute effort

☐ Focus on tasks and timetables
☐ Stated goals and outcomes
☐ Emphasis on coming to closure on decisions
☐ Enjoy finishing tasks

☐ Focus on processes and options
☐ Stated general parameters
☐ Emphasis on gathering new information before deciding
☐ Enjoy starting tasks

Now place yourself in our working group. Do you like to have a plan like Jane (J), or stay open to information as you gather it, like Sandra and David (P)? Which approach works for you?

Circle the atmosphere in which you can be most effective:

J (Judging)   P (Perceiving)

Based on the above descriptors, what are the preferences that best describe the places or atmospheres that appeal to you? Use the spaces below to record your four-letter type:

_____	_____	_____	_____
E or I	S or N	T or F	J or P

Not to keep any secrets, Jane finds that preferences for INFJ describe her best; Sandra and David, ENFP.

The next sixteen pages give you a description of each type, providing more details of the places or atmospheres that appeal to each one. If you are uncertain about some of your preferences, read both pages to see if one sounds more like you. For example, if you think your preferences are for IST but are undecided between the J and the P, read both the ISTJ and ISTP pages.[3]

The type pages contain several different pieces of information:

• contributions to the community or workplace (your special way of adding value to teams, organizations, or spiritual communities)

• preferred settings for work or service (your places or settings for enhanced effectiveness)

• leadership style (how you motivate others)

---

[3]To become more clear about your preferences, you can take the MBTI® tool, which is a questionnaire designed to help you sort your preferences on the same four dimensions. Ask your minister or local community education program or call the publisher of the MBTI® tool, Consulting Psychologists Press, at 800–624–1765 (www.cpp.com).

- typical tasks (the responsibilities or service opportunities you find enjoyable)
- typical occupations (a sample of common careers, in alphabetical order)
- suggestions for growth (avenues for personal development)

As you read your type page(s), highlight those statements or descriptions that seem to fit you and put a question mark after things that do not seem to describe you. Note that *within* each of the sixteen types there is great diversity. At the end of the chapter, we will look at what the Bible hints at concerning personality type and delve further into settings preferred by various types.

Use the following questions to guide you as you read through the page bearing the four letters you chose for yourself:

- What factors are important to me as I choose places or settings to work or serve?
- In what ways does my current setting conflict with or enhance my natural style? Where am I and my setting the same/different?
- What factors do I want to seek in new settings to be as effective and satisfied as possible?
- What things can I do to change my current setting or my attitude toward it?

As you discover ways in which your personality type might influence the places or atmospheres you choose to work or serve, record your observations in "My *LifeKeys* Notations," pages 286–287.

ISTJ

Your dominant function is Sensing: Seek settings where factual details and accuracy are important.

Your auxiliary function is Thinking: Seek settings where objectivity and logic are important.

Contributions to Workplace or Spiritual Community

- Being dutiful and responsible conservers of tradition
- Having hardworking, dependable, and pragmatic habits
- Using past experience effectively
- Bringing order and logic to what they do
- Working accurately with details, schedules, and documents

Leadership Style

- Bring a traditional and analytical approach to leadership
- Offer a daily focus on what needs to be done to keep things "ship-shape"
- Use an efficient, factual perspective
- Selected by others to lead because of past trustworthiness
- Follow procedures, emphasizing reliability, stability, and consistency

Common Occupations

- Accountant
- Computer professional
- Dentist
- Electrician
- Math teacher
- Manager/administrator: government, corporate, small business
- Mechanical engineer
- Police supervisor
- School principal

Preferred Atmospheres for Work or Service

- Quiet atmosphere that allows for privacy
- Goals met at a steady pace
- Experienced, committed co-workers
- Focus is on tangible tasks
- Expectations known: clear, well-documented procedures
- Stable assignments and responsibilities

Typical Responsibilities or Tasks

- Individual, behind-the-scenes, hands-on assignments or projects
- Administrative areas, especially organizational, financial, record-keeping
- Managerial or general office tasks to keep things running smoothly
- Oversee or perform routine maintenance responsibilities
- Efforts to establish procedures or document what worked

Suggestions for Growth

- Set priorities and be careful of taking on too much out of a sense of duty.
- Step back from the details, talk with others about the big picture.
- Approach change by naming what is best about the past while being open to what can be improved.
- Allow for mistakes by you or others.

Hold them in the highest regard in love because of their work.
(1 Thessalonians 5:13)

ISTP

Your dominant function is Thinking: Seek settings where objectivity and logic are important.

Your auxiliary function is Sensing: Seek settings where factual details and accuracy are important.

Contributions to Workplace or Spiritual Community

- Finding expeditious ways to handle a project; dispensing with red tape
- Grasping reality to troubleshoot and solve problems
- Contributing quietly, behind the scenes
- Setting an example of authenticity, pointing out hypocrisy
- Sharing a storehouse of facts and details when asked about their *special* interests

Preferred Atmospheres for Work or Service

- Small to medium-sized organizations or pockets of efficiency in bureaucracies
- Minimal rules and requirements, emphasis on autonomy
- Little red tape or roadblocks to efficiency
- Hands-off, egalitarian norms
- Action-oriented co-workers, focused on immediate problems
- Logic and principles are upheld

Leadership Style

- Model crisp, practical, efficient, as-needed leadership
- Use a hands-off style unless situation or people call for more
- Match perseverance, technical orientation, with flexibility and calmness
- Practice non-hierarchical and egalitarian model of authority
- Lead through example and action

Typical Responsibilities or Tasks

- Efforts requiring artisans or craftspeople
- Straightforward, pragmatic, and necessary projects (transportation, repairs, maintenance, etc.)
- Hands-on, physical tasks or venues, such as camp or sports ministries
- Crisis intervention—flood and other kinds of disaster relief
- Set up or maintain technology, computer systems

Common Occupations

- Carpenter
- Construction worker
- Dental hygienist
- Electrical engineer
- Farmer
- Mechanic
- Military personnel
- Pilot
- Probation officer

Suggestions for Growth

- Stay connected to others for personal and spiritual growth—not letting your Introverted side be the only avenue.
- In looking for expedient ways to get jobs done, consciously think about whether your values are honored.
- Be careful of withdrawing from, rather than working on, important relationships.
- Remind yourself that many good things in life defy the rules of logic.

But those who do what is right come to the light so others can see that they are doing what God wants.
(John 3:21 NLT)

149

ESTP

Your dominant function is Sensing: Seek settings where factual details and accuracy are important.

Your auxiliary function is Thinking: Seek settings where objectivity and logic are important.

Contributions to Workplace or Spiritual Community

- Paying attention to what needs doing/fixing right now
- Meeting practical needs in the most efficient way
- Reminding others of the joys of this life, this *present* time
- Solving problems in a straightforward, logical manner
- Finding compromises to get things moving

Leadership Style

- Negotiate, conciliate, or motivate to action
- Bring order out of chaos, managing distractions well
- Find the fastest and most direct way to move a task along
- Offer an uncanny and exquisite sense of timing
- Take charge in crises

Common Occupations

- Auditor
- Business manager, small business owner
- Carpenter or construction worker
- Community health worker
- Craft worker
- Farmer
- Law enforcement
- Marketing or sales professional
- Pilot

Preferred Atmospheres for Work or Service

- Goals are clear yet flexibility exists in how they are met
- Lively, results-oriented co-workers who believe that work and fun can coexist
- Casual, non-bureaucratic organization
- Emphasis on tangible facts, logical processes
- Latest, best resources available to accomplish work efficiently
- Action-oriented, practical focus

Typical Responsibilities or Tasks

- Natural crises and disaster relief
- Activity-oriented organizations or programs, with any age group
- Hands-on projects: production, construction
- Maintenance of physical property
- Efforts where people they know invited them to participate

Suggestions for Growth

- Conquer long-range planning by thinking where you want to be five years from now, then planning backward.
- Be wary of giving the impression that your recreational pursuits are more important than the work at hand.
- Step back from assessing what went wrong to consider the role you may have played.
- Find time for spiritual pursuits in the midst of all your activities.

Anyone who listens to my teaching and follows it is wise, like a person who builds a house on solid rock.
(Matthew 7:24 NLT)

ESTJ

Your dominant function is Thinking: Seek settings where objectivity and logic are important.

Your auxiliary function is Sensing: Seek settings where factual details and accuracy are important.

Contributions to Workplace or Spiritual Community

- Organizing to meet day-to-day concerns
- Using direct experience/memory of what is most efficient
- Demonstrating consistent habits based on principles
- Insisting that "hard questions" be answered and acted upon
- Following through to see that tasks are done correctly, results are seen

Preferred Atmospheres for Work or Service

- Place for everyone/everything and everything in its place
- Past, relevant experience is honored
- Hierarchical structure based on logic of function, role, order
- Leaders seek input but provide direction through a results-oriented plan
- Stable, efficient, and predictable
- With hardworking, task-oriented co-workers who plan times for fun

Leadership Style

- Use a traditional, hierarchical style
- Model preparedness and efficiency
- Define and focus efforts to meet goals
- Marshal people and tasks in a no-nonsense manner
- Make quick, fact-based decisions

Typical Responsibilities or Tasks

- Management and administration—organizing people and projects
- Direct, tangible, need-related efforts
- Working on problematic areas
- Financial management according to goals and schedules
- Team and community projects

Common Occupations

- Government worker, administrator
- Insurance agent or underwriter
- Judge
- Manager or school principal
- Military personnel
- Nursing administrator
- Police officer
- Sales representative
- Teacher: trade or technical

Suggestions for Growth

- Consciously show others how much you appreciate their efforts.
- Rethink tried-and-true methods—where might change be good?
- Study methods that allow you to factor human elements into decisions.
- Take time to reflect on your values, feelings, and the importance of personal and spiritual growth.

Be diligent in these matters, give yourself wholly to them.
(1 Timothy 4:15)

ISFJ

Your dominant function is Sensing: Seek settings where factual details and accuracy are important.

Your auxiliary function is Feeling: Seek settings where personal values and their impact on people are important.

Contributions to Workplace or Spiritual Community

- Providing stability, improving efficiency
- Offering sensible and matter-of-fact attention to daily concerns of people
- Accurately recalling specifics found in conversations and situations— getting the details right
- Adding a sense of dignity and respect to the community
- Honoring commitments; others can rely on them

Leadership Style

- Encourage the best from others
- Organize conscientiously behind the scenes to accomplish tasks
- Enroll people in practical, kind, and cooperative ways
- Lead willingly *if asked*
- Work within systems, structures, and rules

Common Occupations

- Bookkeeper
- Clerical supervisor
- Curator
- Family practice physician
- Librarian
- Medical technologist
- Nurse
- Preschool and elementary teacher or aide
- Religious professional

Preferred Atmospheres for Work or Service

- Secure, predictable, organized setting
- Caring, responsible, courteous co-workers
- Stable, enduring organizations where the emphasis is on serving others, not competitiveness
- Roles and responsibilities are clear
- Commitments honored, past traditions treated sensitively, loyalty rewarded
- Calm, quiet, private atmosphere

Typical Responsibilities or Tasks

- Office administration, financial, and other record keeping
- Places or projects focused on health or medical care for others
- Long-term role in providing practical help to others
- Assist in any task *if* it makes sense
- Service-oriented areas where they can be personal, kind, and sincere

Suggestions for Growth

- Practice working from the facts to several possibilities, concentrating on the big picture.
- Consider taking credit due to you so that you don't miss out on resources for yourself and others.
- Tackle a leadership role that requires your strengths.
- Make sure to take care of your own needs so that you have energy for others.

Pursue righteousness, godliness, faith, love, steadfastness, gentleness.
(1 Timothy 6:11)

ISFP

Your dominant function is Feeling: Seek settings where personal values and their impact on people are important.

Your auxiliary function is Sensing: Seek settings where factual details and accuracy are important.

Contributions to Workplace or Spiritual Community

- Providing caring, gentle, behind-the-scenes help
- Meeting individual needs personally and genuinely
- Offering acts of altruistic charity
- Giving immediate, direct help to people
- Sharing concrete, practical, and precise information when asked

Preferred Atmospheres for Work or Service

- Organizations that contribute to community and/or individual well-being
- Adaptable, flexible, and accepting setting
- Self-employment, small organizations, or pockets of caring in large organization
- Empathetic, cooperative, supportive, harmony-seeking co-workers
- Quiet, private, aesthetically appealing atmosphere
- Emphasis on practical tasks

Leadership Style

- Direct leadership only when no one else will
- Primary responsibility for necessary detail and follow-through
- Considerate, compassionate, tolerant, and forgiving
- Flexible and open to needs of the present
- Lead through praise, not criticism

Typical Responsibilities or Tasks

- Individual efforts that help a team
- Practical and spiritual support to individuals in need
- Nursery, preschool, those with special needs, and elder care
- Craft and artistic endeavors
- Medical, social services, home repair, and other service-oriented arenas

Common Occupations

- Bookkeeper
- Carpenter
- Mechanic
- Nurse
- Office manager
- Physical therapist
- Police detective
- Surveyor
- X-ray technician

Suggestions for Growth

- Consider taking assertiveness training to learn to represent your needs as legitimate.
- Work on establishing boundaries with people so they can help themselves.
- Consider the future ramifications of your interests, activities, and paths.
- When conflicts arise, reflect on ways to work through it rather than avoid it.

Truly I tell you, just as you did it to one of the least of these who are members of my family, you did it to me.
(Matthew 25:40 NRSV)

ESFP

Your dominant function is Sensing: Seek settings where factual details and accuracy are important.

Your auxiliary function is Feeling: Seek settings where personal values and their impact on people are important.

Contributions to Workplace or Spiritual Community

- Reminding others how to appreciate each other and all they have
- Bringing enjoyment to all
- Being generous with time and talents
- Communicating warmth, excitement, and acceptance
- Keeping track of many things at once

Preferred Atmospheres for Work or Service

- Spontaneous yet stable and secure workplace
- Energetic, easygoing co-workers
- Clear roles and responsibilities but room to carry them out with flair or style
- Upbeat, positive, environments—entertainment, hospitality, recreation
- Collaborative team orientation
- Lively, interactive, colorful surroundings

Leadership Style

- Attract others by enthusiasm, optimism, and zest
- Energize people to start a task
- Seek input from all involved before making a binding decision
- Facilitate conflict and crises through a tactful, personal approach
- Link people, practical information, and resources to accomplish tasks

Typical Responsibilities or Tasks

- Action-oriented outreaches or organizations that value spontaneity
- Tangible acts of service: health care, transportation, child care, etc.
- Greeting, visiting, serving people
- Improving workplace or event aesthetics—flowers, food, music, decorations, etc.
- Event planning for community-building celebrations or gatherings

Common Occupations

- Athletic coach
- Child care worker or preschool teacher
- Designer
- Factory or site supervisor
- Office manager or receptionist
- Public health nurse
- Religious educator
- Respiratory therapist
- Transportation worker

Suggestions for Growth

- Make sure that co-workers understand your serious side.
- Consider honing your project and time management skills.
- Avoid being trapped by what others perceive as urgent by using your values to clarify your own needs.
- In evaluating situations, consider new interpretations to get at the big picture.

A cheerful heart is good medicine.
(Proverbs 17:22)

ESFJ

Your dominant function is Feeling: Seek settings where personal values and their impact on people are important.

Your auxiliary function is Sensing: Seek settings where factual details and accuracy are important.

Contributions to Workplace or Spiritual Community

- Preserving traditions from one generation to the next
- Offering a service orientation, warmth and caring
- Making people feel welcome and valued—gracious and giving to others
- Knowing what matters for people and organizations
- Handling tasks efficiently, promptly, and accurately

Leadership Style

- Use take-charge yet take-care style
- Concentrate on relationships and coalitions to accomplish tasks
- Seek others' opinions and invite them into direct service
- Accomplish tasks through cooperative, consensual, and timely plans
- Attention given to each person involved

Common Occupations

- Child care worker
- Cosmetologist
- Dental assistant
- Elementary or secondary schoolteacher
- Home economist
- Nurse/nurse administrator
- Office manager or receptionist
- Religious educator
- Speech pathologist

Preferred Atmospheres for Work or Service

- Stable, efficient settings that value loyalty, teamwork, and sensitivity
- Rewards for conscious attention to detail, time frames, and follow-through
- Practical systems and structures oriented toward people as well as goals
- Conscientious, cooperative, friendly co-workers
- Facts and values are both considered
- Decisiveness is honored

Typical Responsibilities or Tasks

- Management or administrative roles in settings of any size
- Responsibilities directly related to serving people or the community
- Event planning—family-oriented, social, youth, or educational events
- Elderly, sick, shut-in visitation
- Organization of medical or social services—food shelves, day care, shelters, recovery groups, etc.

Suggestions for Growth

- Listen more to avoid assuming what people or organizations need.
- Work on logic skills and managing conflict rather than avoiding it.
- Put yourself first occasionally; clarify when others should help themselves.
- Reexamine your tried-and-true assumptions for work, spiritual practices, and relationships.

For I am not seeking my own good but the good of many, so that they may be saved.
(1 Corinthians 10:33)

INFJ

Your dominant function is Intuition: Seek settings where insight and imagination are important.

Your auxiliary function is Feeling: Seek settings where personal values and their impact on people are important.

Contributions to Workplace or Spiritual Community

- Understanding the feelings and motivations of others
- Finding creative ways for people to accomplish and enjoy tasks
- Modeling integrity and follow-through
- Lending future-oriented ideas to planning and development
- Offering insights about how individuals and systems interrelate

Preferred Atmospheres for Work or Service

- Meaningful, service-oriented vision
- Considerate, harmonious co-workers who share similar values
- Rewards for individual integrity, creativity, and insights
- Private space for quiet and reflection
- Organized so that processes are mindful of the needs of people
- Opportunities for individualized approaches

Leadership Style

- Add emphasis on mutual trust
- Work toward cooperation rather than demand it
- Facilitate, including others' ideas as appropriate
- Develop shared mission, goals, and plans using inspirational approach
- Apply dedicated effort until their dreams become reality

Typical Responsibilities or Tasks

- Efforts to help others grow and develop
- Spiritual direction or one-on-one counseling
- Words, oral or written, to influence outcomes for people
- Small group leadership for study or support
- Task forces that concentrate on what could be

Common Occupations

- Architect
- Education consultant, teacher
- Fine artist, writer
- Librarian
- Marketing
- Psychiatrist or psychologist
- Religious professional
- Scientist
- Social worker

Suggestions for Growth

- Be more open to asking others for help.
- Work on political savvy to better advocate for your ideas or talents.
- As you work on new ideas, solicit practical feedback and critique from others to gain their insights and support.
- Seek help in planning your leisure time from someone you trust who lives more for the moment.

Therefore encourage one another and build each other up, just as in fact you are doing.
(1 Thessalonians 5:11)

INFP

Your dominant function is Feeling: Seek settings where personal values and their impact on people are important.

Your auxiliary function is Intuition: Seek settings where insight and imagination are important.

Contributions to Workplace or Spiritual Community

- Bringing a compassionate, caring, and personal focus
- Adding a spirit of harmony
- Reminding others of their values and the worthiness of striving to meet them
- Providing a positive vision for the future
- Enriching others with creative ideas

Leadership Style

- Facilitate people and processes
- Persuade through conviction and inspire others to do what is right
- Partner with individuals to help them reach their fullest potential
- Provide integrity, interpersonal sensitivity
- Offer unending, unobtrusive personal effort

Common Occupations

- Counselor
- Education consultant
- English or fine arts teacher
- Fine artist
- Journalist
- Psychologist
- Religious educator
- Social scientist
- Writer, editor

Preferred Atmospheres for Work or Service

- Values, as inspiration and motivation, are upheld and acted out
- Service to a larger, common purpose
- Pressure is low but standards are high
- Artistic spaces for quiet and reflection
- Friendly, committed, values-oriented co-workers
- Flexibility and creativity emphasized over routine and structure

Typical Responsibilities or Tasks

- One-on-one counseling/coaching, partnering for prayer or encouragement
- Deep, solo work on a cause or vision they believe in
- Leadership in changes that act out their values
- Efforts that allow for unique expressions through particular skills or gifts
- Small group facilitation, teaching, or writing to influence community values

Suggestions for Growth

- Step back from your own values—are those of others appropriate given their circumstances and experiences?
- Avoid the trap of perfectionism— decide before you begin how well a job needs to be done.
- Practice saying no, accepting that you can't please everyone.
- Develop logic/analysis skills to avoid sounding too idealistic.

Do not conform any longer to the pattern of this world, but be transformed by the renewing of your mind.
(Romans 12:2)

157

ENFP

Your dominant function is Intuition: Seek settings where insight and imagination are important.

Your auxiliary function is Feeling: Seek settings where personal values and their impact on people are important.

Contributions to Workplace or Spiritual Community

- Initiating and promoting ideas to help others grow
- Adding vision, warmth, and enthusiasm to community undertakings
- Connecting resources, especially people and ideas
- Valuing widespread interests and relationships
- Sparking a sense of excitement and adventure

Preferred Atmospheres for Work or Service

- Stimulating, forward-looking creative team environment
- Flexible, imaginative co-workers focused on possibilities
- A variety of people, tasks, and perspectives
- Work and fun coexist or are interspersed
- New, challenging pursuits are brainstormed and launched
- Room for spontaneity, friendship, flair

Leadership Style

- Bring personal charm and charisma to get others started
- Motivate and encourage people to do their best
- Advocate for the less fortunate
- Provide ingenious ideas
- Promote and speak for worthy causes

Typical Responsibilities or Tasks

- Service-related projects that allow for building relationships
- Networking service organizations/ groups, especially those with a creative focus
- Youth work
- Music, drama, public speaking, promoting
- Leadership at the start of new efforts

Common Occupations

- Artist, musician, actor
- Consultant
- Counselor, social scientist
- Dental hygienist
- Journalist
- Public relations
- Research assistant
- Religious professional
- Teacher

Suggestions for Growth

- Use your values to set boundaries and avoid over-commitment.
- Pay attention to your practical personal, physical, and emotional needs. Know your limits.
- Ask someone with project management skills to help you set timelines and make decisions.
- Temper your natural enthusiasm for new ideas, leaders, or fads. Check their claims against your values.

Whatever is true, whatever is noble, whatever is right, whatever is pure, whatever is lovely, whatever is admirable—if anything is excellent or praiseworthy—think about such things.
(Philippians 4:8)

ENFJ

Your dominant function is Feeling: Seek settings where personal values and their impact on people are important.

Your auxiliary function is Intuition: Seek settings where insight and imagination are important.

Contributions to Workplace or Spiritual Community

- Monitoring values and integrity
- Supporting others with warmth and encouragement
- Believing in the positive nature of people
- Inviting others to live up to their ideals
- Articulating messages that others want or need to hear

Preferred Atmospheres for Work or Service

- Community or social service orientation with strong ideals
- Sociable co-workers who focus on improving things for the common good
- Harmonious, empathetic, supportive, creative environment
- Clear organizational structures that bring results yet respond to people's needs
- Participative, open, supportive systems
- Room for personal growth, self-expression

Leadership Style

- Organize, small or large scale, using the best people have to offer
- Plans for the future needs of the organization or community
- Model of exemplary behavior
- Influence through participation, personally digging in on task at hand
- Praise and enthusiasm to motivate others

Typical Responsibilities or Tasks

- Structuring projects or tasks to target major needs
- Public speaking or teaching for adults or children
- Creation of inclusive atmospheres where each person is valued
- Activities that provide a sense of harmony and fun
- Facilitative and leadership opportunities

Common Occupations

- Actor, musician, artist
- Consultant
- Counselor or therapist
- Designer
- Home economist
- Optometrist
- Religious professional
- Teacher
- Writer

Suggestions for Growth

- Be careful of losing focus on the purpose or logic of a task.
- Check yourself for over-control or exaggerated zeal when deadlines loom.
- Develop conflict management skills that use objective analysis.
- Take care of yourself—take your vacation time, honor your personal needs.

"For I know the plans I have for you," says the Lord, "plans to prosper you and not to harm you, plans to give you hope and a future"
(Jeremiah 29:11).

INTJ

Your dominant function is Intuition: Seek settings where insight and imagination are important.

Your auxiliary function is Thinking: Seek settings where objectivity and logic are important.

Contributions to Workplace or Spiritual Community

- Envisioning systems or adjusting strategies to create a better world
- Breaking new ground, shifting paradigms, and changing the way people think
- Synthesizing diverse information and viewpoints
- Thinking and acting independently from traditional or outmoded ways
- Pushing others toward their goals

Preferred Atmospheres for Work or Service

- Individual initiative is rewarded
- Decisive, intellectually challenging, effective co-workers who take a long-range view of issues
- Room for creativity, independence, and autonomy
- Emphasis on problem-solving, outside-the-box thinking
- Private space for reflection
- Willingness to implement groundbreaking ideas

Leadership Style

- Mastermind change through the power of their ideas
- Challenge self and others to work toward a compelling future
- Develop conceptual designs and models
- Discover patterns and systems which solve complex problems
- Foster coherence of purpose and follow-through

Typical Responsibilities or Tasks

- Projects or roles that require conceptual and analytical skills
- Long-range planning and strategy development
- New approaches to traditions or procedures with wide ramifications
- Growth for others through teaching, speaking, coaching, or writing
- Research and entrepreneurial positions

Common Occupations

- Architect
- Attorney or judge
- Computer professional
- Electrical or chemical engineer
- Management consultant
- Manager
- Scientist or researcher
- Social services worker
- University instructor

Suggestions for Growth

- Share your ideas-in-process and insights to gain support and feedback.
- Schedule time for relationships, develop the art of friendship.
- Practice patience when others don't "see" your vision. Think about what will capture their attention.
- Practice sharing tasks and training others.

I devoted myself to study and to explore by wisdom all that is done under heaven.
(Ecclesiastes 1:13)

INTP

Your dominant function is Thinking: Seek settings where objectivity and logic are important.

Your auxiliary function is Intuition: Seek settings where insight and imagination are important.

Contributions to Workplace or Spiritual Community

- Searching relentlessly for universal truths
- Determining the long-term consequences of any given plan or strategy for action
- Pointing out errors of logic and sentimentality
- Providing clear, analytical frameworks for understanding
- Contributing intellectual insights

Leadership Style

- Gain respect through depth of knowledge
- Conceptualize issues
- Influence through theoretical ideas
- Make decisions from a sound, logical foundation
- Allow for flexibility, independent thinking, autonomy

Common Occupations

- Artist
- Computer professional
- Lawyer
- Photographer
- Psychologist
- Respiratory therapist
- Scientist or researcher
- Surveyor
- Writer

Preferred Atmospheres for Work or Service

- Emphasis on using systems and models to rationally solve complex problems
- Rewards for self-direction, creativity
- Scholarly, competent co-workers
- Maximum flexibility, minimal policies and procedures
- Private spaces and time for thought
- Quiet, with as few meetings and interruptions as possible

Typical Responsibilities or Tasks

- Orderly approach to explore difficult, long-standing issues
- Scholarly or intellectual endeavors
- Conceptualization of new efforts or improvement of ineffective ones
- Examination of long-term implications of current traditions or methods
- Endeavors that tap into core organizational or theoretical issues

Suggestions for Growth

- Practice ways to state your theories and ideas more simply.
- Learn different methods of providing critique; some people need to hear the positive before the negative.
- Pursue at least one social, nonintellectual activity.
- Seek self-awareness classes to help you recognize the value of feelings and emotions for yourself and others.

And this is my prayer: that your love may abound more and more in knowledge and depth of insight.
(Philippians 1:9)

ENTP

Your dominant function is Intuition: Seek settings where insight and imagination are important.

Your auxiliary function is Thinking: Seek settings where objectivity and logic are important.

Contributions to Workplace or Spiritual Community

- Initiating new projects, direction, etc. with enthusiasm and energy
- Meeting challenges proactively
- Providing insight and imagination to tasks and projects
- Exhibiting resourcefulness in dire or complicated situations
- Debating, asking the tough questions

Leadership Style

- Use models and logical systems to meet needs
- Speak out for change
- Organize, operate, and assume the risk for new ideas and approaches
- Challenge and encourage personal and/or organizational achievement
- Influence through cleverness and expertise

Common Occupations

- Actor
- Chemical engineer
- Construction worker
- Computer professional
- Journalist
- Marketing professional
- Photographer
- Psychiatrist
- Public relations professional

Preferred Atmospheres for Work or Service

- Flexible, change-oriented, entrepreneurial efforts or organizations
- Highly competent, effective, competitive co-workers
- Lack of bureaucratic structures
- Strategic, big-picture focus
- Freedom to act or change
- Rewards for risk-taking and innovation

Typical Responsibilities or Tasks

- Liaison among groups or organizations, especially those with a novel or global focus
- New method or system design to improve effectiveness
- Drama, music, public speaking
- Strategy development for new ideas, products, outreaches, or missions
- Marketing, fund-raising, promotion of services and products

Suggestions for Growth

- Get feedback on your style. Look for ways to recognize and include others.
- Take time for reflection and relaxation. What might you need to let go to make room for new opportunities?
- Seek practical, factual advice—what is easily imagined is not always easily achieved.
- Reflect on where bending rules or avoiding convention leads to more trouble than it was worth.

Not that I have already obtained this or have already reached the goal; but I press on to make it my own, because Christ Jesus has made me his own.
(Philippians 3:12 NRSV)

ENTJ

Your dominant function is Thinking: Seek settings where objectivity and logic are important.

Your auxiliary function is Intuition: Seek settings where insight and imagination are important.

Contributions to Workplace or Spiritual Community

- Developing long-range plans for people and organizations
- Understanding how parts relate to whole
- Bringing a logical order to problems
- Offering intellectual and philosophical insights
- Encouraging others to do their best work

Preferred Atmospheres for Work or Service

- Focus on pressing issues or problems, with rewards for meeting them
- Large scale projects, challenges, or organizations
- Efficient structures and people in alignment with master plan
- Dedicated, tough-minded, confident, competent co-workers
- Clear goals, with energy marshaled to meet them
- Logical, orderly, analytical

Leadership Style

- Take charge when a strong leader is needed
- Provide a clear vision
- Use conceptual models to guide action
- Exhibit dedication, concentration, confidence to make steady progress toward goals
- Stand firm on principles against opposition

Typical Responsibilities or Tasks

- Leadership, long-range planning, strategic alignment, visioning
- Organization of systems, structures, products, and people to work together
- Management or administrative tasks, including fund-raising, investing, legal, or personnel matters
- Project evaluation, organizational development
- Adult education in work, community, or spiritual arenas

Common Occupations

- Administrator
- Attorney
- Consultant
- Human resources professional
- Manager, corporate executive
- Marketing or sales professional
- Mortgage banker
- Social services worker
- Systems analyst

Suggestions for Growth

- Keep focused on the needs of people as you strive toward goals.
- Find the person most likely to challenge your views—and listen.
- Learn to factor your values and those of others into your decisions.
- Determine realistic expectations of people and resources as you plan projects and set goals.

Let us not love with words or tongue but with actions and in truth.
(1 John 3:18)

Are Personality Types a Biblical Concept?

People frequently question, "Is it really biblical that we have a personality type? Can't God change who we are?" While there is no specific Bible passage citing that we have been given a certain personality type, looking at people in the Bible provides examples of the preferences. The lives of biblical people indicate that much of our personality is as inborn as the color of our eyes or the size of our feet. Let's look at the apostle Paul as an example of what we mean.

We have just a few glimpses of Paul prior to his conversion to Christianity—the time when he was known as Saul. In the book of Acts we find him

- waging a campaign against the church, getting letters from the high priest to grant him legal authority to persecute Christians (Acts 9:1–2);
- standing by at the stoning of Stephen, approving of the crowd's actions (Acts 7:57–60);
- dragging Christians off to prison himself (Acts 8:3).

From these texts, we get hints of a man of action, probably with a preference for Extraversion. Not content to merely criticize or plot against the Christians, he was leading the frontal attack!

We can also infer that Paul had a preference for Intuition, with his big-picture approach to destroying the church. His scholarship and standing, often evident in those with a preference for Thinking, gave him access to government officials—and credibility when he spoke. Finally, his quickness of action may point toward a Judging lifestyle—planned and conclusive in its results.

Paul's conversion to Christianity brought about drastic changes in his life. The man who once led the persecution of the early church was now its foremost advocate, devoting his life to spreading the new faith. As profound as this change was, however, look at his actions and see if they are still consistent with what we surmise were ENTJ preferences:

- He traveled, spoke, and taught to spread the faith widely (E).
- He had a big-picture strategy for spreading the gospel by speaking first to the Jews and then to the Gentiles (N).

- He argued effectively for the new religion using the logical methods of the Jewish faith (T).
- He was decided in his beliefs, actively seeking closure on many of the debated issues facing the young church (J).

Can you see the same visionary ability in his methods of preaching first to the Jews and then to the Gentiles? The same boldness and knowledge that gave him confidence with the greatest authorities of his day? The same sureness in his positions? The same desire to bring closure to issues and debate? These are the essence of Paul's personality type—the personality preferences he used so effectively in opposing the church also eventually helped him be one of its most effective advocates. His probable ENTJ style that drove him to attack the church now allowed him to pen the words of his new conviction:

> For I am convinced that neither death nor life, neither angels nor demons, neither the present nor the future, nor any powers, neither height nor depth, nor anything else in all creation, will be able to separate us from the love of God that is in Christ Jesus our Lord. (Romans 8:38–39)

As a likely ENTJ, Paul probably would have found it awkward to embrace a quiet role in the early church. His personality type and gifts catapulted him to the forefront of whatever he was doing. He was the type of leader required at the time, targeting the big picture—the whole civilized world—to spread the good news of Christianity.

People with ENTJ preferences, however, show just one of a variety of leadership styles God can use. A study of Mother Teresa, for example, hints that she may have gained energy more through solitude or one-to-one ministry (Introversion). Her focus on one individual at a time, not poor people in general, points to Sensing. Her decision-making style seemed to be based more on her values (Feeling). Finally, her "go where she was led" style of living may indicate a Perceiving preference. A possible type for Mother Teresa, ISFP, is exactly opposite to Paul's possible ENTJ style, yet Mother Teresa's ways of leading and caring have inspired people around the world.

For each of us, personality type plays a key role in finding the places where we can be most effective. In an old story, a person asked his rabbi how to become acceptable to God. The rabbi replied, "We become acceptable not by being more like Moses but by becoming who God meant *us* to be." Personality type is a tool to help you understand yourself, those around you, and the settings that bring out your best. This understanding enables us to respect those whose needs are different from ours even as we respect ourselves.

A Few Questions and Answers About Personality Type

- **Am I born to be a certain personality type?**

    While most research indicates that type is inborn, outside factors can influence our preferences. For example, we might be born into a family or culture that does not nourish a particular type. If you are the only Feeler in a family of Thinkers, you may be conditioned to find logical support for decisions. If you are the only Thinker in a family of Feelers, you may learn considerate ways to express your objective analyses.

    In addition to family, outside factors such as culture, work settings, or life experiences can influence our expression of personality preferences. Some people therefore may find it hard to select what God truly *meant* for them to be as opposed to what others thought they *should* be.

- **Can I work to change my personality type preferences?**

    Yes, you could with some difficulty, just as you can learn to write with your non-preferred hand. But your preferences celebrate who you are. No preference or type is better than another, just different. While we all can take cues from each of the preferences and learn to use them when appropriate, it makes more sense to concentrate most of our energy on working out of what comes easiest to us. Then we can use our non-preferred style when it is appropriate—for example, noticing spelling and grammar *details* (S) when writing a forecast of future marketing possibilities (N). In summary, if we are all gifted but in different ways, then the best type to be is the one you were born to be!

- **Are all people with the same personality type preferences alike?**

    While there are some similarities among people of the same type, type doesn't explain *everything* about you or anyone else. For example, while David and Sandra as ENFPs are attracted to rather global schemes for helping others, Sandra does not share David's interest in science. Further, type does not measure ability or competency in any area. It does, however, do an excellent job of helping us understand ourselves, appreciate others, know the work/service setting that is best, and make sense of some of our life choices.

- **People with my personality type preferences have trouble with time management (or interpersonal niceties or accuracy, etc.). Can I use my type as an excuse?**

Blaming your personality type preferences is a poor excuse for any inexcusable behavior! Further, your type doesn't "cause" any behavior.

Personality type instead can be used as a framework for growth. You can look at areas where other people with your personality preferences have both excelled and struggled, read about their insights into those trouble spots, and then put the information to use in working on your own blind spots or developmental needs. For example, someone with a preference for Perceiving who constantly struggles to finish projects might learn to set deadlines for each step of a process rather than focusing on a single completion date. A person with a preference for Introversion may analyze whether speaking out earlier may be more appropriate and effective in some interactions.

- **Should I base my career on my type?**

Personality type should not necessarily discourage you from choosing an area in which to work. Research any given field, work setting, or task, and if it still appeals to you, enter it. If few others with your type preferences enter that field, you may find that your perspective on many things differs from the majority of your co-workers. Entering an occupation with this knowledge is far different from *not* understanding why you might feel like an outsider.

The person whose personality type preferences are atypical for a given setting or profession can often bring new insights to everyone. Jane, for example, in her first job as a bank examiner was one of just a few Intuitives in a profession that appeals more to people with a preference for Sensing. Her Intuition helped her make a few suggestions that streamlined the tried-and-true examination process, but she also felt different from most of her co-workers who were more comfortable with that setting and the tasks it involved.

Using Type to Find the Settings That God Has Caused to Appeal to You the Most

You may have noticed references to *dominant* and *auxiliary* at the top of your type page. Within each psychological type, Jung saw a hierarchy for personal development. Each personality type has a *dominant* function, the one that develops first and is usually easiest for people of that type to use. Because of this, your dominant function can be the greatest source of your gifts. In the chart on the following page, find your personality type. The dominant function (S, N, T, or F) is listed as "1." Sometimes people are so accustomed to their dominant function that they overlook its power or the fact that others might truly marvel at what to them seems only natural.

The *auxiliary* function, or number "2" function in the chart and on your type page, also develops early in life and provides necessary *balance* in the way you live. If your dominant function involves the way you take in information (either Sensing or Intuition), then your *auxiliary* involves your way of making decisions (Thinking or Feeling) and vice versa. Sensing or Intuition as an auxiliary keeps a dominant Thinking or Feeling person from making decisions without gathering enough information (often the route to close-mindedness). And, an auxiliary of Thinking or Feeling can help a dominant Sensing or Intuitive person focus and act on what information they pay attention to (an inadequate Thinking or Feeling auxiliary can be the route to aimlessness and procrastination).

Your dominant function is a good starting place for understanding the places or settings that will appeal to you. Considering the atmospheres that appeal to your auxiliary function is also helpful.

Enter with caution those settings that require much use of your third and fourth functions, as listed in the chart. These last functions for your type often lag in development and are sometimes not experienced fully until the second half of life, if at all.

ISTJ	ISFJ	INFJ	INTJ
1. Sensing	1. Sensing	1. Intuition	1. Intuition
2. Thinking	2. Feeling	2. Feeling	2. Thinking
3. Feeling	3. Thinking	3. Thinking	3. Feeling
4. Intuition	4. Intuition	4. Sensing	4. Sensing
ISTP	ISFP	INFP	INTP
1. Thinking	1. Feeling	1. Feeling	1. Thinking
2. Sensing	2. Sensing	2. Intuition	2. Intuition
3. Intuition	3. Intuition	3. Sensing	3. Sensing
4. Feeling	4. Thinking	4. Thinking	4. Feeling
ESTP	ESFP	ENFP	ENTP
1. Sensing	1. Sensing	1. Intuition	1. Intuition
2. Thinking	2. Feeling	2. Feeling	2. Thinking
3. Feeling	3. Thinking	3. Thinking	3. Feeling
4. Intuition	4. Intuition	4. Sensing	4. Sensing
ESTJ	ESFJ	ENFJ	ENTJ
1. Thinking	1. Feeling	1. Feeling	1. Thinking
2. Sensing	2. Sensing	2. Intuition	2. Intuition
3. Intuition	3. Intuition	3. Sensing	3. Sensing
4. Feeling	4. Thinking	4. Thinking	4. Feeling

Note your top two preferences and then seek settings that honor them:

> *Sensing:* Places where factual details and accuracy are important
> *Intuition:* Places where insight and imagination are important
> *Thinking:* Places where objectivity and logic are important
> *Feeling:* Places where personal values and their impact on
>   people are important.

Now look at your third and fourth preferences. These third and fourth functions are often clues to the settings that people of that type may automatically avoid because of difficulties with being at their best. For example, enter with caution the settings that utilize your fourth function:

> *Sensing:* Places where factual details and accuracy are important
> *Intuition:* Places where insight and imagination are important
> *Thinking:* Places where objectivity and logic are important
> *Feeling:* Places where personal values and their impact on
>   people are important.

On the page that describes your type (pages 148–163), the Suggestions for Growth relate to developing your third and fourth functions.

Letting Personality Type Structure Your Search

As you try to find the settings that are most appealing to you, your personality type preferences can aid your search process. Here are some guidelines for finding the settings that respect your particular preferences:

If you have a preference for Extraversion, to find the right setting for you:

- Visit different sites.
- Talk to friends who operate in an environment you'd like to try.
- Use your network of family, friends, church members, colleagues in your profession or work, etc.
- *Remember,* however, to listen as much as you talk and watch overextending yourself since Extraverts often mistake activity for results. (Too many visits, conversations, networks, etc., can leave you unfocused.)

If you have a preference for Introversion:

- Do Internet or library research about settings you find appealing.
- Journal or reflect on the factors that can contribute to your finding your niche.
- Find a mentor or guide to assist along the way.
- *Remember,* however, that when the time is right, you'll need to act and perhaps move beyond your comfort zone to reach out to others who can help you. Be careful to consider how you can "sell" yourself once you've found a setting that fits you.

If you have a preference for Sensing:

- Collect specific information about what settings are available to you right now that match your education, experience, economic and family needs.
- Use what you have learned from your past about what works and doesn't work for you.

- Visit sites and arrange interviews to gather firsthand information and actual experiences.
- *Remember,* however, to be willing if need be to take a risk and try something new even if you don't have 100 percent of what is required (80 percent will generally do!). Try not to let security needs force you to settle for less than what you want. Consider the long-term implications both for staying where you are and for going to something less known.

If you have a preference for Intuition:

- Brainstorm all the possibilities that match with your future aspirations and dreams.
- Try out—even if only in your mind—some farfetched ideas or unusual opportunities.
- Don't worry about staying on one track, as your penchant is for change and novelty.
- *Remember,* however, not to stretch credulity too far by overlooking important requirements or getting caught up in too many possibilities.

If you have a preference for Thinking:

- Evaluate several settings using a matrix listing criteria important to you—commute time, economic and family needs, potential career growth, and so on.
- Use a system of pros and cons to analyze various settings available to you.
- Explore new competencies you'd like to acquire through different opportunities.
- *Remember,* however, to consider your own personal needs and values and those of the people who are most important to you. Factor in your subjective response as well.

If you have a preference for Feeling:

- Think of people you admire or would like to emulate. Where possible, seek them out to hear about what they like in their setting and how they found their niche.
- Factor in your key values to see if they are in harmony with this particular setting.
- Find a supportive friend who will provide a listening ear as you search.

- *Remember,* however, that Feelers need harmony and a purpose beyond the paycheck to be most productive. Be sure to please *yourself* as well as your significant others in your selection.

If you have a preference for Judging:

- Create an organized plan, complete with a "to do" list, to examine what potential setting would work best for you.
- Make a timetable that has step-by-step activities to help narrow down the options.
- Work through a successful process such as *What Color Is Your Parachute?* or *The Path* (see Suggestions for Further Reading, page 283).
- *Remember,* however, not to hone in and decide too quickly, without thorough exploration of what is available to you. Ask yourself, "Have I asked enough questions, gathered enough data, and stayed open long enough in this process?"

If you have a preference for Perceiving:

- Give yourself a generous length of time to gather information and explore options.
- Take "detours" in your process to see if anything interesting turns up.
- As new information comes along, capture it and see what it tells you about the setting where you'll most clearly thrive.
- *Remember,* however, that others may have trouble with what could seem to be (or actually is!) procrastination. Ultimately, the situation may decide for you!

Now for a challenge: For a well-rounded approach, read all of the above and do what you prefer, but add pointers from your non-preferred areas as well.

Sample Settings by Preferences

The following chart includes some key elements of settings that appeal to each of the personality type preferences. The words in parentheses indicate significant correlations with the life gift interest areas discussed in chapter 2 (Realistic (R), Investigative (I), Artistic (A), Social (S), Enterprising (E), Conventional (C)).

Extraversion
(Social, Enterprising)
Settings where they can:
- Be involved in many things at once
- Change tasks and variety to maintain interest
- Keep up a network of contacts
- Discuss information and ideas
- Share thoughts or feelings
- Work within a team

Introversion
(no RIASEC correlations)
Settings where they can:
- Work without interruption
- Concentrate on the task at hand
- Prepare in advance to discuss ideas or plans
- Take an in-depth approach
- Have time and space for quiet reflection
- Engage in small group or one-on-one interactions

Sensing
(Enterprising, Conventional)
Settings where they can:
- Observe and engage the five senses
- Focus on the here and now
- Follow a clear path to rewards
- Succeed with credentials other than academic ones
- Engage in hands-on experiences, immediate interactions
- Be rewarded for experience and seniority

Intuition
(Artistic)
Settings where they can:
- Work with and create new ideas
- Make connections, see relationships among things
- Think and act on future possibilities
- Concentrate on big ideas rather than facts or details
- Push for change rather than stick to what is
- Be rewarded for sharing hunches and imaginative ideas

Thinking
(Realistic, Investigative)
Settings where they can:
- Problem-solve, concentrate on tasks
- Have clear and definite principles
- Work within or create efficient, logically structured systems
- Be competent, clear-thinking, and analytical
- Be more task oriented than people oriented
- Be rewarded for exceeding task requirements

Feeling
(Social)
Settings where they can:
- Be warm and caring toward people
- Instill trust and cooperation
- Work toward obtaining group harmony and consensus
- Learn about people's values, opinions, and reactions
- Build social relationships into their work
- Be rewarded for meeting people's needs

Judging
(Social, Conventional)
Seek settings where they can:
- Trust schedules, goals, and deadlines
- Plan their work and work their plan
- Organize and accomplish tasks
- Bring decisions to closure
- Avoid surprises, last-minute changes, or scrambles
- Count on others to follow through

Perceiving
(Realistic, Artistic)
Seek settings where they can:
- Avoid structure, routine, and repetition
- Stop to enjoy the moment
- Concentrate on processes more than end products
- Stay open to experiences so as not to miss anything
- Set their own pace and hours
- Tackle tasks when inspired

Prayer

Dear God, It is great to know that each personality type has its place and that through Your Grace You can use us as we are. Help me to learn as much as I can about how I operate best and the settings in which I am most comfortable and productive. Help me to discover how my personality can shine for Your purposes. Amen.

For Journal or Discussion

1. Was it easy or hard for you to identify your personality preferences? Why do you think that was?

2. How do your current settings support/not support the preferences God gave you?

3. Reread the suggested areas for growth on your personality type page. Which might you work on right now? What might you do to get started?

4. Think about the style of leadership people of your type offer. In what settings might it be most effective? Are there settings where it is hard for you to take a leadership role? Why?

5. What about the "servant style" of your personality type? What contributions do you make? What areas of growth might make you even more effective?

LifeKey #5

Seek the values that strike the right chord with God.

CHAPTER 5

VALUES—CHORDS THAT
TOUCH YOUR SOUL

We choose—either to live our lives or to let others live them for us. By making and keeping promises to ourselves and to others, little by little we increase our strength until our ability to act is more powerful than any of the forces that act upon us.[1]
—Stephen Covey

Think about your favorite music, whether it is jazz, rock, or symphonic. If the notes of a chord are played correctly, *harmony* results. If the wrong notes are played, you hear disharmony or *discord*—a word that applies not only to dissonance in music, but to conflict or lack of agreement among people or ideas.

Some places or situations harmonize with what we believe in or value. They play our kind of music. At other times, though, discord swirls around us—not just in music but at work, church, or home—without our being sure of the source of the bad notes. Identifying what you value highly can help you sort the right notes from the ones that make you want to cover your ears.

Pete, for instance, hadn't been happy at work for a long time. He'd originally interviewed for a position in new product development. However, within months of being hired, the job was re-engineered. Day after day he found himself glued to a computer, tackling an overflow of administrative tasks from his boss—and reviewing legal contracts to find inconsistencies, of all things.

One week Pete's prayer group decided to do a values exercise

---

[1]Stephen Covey, A. Roger Merrill, Rebecca R. Merrill, *First Things First* (New York: Simon & Schuster, 1994), 70.

together. Pete wasn't wild about the idea, but as he began sorting the little values cards, he became absorbed in the choices he was making.

"Accuracy—I have to value that in my job. And, being of service to others. Competency—I want to do things right. And, I want my religious beliefs to be well thought through. . . ." A moment later, Pete drew a quick breath. His friends looked up at him. Pete said eagerly, "This tells me what's wrong with my life right now! You know, most of the values I placed under 'These are very valuable' are there because my job *forces* me to be that way. If I set work aside, the order changes drastically. Look, creativity has been knocked right out of my priorities. The same with my friendships—I'm simply too busy! Sorting these values cards points to exactly why I'm so miserable in this job."

What Are Values?

What do you value? Think of the things that

- feel important to you
- define your fundamental character
- supply meaning to your life and work
- influence the decisions you make
- compel you to take a stand
- describe atmospheres where you can be productive.

You may not know what you value until an event, circumstance, or person comes into direct conflict with that value—or, until you purposefully try to identify what is important to you, as Pete and his prayer group did. Values are another *LifeKey* that provide clues to who you are, why you're here, and what you do best. At the end of this chapter, you'll find the card-sorting exercise.

Values can unite people with diverse backgrounds and situations. Let's look at one rather famous values statement:

> We hold these truths to be self-evident; that all men are created equal; that they are endowed by their creator with certain unalienable rights; that among these are life, liberty, and the pursuit of happiness. . . .

When Thomas Jefferson penned these words in the Declaration

of Independence, he assumed that those he represented (people living in the British-American colonies without governmental representation) agreed with him that the rights to life, liberty, and the pursuit of happiness were of such high value that people would be willing to die for them. These shared values pulled together the ragtag Continental Army, sustained it through years of fighting and deprivation, and allowed it to outlast the army of the British, one of the finest in the world. Teaming up with people who hold similar values to yours can make it easier to overcome difficulties as well as find purpose and meaning in what you do.

Yet even as you skimmed the above words, you might have questioned whether what Jefferson penned catches the essence of what is most valuable in life *today*. As times and circumstances change, so do people's values. No matter where we live, we will find neighbors and fellow citizens whose values clash with ours.

Within the Christian faith, there are certain values with which few would quibble—we are to love God above all else and love our neighbors as ourselves. Yet there are other values that people of faith may disagree about, including that value's meaning and importance. And while our core Christian values may be similar, varying life circumstances may affect how we prioritize other values. If you are facing job transition, for example, you may place a much higher value on security than you did even a year ago. Our values may encourage us to choose *different* but *acceptable* paths.

Do We Really Have the Option to Order Our Values?

We have discovered that God has given us life gifts, spiritual gifts, and personality types. While the Bible has a lot to say about values, God's purpose is to have an impact on how we define, prioritize, and live out our own personal values. This is in contrast to life gifts (which are to be developed), spiritual gifts (which are to be discovered), and personalities (which are to be understood).

From the Declaration of Independence, for instance, we might assume that liberty or freedom is highly valued in America. Indeed it is, even two hundred years after the document was written. Many of us would define freedom as the ability to do as we please. From a biblical perspective, however, that is not freedom, but often the road to ruin. Biblically, true freedom releases us to follow Christ, not to run after our own desires.

While there are definitely values by which all Christians must abide, when faced with certain situations, two individuals can meet similar challenges with different responses that are biblically sound as well as reflective of who they are and what they value most.

The book of Ruth, for example, tells the story of a Moabite woman. Ruth and her sister-in-law, Orpah, had the good fortune to marry into a kindly family of foreigners from Judah. This family had settled in Moab to escape the famine in their homeland. When the husbands of Ruth and Orpah died, their mother-in-law, Naomi, had no more sons for them to marry, as custom would have dictated. The culture left the two young women free to return to their own families.

Naomi wanted to return to Judah, having received word that the famine was finally over. She suggested that Ruth and Orpah head back to their parents' homes, believing that they would be happiest there, but they begged to remain with her. When she reminded her daughters-in-law that their chances of remarriage were slim if they stayed with her, Orpah agreed to go home, but Ruth refused:

> "Look," said Naomi, "your sister-in-law is going back to her people and her gods. Go back with her."
>
> But Ruth replied, "Don't urge me to leave you or to turn back from you. Where you go I will go, and where you stay I will stay. Your people will be my people and your God my God" (Ruth 1:15–16).

This was a very painful decision for both daughters-in-law. Orpah obviously loved Naomi, placing a high value on the relationship they had built, but her final decision rested on other values: perhaps her family of origin, the geographic location where she had lived almost all her life, or cultural traditions. The Bible expresses no opinion on the way Orpah prioritized her values. She is portrayed as a caring individual who found the decision of whether or not to leave Naomi a difficult choice.

Ruth held a different set of core values. To her, maintaining the relationship with her mother-in-law and the religious beliefs she had accepted outweighed the loss of her homeland and culture.

We know that Ruth's decision ultimately led to security in a new marriage, a marriage that established the family line that led to the birth of King David. We don't know whether Orpah found happiness, but the Bible does *not* express that Orpah made a bad choice. Ruth and Orpah's values were different, bringing them to choose different futures.

Why Clarify Your Values?

In the movie *Chariots of Fire,* Olympic runner Eric Liddell tells his sister, "Jenny, when I run, I feel God's pleasure." Both Eric and Jenny planned to be missionaries, but they disagreed about the values a missionary could hold. Jenny believed that running took Eric away from God's work. Eric felt that God would honor his values for physical fitness and competition in that phase of his life, provided he also valued highly his religious beliefs.

Eric willingly paid a price for his faith, refusing to compete in the 100-yard dash at the Olympics because it was scheduled for Sunday morning. In the end, he won a gold medal in a different event. Eric's success in athletics later provided a platform for evangelism—others saw him as a down-to-earth Christian rather than a "holier-than-thou" missionary. Eric knew what he valued and was able to make his decisions confidently.

In the same way, recall that Pete, who no longer found his work satisfying, clarified which values mattered most to him. The process allowed him to identify a mismatch of personal and workplace values. He put to work his newfound self-awareness as he searched for opportunities in other departments and finally in other companies where his personal values, especially for creativity and friendship, were honored.

Knowing your core values can clarify your choices and help you understand which activities or settings are right for you. Here are some examples:

- "When I realized how much I valued independence, I left the work situation where I had little influence over my own future and started my own business."
- "Once I understood how important my extended family was to me, I restricted my job search to this region of the country."
- "With my high priority for knowledge, especially my desire to obtain a higher academic degree, I sought employment with a company that had a tuition reimbursement program."
- "I didn't realize how important variety is to me—now I try to

avoid standing committees. Instead, I volunteer for one-time needs."

Knowing your values can help you answer questions like: "What gives my life meaning?" "In what ways do I influence others?" "What is worthwhile work for me?" "What deep issues of the soul do I need to clarify?"

Values are one more *LifeKey* to help you understand where you can best use what God has given uniquely to you. They make clear how and where to use your spiritual gifts and life gifts. They add to your understanding of why certain vocations or service opportunities would be better choices for you. Being in charge of the children's Christmas program, for example, may fit your life gifts for creativity and management, your spiritual gifts of leadership and administration, and your passion for children's ministry—*but* if you value accuracy and control, you will be doomed to frustration as the "little lambs" wander off and the Wise Men forget to carry their gifts to the manger.

Shouldn't My Values Remain Constant?

Taking stock of values isn't a one-time event. Our values aren't static even in one season of life. In college, David worked as a lab technician during the day, conducting experiments on viruses that caused life-threatening illnesses. Because the studies used live viruses, the lab placed an *extremely* high value on accuracy. At night, he worked as a busboy in a restaurant where he was judged on speed—how fast David could clear tables and bus dirty dishes. The restaurant soon fired him because the day job had so conditioned him to meticulousness that he separated the silverware and neatly disposed of napkins—in short, David was the slowest busboy they had ever seen! What was of most value during the day was of little value at night.

Many of us find that our lives take us to different arenas that applaud different sets of values. Your family may value service while your workplace values prestige. You may value tradition while the organizations to which you belong value flexibility or variety.

Sometimes these conflicts are manageable. Sometimes a conflict is so severe that we *must* make adjustments to the situation or leave outright. And sometimes we choose to change what we value.

Unlike life gifts or spiritual gifts, not all of our values are God-given, nor are they with us from birth. For example, many of us place a much higher value on religious beliefs now than we did as children. Good change! The importance of physical fitness comes and goes for others of us. If you came from a dysfunctional family, perhaps maintaining your self-respect is of utmost importance to you.

Conflicts around values can also be internal—our major values can collide when we least expect it. One family did not realize how strongly they valued loyalty until they concluded that their church no longer met the spiritual needs of their children. They firmly believed that they as members should be working to change the church, not desert it, yet they also valued passing on their faith beliefs to their children. It took several months for them to determine in this situation which values held more weight for them.

Our purpose here is not to change your values, but to give you a framework for viewing them clearly, for seeing how they might be conflicting in various arenas of your life, and for understanding how your values fit the roles your life calls you to play. Few individuals are lucky enough to escape values conflicts. The rest of us live in tension since few of these conflicts are easily resolved. Sometimes a conflict is so complicated that seeking help is wise. You might simply talk through the problems with a friend; in other cases a minister or counselor might bring clarity.

Your goal is to be able to use your values as markers for navigating through life. Does that seem too vague? Even with no landmarks in sight, sailors of old could navigate vast oceans simply by marking the location of the North Star and then using it to determine the direction to steer their ship. Think of your values as "true north," always ready to provide direction as to which way to steer your life. They perhaps can form the basis for a personal mission statement. (See Writing a Personal Mission Statement, on page 251.)

Are These the Values God Wants Me to Have?

The next question is whether the "true north" of your values is pointing you in the direction God would have you go. As we said earlier, God wants to influence your values. Each of the values cards that you'll find at the end of this book references a Bible verse that illustrates how God views that value. For your top values, you might wish to dig deeper. By using a topical Bible, for example, you might find the following verses on advancement:

> Do you see those who are skillful in their work? They will serve kings; they will not serve common people. (Proverbs 22:29 NRSV)
>
> Whoever becomes humble like this child is the greatest in the kingdom of heaven. (Matthew 18:4 NRSV)
>
> You are those who have stood by me in my trials; and I confer on you, just as my Father has conferred on me, a kingdom. (Luke 22:28–29 NRSV)

Thus the Bible has verses that affirm honing your skills to rise as high as you can—working for kings—but also indicates that humility and servanthood are the keys to advancement in the kingdom of God.

Sorting your values can sometimes help you find "true north" for career dilemmas. Karen, for example, knew that her people skills were better than the administrative skills her job called for, but when she made a few mistakes, she thought she wasn't being diligent enough. After perceiving that her top value was serving others, Karen understood her struggle. Her current job didn't let her help people directly, and she therefore sometimes found it hard to concentrate. Although she couldn't change jobs right away, Karen developed some new procedures to catch her own mistakes and took a volunteer counseling position that fulfilled her values. She didn't need to change her values, but needed to make changes to her life so that they were honored.

Sometimes you discover "true north" by considering what the Bible has to say about values that aren't important to you. Note your level of comfort as you prioritize them. Are you missing any values that God might want you to hold? Is your lack of concern for any value keeping you from the path that God would have you follow? In one of our seminars, a participant reflected:

> I attended *LifeKeys* because I was dissatisfied with my job in the marketing department of a large corporation. There weren't enough promotion opportunities, and I felt that my creativity wasn't honored—I spent most of my time working on other people's ideas. When I finished sorting my value cards, I recorded my top eight values—and left the room! In putting

achievement, advancement, creativity, and so on as my most important values, I had sorted my family out of what I value most.

I spent over an hour thinking through what I really valued. Getting promoted isn't as important right now as time with my four kids. My current job is just what I need for the next five years. When the children are older, I'll still have the chance to find a more challenging, fulfilling position.

What If We Missed "True North"?

As we ponder our values, examining whether our lives reflect the priorities we want to hold closely, many of us sense a huge gap between who we are and who God wants us to be. We wonder if we can ever find and stick to the best path.

Paul makes it clear that mature Christians acknowledge that they are not perfect:

> Not that I have already obtained this or have already reached the goal; but I press on to make it my own, because Christ Jesus has made me his own. Beloved, I do not consider that I have made it my own; but this one thing I do: forgetting what lies behind and straining forward to what lies ahead, I press on toward the goal for the prize of the heavenly call of God in Christ Jesus. (Philippians 3:12–14 NRSV)

Paul says that this is the mature view: We are to acknowledge our shortcomings, but nevertheless let go of them so we can continue to strive toward the goal of becoming all Christ intended for us to be. We are to let go of discouragement and instead sense the unending forgiveness God sends our way. Our Creator loves us even though we will never quite measure up to the full potential of our design.

Were you ever involved in sports? If you were, you probably had at least a few games or meets where your performance just didn't measure up to how well you did in practice. Good coaches don't tear you apart when that happens; instead, they help you find key factors that will improve your performance the next time. God wants to help you identify the values that can be *LifeKeys* for you. In fact, rest assured that if you take the time, God stands ready to guide you, encourage you, and help you find those good works prepared in advance for you.

Prayer

Dear God, In this complex world, it is hard for me to know what I value, let alone what You would have me value. I understand that we need not all hold the same values, but I want so much to know Your will for me in this area. Help me listen to no one but You as I clarify what is most important to me. Show me how to work these values into the decisions I make about how to live, where to work, and how to serve You. If I find conflicts, Lord, please guide me in resolving them. Amen.

Exercise: Clarifying Your Values

At the end of this book you will find a set of fifty-one values cards, each listing a separate value and its definition. There are some blank cards if you think of a value that we didn't include.

1. Find a place where you can lay out all of the cards.
2. Place the heading cards (*These are very valuable to me, These are valuable to me, These are not very valuable to me*) in a row at the top of your workspace.
3. Place the prompt card (*As I make important decisions, this is how I would value _____*) in a place where you can easily refer to it as you sort the cards.
4. Filling in the blank on the prompt card with each value, quickly sort the values cards into the appropriate columns, laying them out so that you will be able to view all of the cards in one glance. Do this *rapidly*, following your feelings or instincts rather than trying to analyze each one thoroughly.
5. Place no more than eight cards in the "These are very valuable to me" column. This could be a difficult task!
6. Next, rank the cards within the "These are very valuable to me" column, placing the value that is of most importance to you at the top of that column.
7. Copy the values in the way you have sorted them onto the Values Summary (page 187). You will now have a record from which to complete the exercises.
8. Record your top eight values in "My *LifeKeys* Notations," pages 286–287.

Values Summary

Copy the values from your values card sort onto this page in the order you gave to them. This will give you a working record to use for the exercises. (You need not order the second or third column, but most people find it helpful to record where they placed each value.)

Date: _____

These are very valuable to me	These are valuable to me	There are not very valuable to me
1. _____	1. _____	1. _____
2. _____	2. _____	2. _____
3. _____	3. _____	3. _____
4. _____	4. _____	4. _____
5. _____	5. _____	5. _____
6. _____	6. _____	6. _____
7. _____	7. _____	7. _____
8. _____	8. _____	8. _____
	9. _____	9. _____
	10. _____	10. _____
	11. _____	11. _____
	12. _____	12. _____
	13. _____	13. _____
	14. _____	14. _____
	15. _____	15. _____
	16. _____	16. _____
	17. _____	17. _____
	18. _____	18. _____
	19. _____	19. _____
	20. _____	20. _____
	21. _____	21. _____
		22. _____

Values Exercises

Choose at least one of the following exercises to complete. More can be found in *LifeKeys* Applications, pages 255–282, with specific applications for first career, volunteer work, midlife changes, and retirement.

1. What do your top values mean to you? Rewrite your list of eight most important values. Without looking at the cards, write your own definitions for each of these. Any thoughts about what you have written?

My top eight values	My own definitions
1.	
2.	
3.	
4.	
5.	
6.	
7.	
8.	

2. To evaluate whether your life reflects your values, pull out your calendar and think about the past week. Write out your activities below as they correspond to your top eight values.

Value 1 _____

Value 2 _____

Value 3 _____

Value 4 _____

Value 5 _____

Value 6 _____

Value 7 _____

Value 8 _____

Set one or two goals to bring your lifestyle more in line with your values.

Which values are under your control? Where do you feel help-less in matching your lifestyle with your values?

Are any of your values in conflict with others?

3. To evaluate your current work/service environment, re-sort the cards, choosing the eight values you believe are most important

in that place. Are there any conflicts between your lists? (This can also be useful for family discussion or team building.)

Do values explain any conflicts or tensions you feel? How might this be resolved? You may need to talk through alternatives with someone you trust.

4. Assume that you have found a job or service opportunity that fits with your life gifts, spiritual gifts, personality type, and passions. What is the atmosphere needed for it to mesh with your top eight values?

5. Imagine that a biographer is about to write your life story. As the writer speaks with one of your friends, a co-worker, and members of your family, what values would you like them to say you held highest?

Friend:

Co-worker:

Family member:

Are there any conflicts?

Are there changes you need to make to hold these values?

For Journal or Discussion

1. Think of someone you view as a role model. Look through the list of values and think about which ones they might hold as their top eight. In what ways would you want to emulate their values?

2. Choose one of your top eight values and ponder how and why it became important to you. How might you influence values in others?

3. What values do you wish to see upheld in your family? Workplace? Place of worship? In what ways might you work toward seeing those values in action?

LifeKey #6

You are called to serve where you can harmonize with God's song in your heart.

CHAPTER 6

PASSIONS—WHAT GOD PUTS IN YOUR HEART

I loved drama and music and puppetry and I liked television and I liked philosophy and religion. But the moment I realized that all of those could be used in the service of children and their families, that's when I knew who I was.[1]

—Mister Rogers

"Lyda Rose, I'm home again, Rose . . ." Was this beautiful song from *The Music Man* your introduction to barbershop music? Do you remember that the four town council members who sang it hated each other—until Professor Harold Hill showed them how to sing in harmony? These four, who had previously quibbled about everything, now couldn't bear to be apart, so great was their delight in their music. They sang on the courthouse steps, in the town square, in the street, and at the stable, enjoying the harmony so much that they forgot their intent to tar and feather Professor Hill.

These men had a passion: a desire or purpose that brought them joy, helped them overlook their differences and difficulties, and brought its own rewards.

Webster's defines passion as a powerful emotion: "Passion, fervor, ardor, enthusiasm, zeal." The word *enthusiasm* comes from the Greek phrase *en theos*, "with God." Thus if you are *enthusiastically* pursuing a passion that God has put in your heart, you are doing it *with God!* You've found those good works God prepared in advance for you. Your enthusiasm provides the energy and stamina

---

[1]From a radio interview on *Fresh Air*, National Public Radio. Retrieved from *www.npr.org/dmg/audioplayer.php?prgCode=FA&showDate=28-Feb–2003&segNum=3v*

you'll need to persevere. Think of what can happen when God places these motivations in your heart.

Passionate People in Action

Think, for example, of Nehemiah, who was just one of the thousands of Jewish exiles living in Babylon. When Nehemiah heard that Jerusalem still lay in ruins, he fasted, wept, and prayed for several days—and then took action. He gained permission from his captors to lead a party back to Jerusalem to rebuild the city walls. Once there he formulated his plan: "I set out during the night with a few men. I had not told anyone *what my God had put in my heart* to do for Jerusalem" (Nehemiah 2:12, emphasis ours).

The rest of the story is full of drama. The workers hauled stone with one hand while carrying swords in the other to fend off attackers. They stood guard over their progress at night and worked by day. Conspirators hired false prophets to discredit Nehemiah, but he and his workers rebuilt the walls in just fifty-two days! Through it all, Nehemiah was convinced that he was *en theos,* carrying out God's designs.

The Shapes and Sizes of Passions

Few of us are called to rebuild a city, but what might God put in your heart? Just as we saw with spiritual gifts, some people act on their passions in leadership roles while others serve one-on-one. God needs passions in all shapes and sizes. At a church in Seattle, for example, David helped people start ministries that God had placed in their hearts. One man, a computer expert, wanted to network all the homeless shelters in the city so that people could easily find a safe place for the night. Another woman, a retiree, wanted to bake cookies for all of the latchkey children who lived on her apartment building floor so she could serve as an on-the-spot checkpoint so that their parents could know they'd arrived home from school safely. Neither passion is more or less important, but instead, each one fit the volunteer's *LifeKeys.*

You may be given a small passion *in the eyes of the world,* like maintaining a pick-up basketball court in the church yard so that neighborhood kids feel welcomed by the church. Know that *in God's eyes* no passion is small. Or you may be given a passion that targets thousands, such as ending gang wars in a city. Remember, God asks some of us to help one person at a time and others of us to marshal support for widespread efforts. It isn't the scope of your passion that counts, but whether or not it is from God. The world can use all kinds of help.

Instead of worrying about the size or scope of your passion, ask, "What are those good works God planned in advance for *me*?" Now that you understand who you are and what you do best, you can find the intersection between your special design and what God most wants done.

Marlys, a friend of Jane's, might not understand why we consider her a modern-day Nehemiah, but she acted on what God put in her heart. Marlys had learned how much God loved her when she was left to raise her three girls alone. When she retired from teaching, her passion became helping others experience God's love as she did.

One day her friend Sophie asked to explain a new refugee outreach project to Marlys. When they met, Sophie told her, "The refugees in this camp have nothing but the clothes they were wearing when the armies approached their villages. One of our missionaries invited each family to write a letter that detailed their needs. I suppose we could just ship food and clothing in bulk, but I would love to answer the letters personally and send each family a box prepared *just* for them."

"How many families are there?" asked Marlys, as she gazed at the photos the missionary had taken of the tents, the dirty stream that was the camp's only water supply, and the children dressed in ragged clothing.

"We have letters from 1,200 families. Two of the teachers at my school started translating them from Spanish. The women's group at my church held a clothing drive that took care of one-third of the families' needs. With two-thirds more to go, I'm talking with other churches and people like you to help out with the rest. We need to respond as soon as possible—the letters are already a few months old."

Upon seeing the photos and hearing about the plight of these families, Marlys acted with enthusiasm on her passion. She didn't hesitate but a moment. "Give me four hundred of the letters. I know a few people who speak Spanish . . ."

Sophie stared at her. "Some of the families have a dozen children," she warned.

"Oh, I won't try to do this alone."

Distributing flyers and then collecting clothing in her own neighborhood produced enough donations to make Marlys's small basement look like an overstocked thrift store. When her grown children saw her efforts and her needs, they quickly canvassed their own neighborhoods. Her granddaughters convinced a group of teenage friends to spend an entire Saturday cleaning and sorting toys as well as packing the boxes to be shipped. With the help of her prayer group, friends, and neighbors whose curiosity was aroused, Marlys's basement soon became a temporary storehouse for four hundred neatly packed, individually labeled boxes of love.

Marlys called Sophie and happily reported, "The boxes are ready to go. Does that take care of all the letters or can I do more?" When letters arrived from another camp, she started again, with enthusiasm, knowing she was acting "with God."

How Did They Know What God Had in Mind?

In building the walls of a city or preparing a shipment of boxes to refugees, both Nehemiah and Marlys were ready to act on what God put into their heart. But how did they know what God had in mind for them?

1. They were already in a relationship with God.

Many Christians, when first starting out on this path of discovering their passions, focus too heavily on trying to discern God's will rather than on trying to get to know their Creator. Marlys, Nehemiah, and countless others who have learned to serve *en theos*, first spent time in prayer, study, and worship until they understood God's purposes.

Note that we are called human *beings*, not human *doings*! So many of us have been judged all of our lives by what we *do* that it is hard for us to imagine a God who wants us to *be*. King David, described by the prophet Samuel as a man after God's heart, described his intense longing for time with God:

O God, you are my God;
I earnestly search for you.

My soul thirsts for you;
My whole body longs for you.
(Psalm 63:1 NLT)

We're designed to yearn for God. Jesus called himself the vine and us His branches. Branches need time to grow strong before they can bear fruit. In the meantime, branches are called to "abide," to wait while remaining in the same place. When we are ready, God can guide us in bearing fruit. Do you need to know God better?

2. They were able to recognize God at work.

Both Marlys and Nehemiah were already looking for ways to be God's hands for others. Hearing God's voice, however, is seldom easy for anyone—Paul in writing to the Corinthian church spoke of seeing now only dimly through a mirror. Waiting for clear direction can also be dangerous. Even when God gives it, people often misunderstand! As a boy, Samuel didn't recognize God's voice calling him in the night (1 Samuel 3). His master, Eli, identified the voice as God's.

We all struggle today with hearing God's voice. One father was torn between wanting to serve on a mission trip and being reluctant to take an entire week of vacation away from his family. As he was debating what he should do, his boss called him in and said, "You've been working too hard—have an extra week off this year." (Have you *ever* heard of this happening?) He *still* wasn't sure if he should go on the mission trip. Most of us go through seasons of our lives without a clue about which way to turn. Yet we are promised, "Do not be conformed to this world, but be transformed by the renewing of your minds, so that you may discern what is the will of God—what is good and acceptable and perfect" (Romans 12:2 NRSV).

God's revelations to you have a pattern: first comes discovering who God is, then growing in maturity and fruit, and finally, discerning God's will for you.

3. They already understood how their *LifeKeys* could be of use to God; they didn't have to stop to analyze the fit.

When an opportunity to act *en theos* arises, people who have taken stock of their own abilities—without pride or false humility— know what to do. One of our motivations for *LifeKeys* is to help people reach the point where they can recognize their passions;

first, they need to explore what they are capable of doing.

George Barna once surveyed American adults to determine whether they knew their spiritual gifts.[2] Of those who had heard of spiritual gifts, fewer than a third could correctly name even one gift. Less than a quarter could name a single one of their own spiritual gifts. No wonder it is hard to dream! That is why we ask you to consider your passions only after you understand your other *LifeKeys*. Now that you have discovered the unique ways God has gifted you, we hope it will be easier for you to find those places to serve that have your name all over them.

Even with the motivation that their passions provided, however, neither Nehemiah nor Marlys faced an easy task. Both spent a great deal of time praying, gathering information, locating resources, and planning how they and others could best accomplish the work.

How Do I Find My Passions?

We hope that by now you have a basic understanding of who you are (personality and values) and what you do best (your life gifts and spiritual gifts). The remaining big question is why you're here. Which specific tasks, projects, or causes hold for you the most pull or energy? Where can you be *en theos,* enthusiastic, with God?

There are as many answers as there are people. For some of you the answers come easily. Are your shelves filled with books on gardening? Do seed catalogs flood your mailbox while you wait for those warm days to dig the soil and start your garden? Before you say, "Well, gardening isn't a God-given passion," think of the places where God could use a good gardener. Perhaps an elderly neighbor longs for help with her window boxes. Or the church landscaping needs attention. Or a sick individual's spirits could be lifted with flowers from your garden.

What if new product development and marketing hold your interest? When you're working on a fresh idea, hours go by in between glances at your watch. You eagerly make and return phone calls in hopes of finding prospective customers because you know they will benefit from your product. Besides, a successful product

[2]News Release, Barna Research Group, Ltd., Glendale, Calif. "Most Christians Are Oblivious to Their Spiritual Gifts" (October 3, 1995).

creates more jobs. If this is you, your passions for developing and marketing new things may tie in with God's needs for promoting and recruiting. From helping others to see how they can benefit by teaching Sunday school to promoting educational opportunities, God could put many things in your heart.

Again, passions come in all colors, shapes, and sizes—one size definitely does not fit all. Your passions may be focused, as was a women's group who baked birthday cakes for residents at a nearby nursing home. Or your passions may be as broad as the religious organization that ran the nursing home.

So how do you find passions? Some people are "dreamers"— they easily think of ways to be *en theos* and may struggle to narrow down what to do next for God. But people find passions in at least three other ways:

- **Are you a "one talent" person?**

  Are you an "I'm pretty happy any time I'm building (cooking, painting, driving)" person? Your passions may center on a specific life gift or interest, whether it be teaching, singing, accounting, or backpacking. Your path to enthusiasm may be finding different arenas that need your skills—like a friend of ours. She's used her "one talent" artistic life gift to design angels sold as fund-raisers, paint murals in the church nursery, and lead support groups for women just released from prison, using craft projects as ice breakers.

  This doesn't mean you accept every offer that comes your way. For example, one person with the gift of administration and a love for cooking organized church dinners out of a passion to increase fellowship in the church. Another with the same gifts organized delivery of meals to a family in crisis out of a passion to help those who grieve. Same gifts, different passions. Neither of them felt called, that is, felt enthusiasm, to fill the role of the other.

- **Are you a "make me an offer" person?**

  Would you like some options or a chance to try something before signing up? If asked, "What excites you?" does your mind project a blank screen? Or are you so busy in this season of life that you cringe at the thought of trying to envision your passion?

  You may enjoy linking up with visionaries—people who

have the idea, plan, and passion for a given service—who need more help to make their vision a reality. This book came about because David made "an offer" to Jane and Sandra. When David conveyed his vision for what became *LifeKeys*, Jane thought that perhaps her consulting skills and passion for writing might be needed. Sandra, already involved in helping others find places or positions that were a good fit, had longed to add a spiritual dimension to her efforts.

Frequently the "make me an offer" folk become very passionate about the project as well (here we are, David, Jane, and Sandra, still working on *LifeKeys* more than a decade later!). If you try a few offers or come up with some yourself, God can begin to direct you and guide you into areas where you will find great excitement.

- **Are your passions right under your nose?**

What about the heartfelt desire to be the best parent/friend/employee you can be? The most considerate neighbor? A competent coach? A teacher who makes a difference in the lives of those entrusted to him or her? You may not need to look any further than your current activities to uncover your passions.

If this describes you, then envision discovering your passions as digging deeper. One of David's friends was named Oilman of the Year back in the 1970s. David congratulated him, saying, "You must be one great prospector."

"No," he replied. "Last year I went back to forty-three existing oil fields and dug deeper. We hit new wells in all but one of those."

What can you do to dig deeper where you are? Or to help people who are similarly situated? One man changed the atmosphere in his office simply by taking the first reconciling step of having lunch with the three co-workers he liked least. When he showed that he cared, they passed on the same kindness to others. In an amazingly short space of time the office changed from a hostile, backbiting organization to a place of camaraderie.

Note that God can put passions into our heart in any arena, not just in the church or with the disenfranchised or through outreach programs. One of the early participants in our class said, "I've always had a passion for politics but have never made room for it—until now!" He became very active in the grass-roots efforts of his political party, trying to bring the values of his faith to this arena.

In other words, in many instances people don't need to search very hard to find a passion that they can act upon *en theos*—with God. Start by reviewing your discoveries about yourself through your life gifts, spiritual gifts, personality type, and values. Then begin a conversation with God about what you might do right where you are.

But My Plate Is Too Full to Add Passions!

If you find yourself a bit reluctant to *even begin* looking for passions, knowing full well that your life is too busy as it is, believe us, you have a lot of company. While it is true that Jesus compelled us to feed the hungry, welcome strangers, clothe the needy, care for the sick, and visit those in prison (Matthew 25:35–36), this may not be the stage of your life where you can do all of those at once.

The Bible is full of people who waited *a long time* for their chance to act. Jesus was probably thirty when he began His ministry. After his conversion, Paul spent about ten years in a small town before beginning his missionary travels. David is described as a youth when Samuel anointed him king; he was thirty before he finally became king of all Israel.

Or consider Esther. She concealed her Jewish background when she was chosen as a possible wife for the king of Babylon. Then a chance arose for her to influence the king to change his decree that all the Jews be killed. Her uncle Mordecai told her, "Who knows? Perhaps you have come to royal dignity for just such a time as this" (Esther 4:14 NRSV). Who knows for what purposes God might be preparing you?

If this is a season of waiting, consider what you can do to ready yourself for the next season. Do you need a deeper understanding of Scripture, better organizational skills, or a network of people who have done similar things? Would taking a class help? Should you be saving money for a van to use in future ministry? Are there ways your family could join you in your passion, thereby allowing your family to be *en theos* together?

Finally, God has places for you to be *en theos* no matter what your schedule. Look for ways to serve where you are:

- If your house is constantly overrun by neighborhood children, could your passion be teaching children how to be kind to one another?
- If everyone at your law office is overworked, could your passion be setting policies and billing structures that allow for more balance in life?
- If you are busy all day long, could your passion be to act as a kind and considerate person toward each customer/friend/relative you meet?

If you don't see yourself as a dreamer, a one-talent person, or in any of our other scenarios, perhaps this is the time for you to deepen your relationship with your Creator in preparation for those passions yet to come. Use this season to grow in trust, yet ponder this: If God gives you a passion, are you ready to say, "Yes, of course!" Believe that God loves you enough to place the right passions in your heart.

So often, though, we misunderstand what God is asking of us. Remember the Bible story of the ten talents? A rich man gave five talents to one servant, who traded and earned five more. A second servant received two talents, which he doubled as well. To these servants the master said, "Well done. You have been trustworthy in a few things; I will put you in charge of many things."

A third servant, given just one talent, feared that he might lose it. He hid it away because he believed his master to be harsh. When the master found out that this last servant hadn't even bothered to put it in the ancient equivalent of an insured interest-bearing account, he became angry at the servant's over caution. The master then took from the servant the one talent and gave it to the servant with the ten talents (Matthew 25:14–29).

The tragedy of the third servant is that he misunderstood. His master was benevolent, giving this servant no more than he could handle, yet the servant was afraid to try. Are you guilty of viewing God as harsh? God isn't waiting to punish us for erring while trying to use our gifts. Instead, we believe God grieves when we are afraid to try.

We are not to worry about how capable we are; we are simply to make the most of whatever we have. We have all been given a special package of gifts to use for God's glory. God wants to show you those good works prepared in advance for you so that someday you too will hear the words "Well done, good and faithful servant."

Can Passions Change?

Yet even God-given passions may change as your life changes. A person just launching a career may no longer have the passion to lead the Bible study that was so rewarding while in college; the old passion may be replaced with a new one of being a responsible employee with godly principles. Similarly, a couple with young children may need to take a break from working with the church youth group; the desire to lay their own foundation for good parenting could fill their hearts. Or a person experiencing illness or a life crisis may need to concentrate on renewing his or her own spiritual resources first; the desire to grow in faith in order to serve better in the future may be a person's most urgent God-given passion during recovery.

Occasionally God calls for a complete redirection of our passions. One much-in-demand evangelist was booked up to four years in advance. When his high-school-age son started to neglect schoolwork and in general cause his parents to worry, the evangelist canceled *all four years* of engagements. His passions refocused to include more time with his family; together they moved hundreds of miles away so the evangelist-father could take a job with a parish church. The son, who quickly settled down again once his father was close at hand, went on to establish his own ministry of evangelism that grew to reach many more people than his father had. Neither passion pursued by the father was better; evangelizing while traveling or within a parish are just different ways of serving God.

Sometimes God even changes your passions in ways that don't seem very *en theos* to you or to those around you, but life can bring surprises. A friend of David's, a banker who retired because of health problems, confided to a friend that he had always wanted to be a disc jockey. The friend knew the head of a Christian radio station who made a deal with the banker: "You can have a go at being a DJ if you'll take over as my financial manager." While the banker found he lacked the necessary life gifts to succeed on the air, he became a vital part of the station's management team.

How Can I Know If a Passion Is Right for Me?

As you contemplate what your passions might be, an obvious question is how to be sure a passion is from God and not an obsession flowing from some other source.

Even on a small scale, passions need to be tested. For example, one couple with a special needs child volunteered to work with a church committee to reach out to other families with special needs children. The couple seemed genuinely interested in helping others, but the pastor was uneasy with their participation. Through her counsel, the couple realized that they were still too bitter about their own situation to work well with other families. The minister helped them find a different ministry where they were better able to use their gifts.

Test your passions in the same way you test other decisions:

- Would Scripture prohibit you from acting on this passion?
- Do those who understand your gifts and talents believe this passion is a good fit for you?
- Do the trusted people around you see this passion as a possibility grounded in reality? As we will discuss below, however, sometimes God enables us to stretch beyond our "normal" capabilities.
- How well do you understand your motives? Could they possibly be too self-serving?
- As you pursue this passion, does your motivation increase or decrease the more you work with it?

There Is NO WAY I Have All the Gifts Needed for This Passion

If you feel like you don't have what it takes to follow through on what God has put in your heart, there are two things to keep in mind:

- Sometimes God works with a person for a time in a new and more focused way. For example, before Saul became king, Samuel revealed to him, "The Spirit of the Lord will come upon you in power, and you will prophesy with them; and you will be changed into a different person. Once these signs are fulfilled, do whatever your hand finds to do, for God is with you" (1 Samuel 10:6–7).
- Sometimes the gifts you need are in the people around you. Marlys didn't pack all of those boxes or translate all of the let-

ters herself. Nehemiah didn't build the walls single-handedly. Even if you are missing abilities that you believe are crucial, start to share your dreams with others, asking God to let them know if they are to join in. If you become convinced through the discerning questions above that a passion *is* from God, seek guidance as to how to carry on with it, whether or not you can do it alone.

Keep Moving

One of the biggest dangers in this whole process is analysis paralysis—never getting started on those good works because you're worried about discovering *just* what God has in mind for you. Again, start with examining how God has designed you. Add in where you see God at work, and you can't be too far from the place God has in mind for you. Don't become paralyzed by looking for only one "right" spot to serve. Many, many passions start as small inklings; it's only when you're in the middle of the *en theos* experience that you might really grasp the breadth of what God has planned.

One woman was very hesitant to lead a new support group, and did so only when a friend agreed to co-lead it. The woman soon discovered that she had the spiritual gift of *shepherding* and found her leadership role very natural, very *en theos*. Her passion grew, as did her efforts. However, if God at the beginning had let her see her future role as the organizer and leader of an entire small group ministry at a large church, she probably would have said, "Sorry, God, wrong person." Because she had trusted God enough to take that first step, God was able to work through her.

Remember Marlys as she was *en theos* with her passion to help others? She trusted God, she knew her own gifts, she saw God at work, and she signed up to help. Discovering what God has put in your heart—what your passions are—can bring the greatest contentment imaginable. Picture God waiting to put a new song in your heart, a song that comes from acting upon the passions that God designed just for you.

Prayer

Dear God, I want to serve en theos, *with You, but this is unknown territory. Help me remember that discovering what You have put in my heart can bring me the greatest contentment possible. You do not call all of us to be leaders or to care for children or to go to the mission field, but instead, You call each of us to the tasks for which You designed us. Be my guide as I work to uncover my passions. Amen.*

What Can I Do En Theos, *With God?*

We talked about four different approaches to discovering passions. Think about which approach might best suit you and turn first to the questions for that approach:

- **The "one talent" approach**—those people who look for chances to use a specific life gift or spiritual gift in a variety of arenas where they can become *en theos* with God.
- **The "make me an offer" approach**—those people who know their life gifts and spiritual gifts and are excited about teaming up with leaders who have vision for new or existing possibilities.
- **The "right under your nose" approach**—those people who might act on passions right where they are.
- **The "dreamer" approach**—those people who find this process easy and exciting and are ready to simply dream about what they might do for God.

Take time to answer these questions. Realize that many passions develop over months or even years (remember, we are allowed time to abide as we learn more about God). If this is your first experience in discerning what you might do for God, give yourself *ample* time!

And, we suggest that you not try to answer all of the questions, even in the section that suits you best. Instead, start with one or two questions—unless you are *highly* motivated.

For the "One Talent" People

1. Look at the life gifts and spiritual gifts you recorded in "My *LifeKeys* Notations" (pages 286–287). Which of these could you use right now, *en theos,* with God?

2. The following list is meant to trigger your own thoughts. It is by no means exhaustive or all-inclusive—seriously try to think of *other* areas. Which skills might you enjoy using?

_____ Artistic expressions	_____ Mathematics
_____ Car repairs	_____ Office administration
_____ Carpentry	_____ Organizing events/
_____ Coaching athletics	parties
_____ Computers	_____ Photography
_____ Cooking	_____ Sewing
_____ Crafts	_____ Speaking
_____ Driving	_____ Storytelling
_____ General management	_____ Teaching
_____ Graphic arts	_____ Time management
_____ Home repairs	_____ Travel
_____ Interior design	_____ Word processing

What other areas can you add?

For the "Make Me an Offer" People

1. In the space below, write down the passions or interests of people you know who are already *en theos*. How could you help them accomplish their dreams? (Remember, sometimes the project may not be as important to you as the character of the person in charge.)

2. Find out what ministries and missions your church actively

supports. Which of these are of interest to you?

3. Get a list of the most recent volunteer opportunities available at your church or at another organization that seems appealing to you. Some churches have notebooks or databases with descriptions of available opportunities. Take time to review it for ideas. Write down which tasks interest you.

4. Contact the formal or informal leadership of your spiritual community in areas that seem attractive to you (for example, adult education, outreach, member involvement, music, etc.). Ask about their volunteer needs.

For the "Right Under Your Nose" People

1. List below the roles you play or have played during the past three years. Examples include employer, employee, parent, child, teacher, neighbor, citizen, patient, counselor, customer, etc. What concerns arose for you in those roles? Which concerns could you act upon?

2. Are there places where it is easy for you to serve in this season of your life? What activities do you already take part in that

could offer further opportunities for service that you would enjoy?

3. For the issues listed on the following chart, or others that concern you, where could you help right now?

Age group:

- ☐ Children
- ☐ Teens
- ☐ College/young adults
- ☐ Singles
- ☐ Young marrieds
- ☐ Parents of young children
- ☐ Parents of teens
- ☐ People approaching mid-life
- ☐ Empty nesters
- ☐ Seniors

People with practical needs:

- ☐ Education (or tutoring)
- ☐ Finance/budget issues
- ☐ Nursing/health care assistance
- ☐ Housing needs
- ☐ Immigration issues
- ☐ Legal advice/concerns
- ☐ Maintenance or repair needs
- ☐ Parenting concerns
- ☐ Prayer ministries
- ☐ Workplace issues

People with counseling needs:

- ☐ Substance abuse
- ☐ Marital counseling
- ☐ Families experiencing relationship problems/grief support
- ☐ Spiritual direction/discipleship
- ☐ Parents of special-needs children
- ☐ Support groups
- ☐ Terminal illnesses
- ☐ Mental health issues

Ministries to specific populations:

- ☐ Business and professional men or women
- ☐ Community/neighbors
- ☐ People with disabilities or illnesses
- ☐ Ethnic groups
- ☐ Refugees
- ☐ International students
- ☐ Missionaries
- ☐ New church members
- ☐ Unemployed
- ☐ The disenfranchised

Other:

4. As you look through your life gifts and spiritual gifts, how could you expand using them, finding new ways to minister to others?

For the Dreamers

1. If you had no fear of failure and limitless time and resources at your disposal, what would you do (after your trip around the world!)? What are some of the longings of your heart that you would finally be able to address? What "dreams" continually cross your mind?

2. If you could do some of the things you either feel you *should* do or have *wanted* to do for a long time, what would these be?

3. Name three people who have accomplished something that you would like to do. Because of their example, toward what causes or purposes might you like to turn your efforts?

Name of person	What they did	What I might do
1.		
2.		
3.		

4. Who is the one person who has made the strongest positive impact on your life? Why do you believe that person had such a powerful influence on you? As a result of his or her influence, where might you like to invest your time and effort?

For Journal or Discussion

1. Try to summarize in a few sentences two or three possible passions you believe God may have put in your heart where you could act *en theos*. Choose one of these and try to be specific as to how you might act on this passion.

2. If stuck, list nine or ten things you've really enjoyed—work, hobbies, volunteer activities, etc. How did you get involved? How do you *really* find your passions? "Right under your nose"? "Make me an offer"? "One talent"? "Dreamer"?

3. Sometimes it's difficult to discern whether you really shouldn't pursue something or if you're merely making excuses. Name something that you feel passionate about but unable to do. Journal or discuss with others the reality of pursuing it. Include passions you're already acting on but are questioning whether to continue.

4. Reflect on people in your life who were unable to complete a passion. Perhaps they died young or met an insurmountable roadblock. Are there ways to carry on their passions if you are motivated to do so? In your own life, is there anything you don't want to leave undone?

LifeKey #7

Keep in step with God's syncopation for your life.

CHAPTER 7

LIFE CHOICES—
ORCHESTRATING YOUR PRIORITIES

*Time is significant because it is so rare. It is completely irre-
trievable. You can never repeat it or relive it. There is no such
thing as a literal instant replay. That appears only on film. It travels alongside us every day, yet it has eternity wrapped up in it.*[1]
—Charles R. Swindoll

By now you've read the bulk of this book—and done a great
deal of discovery and reflection. We hope that with each chapter
the nature of who you are—your life gifts, spiritual gifts, personality type, values, and passions—has become increasingly clear. In
completing the passions exercise, you may even have envisioned an
exciting area of service or ministry that seems a perfect fit, and you
would love to begin. Ready, set, stop!

Stop, you say? Yes! Here's why. Most people who work through
these materials with us benefit from reflecting on how that new
good work will affect the rest of their lives. Many bewail, "It may
be exciting to understand my life gifts and spiritual gifts, but how
can I possibly find time to use them for God's purposes? I'm
already working two jobs just to pay off college debts and keep my
apartment." Or, "I don't have enough time for my children as it is."
"I haven't even taken a vacation in two years."

LifeKeys helps you discover who you are and what you do
best—intensely useful information. You can use it to appreciate
how God has designed you and those close to you. It will help you

---

[1]Charles R. Swindoll, *Living on the Ragged Edge* (Dallas: Word Publishing, 1985), 68.

sharpen your job skills, discover new leisure activities, and find meaningful places of service in your church or community. Nevertheless, the usefulness of this information is limited if *time constraints* keep you from putting it into action. So as we move toward a complete picture of orchestrating a life of harmony, let's take a look at time and busyness.

We know deep within us that the world is an incredibly busy place—and that our busyness is only getting worse. A few decades ago futurists predicted that the advent of computers would shorten the average work week. Instead, today people find that on top of the forty-plus hours they work, they can continue to be "at work" via cellular phones and laptop PCs. The virtual office of modern technology compels us to bring our jobs wherever we go. And go we do—if not physically, then through fax and e-mail. With instantaneous worldwide communication we can close a deal or answer inquiries twenty-four hours each day.

On the home front, the latest labor-saving devices simply raised the standards for entertaining, parenting, and home maintenance. Home-baked bread? Sure. Crisply ironed laundry? Sure. Perfectly manicured lawns? Why not? We all *expect* to accomplish more in less time, but instead we wind up with *no* time. A chance to redirect? Use our gifts for God? Maybe that's okay for others, you think, or maybe after you retire....

Even God took the seventh day to rest, yet people think they can get by without a lull in their schedule. With everything open on Sundays, we face a smorgasbord of *productive* activities. Because we can now do our work seven days a week, many of us lose the respite the Sabbath was meant to provide. Why relax? Why refocus on God? By filling up each day of the week, we often lose perspective on the whole of our lives. Gone is a weekly, ever-repeating opportunity to reflect and to reorient our direction. Schedules now dictate our lives so completely that we forget we can choose to change.

Is this hectic pace the life Jesus had in mind for us when He promised, "I came that they may have life, and have it abundantly?" (John 10:10 NRSV).

We are well aware that you can attend lengthy seminars, read books, and buy day planners to learn how to manage your time. Our objective is not an alternative time management system—instead, we hope to help you consciously examine what we call "life choices," providing a perspective for the decisions you face and a chance to reflect on where your time goes. Do your values match how you use your time? Is your time flexible enough to allow yourself to align with God's purposes? Are your current life choices your enemy or your ally?

God's Time

> God made us plain and simple, but we have made ourselves very complicated. (Ecclesiastes 7:29 TEV)

If you were given a three-year assignment of designing and implementing a task force to evangelize the world—without the use of television, newspapers, or radio—how would you begin? Form a committee to design a mission statement? Put together a business plan? Assemble a team of experts? Pinpoint all the critical events and strategize how to head off problems?

This, of course, was the goal of Jesus, but how did He choose to reach it?

Jesus had a strategic plan to carry out this assignment, but it contained none of the common elements we consider so necessary to successful planning. If we look at what He did, we can begin to see the choices God would have us make. Here are some of our thoughts:

1. Put *first things first*—seek the kingdom of God.

> As Jesus and his disciples were on their way, he came to a village where a woman named Martha opened her home to him. She had a sister called Mary, who sat at the Lord's feet listening to what he said. But Martha was distracted by all the preparations that had to be made. She came to him and asked, "Lord, don't you care that my sister has left me to do the work by myself? Tell her to help me!"
>
> "Martha, Martha," the Lord answered, "you are worried and upset about many things, but only one thing is needed. Mary has chosen what is better, and it will not be taken away from her" (Luke 10:38–42).

What does this passage mean? That we should all devote our lives to worship and study? Perhaps a few of us are meant to, but if no one cooked or farmed or nurtured children, life on earth would soon cease to be. Jesus fully expected to receive a meal while at Martha's house.

However, Martha placed the meal preparation tasks before her relationship with Jesus. We often do the same, hoping to squeeze God in between deadlines and phone calls. What Jesus is saying is that our relationship with God takes time, and we need to find it. This relationship would appear to be of far greater benefit to us than it is to God, yet as we can see from the story of Mary and Martha, God desires it as well.

God's intent is not that we go through certain rote, ordained gestures, but that we find a way to escape from the distractions of life in order to spend time with our Creator. *LifeKeys* stresses each person's uniqueness; included in that uniqueness is the suggestion that there is more than one way to be in an ongoing relationship with God. Personality type can help you examine a variety of meaningful ways to spend time with God. The following chart contains suggestions for spiritual practices for each type.

ISTJ	ISFJ
• Traditional Bible study, rituals • Daily devotions, contemplation, and prayer • Looking for concrete examples of God's grace in action • Engaging the senses through communion, music, candles, symbolic objects	• Spiritual direction for insights as to how God is at work • Being in nature to contemplate God's creation • Structured traditional daily devotions and prayer • Reading Bible verses that appeal to the senses—the lilies of the field, a single mustard seed, etc.
ISTP	ISFP
• Volunteering in tangible, practical ways • Exploring spiritual issues with trusted, like-minded others • Reading and reflecting about essential biblical facts and details • Being in nature	• Finding spiritual role models • Being in nature, meditating on God in natural things • Practical classes with a spiritual twist: parenting, getting organized, etc. • Small prayer or study group with close friends

ESTP	ESFP
• Volunteering to make a tangible difference • Experiential prayer—labyrinths, rituals such as Stations of the Cross • Activities in nature, often with friends • Worship in informal settings, active participation	• Group devotions or study time • Looking for concrete experiences of God in daily life • Bible study for practical applications • Vibrant, joyful spiritual gatherings
ESTJ	**ESFJ**
• Blending prayer with everyday activities—driving, exercising, reading newspapers • Structured Bible study with others • Leading pragmatic volunteer efforts • Retreats, rallies, and other spiritual gatherings	• Group Bible study with applications to daily life • Regular spiritual practices • Retreats emphasizing fellowship • Reading/hearing accounts of God in the lives of others
INFJ	**INTJ**
• Journaling and poetic writing • In-depth study of Scripture, religious issues • Using creative imagery to make Scripture come alive • Time alone to reflect, meditate, and pray	• Spiritual direction to address specific issues • Intellectual study, dialogue, or debate on matters of faith • Contemplation, reflection, and meditation • Silent or directed spiritual retreats
INFP	**INTP**
• Studying about compassionate "giants" of faith • Prayer partners and prayer circles • Contemplation and meditation • Inspirational music, books, and symbols	• Intellectually demanding, challenging Bible study • Resources that demonstrate logically the principles of faith • Reflection, prayer, and meditation • Spiritually oriented discussions and debates

ENFP	ENTP
• Group study with ample time for discussion • Singing, acting, dancing, being in nature • Tapping diverse spiritual resources—books, films, insights from other faiths • Spontaneous prayer, perhaps prompted by symbolic reminders	• Joining with others in novel spiritual practices • Joining in major efforts to improve life for all • Challenging, intellectually vigorous Bible study • Studying how faith should influence major issues
ENFJ	ENTJ
• Leading others in spiritual experiences • Directed, reflective times for prayer • Studying the lives of spiritual leaders for insights • Small group for authentically sharing their spiritual journeys	• Crafting logical, biblically based principles • Discussion/dialogue with a respected spiritual leader/expert • Spending time in places of grandeur—cathedrals, forests, oceans, deserts • Intellectual connections between faith and science, art or philosophy

If you get bored with your spiritual practices, look at those for people with the opposite preferences. For example, INFJs would look at the suggestions for ESTPs. Sometimes when we're trying a practice we know the least about, we can't be in charge to the same degree and God can get our attention.

For some people, meaningful time with God may come through bringing to mind a certain verse of Scripture throughout the day. Others may focus their thoughts on God during a daily walk or during an extended period of quiet time only once or twice a week. Still others find that music or dance focuses their thoughts on their Creator.

Talk with others about what has worked for them. Try different approaches. Consider working with a spiritual director to enrich this part of your life. Above all, remember what Jesus told Martha: "Only one thing is needed."

As you schedule your days, keep asking yourself, "What is really required today? Have I made room for the *one thing* that is really needed in the midst of the urgent demands of life?" God is waiting for you. Seek time with God first as you work to make life choices.

2. Know your mission.

Jesus knew His mission—what He was called to Earth to do. In Capernaum, news had spread of His miracles:

> That evening after sunset the people brought to Jesus all the sick and demon-possessed. The whole town gathered at the door, and Jesus healed many who had various diseases. He also drove out many demons, but he would not let the demons speak because they knew who he was.
>
> Very early in the morning, while it was still dark, Jesus got up, left the house and went off to a solitary place, where he prayed. Simon and his companions went to look for him, and when they found him, they exclaimed: "Everyone is looking for you!"
>
> Jesus replied, "Let us go somewhere else—to the nearby villages—so I can preach there also. That is why I have come." So he traveled throughout Galilee, preaching in their synagogues and driving out demons. (Mark 1:32–39)

Jesus knew that His mission was to spread the news about the kingdom of God. That meant that once people had heard His teachings and had witnessed His healings, He moved on.

Have *you* identified *your* mission? As a spouse or parent or child, as a neighbor, as an employee, as a friend? Knowing your mission and taking it seriously will help to determine your priorities.

The process of this book—identifying your life gifts, spiritual gifts, personality, values, and passions—provides the tools you need to craft a mission statement for your life. The Life Gifts Sentence you wrote in chapter 2 is a good start. From there, if you are ready, you can use the questions in Writing a Personal Mission Statement (page 251) to guide you through this process.

A well-defined mission statement spells out your priorities in a way that leads you to say yes to activities and requests that are right for you. A friend put it this way: "I ask myself this: Given my mission, is this a *good* choice for me, or an *excellent* choice? It's best to leave the good choices for others—the excellent ones are all I can handle." She finds that knowing her mission keeps her focused on her priorities.

Priorities are funny; even if you know something is of utmost importance, you will not get to it unless you consciously make time for it. Urgent events (phone calls, persuasive volunteer recruiters, deadlines made by others) tend to keep you from the important. In Capernaum, there were plenty of urgent things for Jesus to do. Surely the people of that village could have kept Jesus busy with healings, debates, and teachings for weeks on end. Had Jesus not been acutely aware of the life choices embodied in His mission, He might have been tempted to stay in just one place that needed and accepted Him. Instead, His mission and priorities led Him to move on.

If you are going to have time and energy for your top priorities you will have to:

- *Know what they are.* Look over your "My *LifeKeys* Notations." What can't you live without? Choose among your priorities as if you were packing a suitcase with limited room—for that is what a calendar is.

- *Look ahead.* Plan monthly or even seasonally, not just daily or weekly. What are your busy times? What can you do to make room for your priorities in the midst of the urgent? Without scheduling in advance, you might miss your children's activities or other important family time. You won't easily find time for friends. You are unlikely to have time for planning a service project or taking part in a ministry unless you firmly plant these events on your calendar. You also need time for *no* schedule— times each month, week, and day that allow you to live spontaneously. Search out how full your calendar should be by reviewing the Judging/Perceiving preferences you identified in chapter 4.

- *Learn to say no to the* unimportant *urgent and postpone the* perceived *urgent.* Look for patterns in the events or activities that interrupt you or that keep you from your priorities. A writer of historical fiction, for example, discovered a pattern of too many phone calls—each of which pulled her mind back to the present and away from the time period of her story. Her solution was an answering machine and a set time each day for returning calls. A minister had to learn to evaluate people's requests to determine if they were as urgent as they claimed and if he was the only one who could respond to them. Perhaps a request can wait until you have more time in your schedule. Maybe you need to say no or offer to find someone else to help out.

3. Know your limits.

In Mark 6:32 we see Jesus attempt to take His disciples to a quiet place for rest after their first preaching tour. The crowds spotted Jesus and followed Him to the remote area He had chosen for prayer. Rather than avoid the crowds, Jesus had compassion on them and willingly taught for the rest of the day. At dinnertime, the disciples wanted to send the crowds away, but instead Jesus fed them through the miracle of the five loaves of bread and two fish. Read what happened when the people had finished eating:

> Immediately Jesus made his disciples get into the boat and go on ahead of him to Bethsaida, while he dismissed the crowd. After leaving them, he went up on a mountainside to pray. (Mark 6:45–46)

Jesus knew when He and the disciples could handle no more. He understood that the spiritual, mental, and physical demands made on our bodies can only be met if we also find time to rest and replenish the spirit. Yes, people came first, but He and His disciples had reached their limit.

Look at the word *recreation*. You need to re-*create* yourself through activities that bring rest to your body, mind, and soul. You may be re-created through time with a book, prayer, a long hike, or a cup of tea with a good friend.

Review your life gifts, those areas that are of interest to you, to see what might be helpful to allow you a place or activity to replenish. Do you make *time* for any of these activities? If not, ponder how you might alter your life choices to nourish yourself so that you can truly nourish others. Taking good care of yourself *must* be one of life's priorities. Without this care, you may fall victim to the many health problems related to stress. When you don't respect yourself and your limits, you lessen your ability to be a truly present help for others. Besides, stressed-out people are crabby, ineffective, and seldom good company.

> So there is a Sabbath rest still waiting for the people of God. For all who have entered into God's rest have rested from their labors, just as God did after creating the world. So let us do our best to enter that rest. (Hebrews 4:9–11 NLT)

4. Simplify your life.

> "Look at the birds of the air; they neither sow nor reap nor gather into barns, and yet your heavenly Father feeds them. Are you not of more value than they? And can any of you by worrying add a single hour to your span of life? And why do you worry about clothing? Consider the lilies of the field, how they grow; they neither toil nor spin, yet I tell you, even Solomon in all his glory was not clothed like one of these. But if God so clothes the grass of the field, which is alive today and tomorrow is thrown into the oven, will he not much more clothe you— you of little faith?" (Matthew 6:26–30 NRSV)

Do you ever look at your possessions as time-takers? First you need to shop for them, then pay for them, learn to use them, store them, clean them, keep them from being stolen, and organize them. Can you program that VCR you purchased to free you from the tyranny of TV schedules? Do you avoid using your time-saving food processor because washing it afterward takes too long?

Think about your schedule or your family's schedule. Are there things that you do only because you *always* have or think you *should*? Perhaps no one would mind cutting a few courses from Christmas dinner if doing so freed the hosts to spend more time visiting with and enjoying their guests. Maybe now is the time to check with family and friends to see if the traditions are still as restoring to everyone as they once were.

God tells us not to worry about our lives, what we shall eat or drink, or what we will wear. This is our directive to seek a simpler life. Jesus followed this directive and had most of the hours of His day available for ministry. However, the Bible does not instruct *all* of us to sell *all* of our possessions to simplify. The book of Acts mentions several early Christians who kept their homes, using them along with their wealth or earnings to help the church. They still had possessions but were willing to share them. The point is to hold things lightly, to keep priorities straight, and not to let your daily tasks and possessions *own* you.

No one can define simplicity for you, since one person's simplicity is another person's nightmare.[2] Buying the cheapest model bike is not simplicity if long-distance cycling is your means of

---

[2]For a stimulating treatment of this topic, see Richard J. Foster, *Freedom of Simplicity* (San Francisco: Harper & Row, 1981).

reducing stress. Choosing secondhand clothes is not simplicity if you feel scruffy or do it only to appear thrifty. And driving a car to its bitter end is only simplicity if the vehicle still safely and reliably meets your family's needs. Any attempt to define simplicity for someone else can quickly deteriorate into legalism. Our point here is this: Take a look at what you have and how you spend your time. See what things keep you from your priorities. Where necessary, simplify.

In his book *Celebration of Discipline* Richard Foster says, "Freedom from anxiety is characterized by three inner attitudes. If what we have we receive as a gift, and if what we have is to be cared for by God, and if what we have is [to be made] available to others, then we will possess freedom from anxiety. *This is the inward reality of simplicity.*"[3]

The apostle Paul found the key to simplicity:

> For I have learned to be content whatever the circumstances. I know what it is to be in need, and I know what it is to have plenty. I have learned the secret of being content in any and every situation, whether well fed or hungry, whether living in plenty or in want. I can do everything through him who gives me strength. (Philippians 4:11–13)

5. Reflect on those who seem to have enough time.

> "You are the light of the world. A city built on a hill cannot be hid. No one after lighting a lamp puts it under the bushel basket, but on the lampstand, and it gives light to all in the house. In the same way, let your light shine before others, so that they may see your good works and give glory to your Father in heaven" (Matthew 5:14–16 NRSV).

Your life choices matter to God. Along with your life gifts, spiritual gifts, and personality type, time is God's gift to you. Good works are waiting for you—no one else can do them for you. But how do you find the time?

Think of people you greatly admire. Where did they get time to accomplish what they did? If you compare yourself to Jesus, whose ministry lasted only three years, you may feel overwhelmed before

---

[3]Richard J. Foster, *Celebration of Discipline*, revised edition (San Francisco: Harper & Row, 1988), 88.

you begin. That's why the pages of *LifeKeys* are filled with stories that are easier to relate to. Still, where did Marlys find the time to pack four hundred refugee boxes? Where did Jeff find the time to build a playground? And how did those church members sew all of those choir robes?

Guess what? You have the same amount of time available to accomplish whatever God chooses for you. For each of us the clock and calendar still tick off the same number of minutes in a day, days in a month, and months in a year. Yes, some of us seem to need more sleep and some of us will live longer, but from an eternal perspective we have more or less the same amount of time.

And each minute that you have comes from God. Are you a good steward of those minutes? Have you learned how to use your time so that someday you will hear, "Well done, good and faithful servant"?

It *is* possible. We have the promise that "He who began a good work in you will carry it on to completion until the day of Christ Jesus" (Philippians 1:6).

Work through the life choices exercises with an eternal perspective. Use your time with God this week to prayerfully examine your schedule, your priorities, and your lifestyle. Reflect on how God might ask you to change it to find time for those good works that await you.

Prayer

Dear God, It would be so much easier if You could be my appointment secretary, saying yes and no and "not now, but later" for me. But I need to learn to live effectively in the here and now. From here on, all my time is Yours. Teach me how to use it, setting aside time for You, time for others, and time to re-create myself, so that I can be ready to do what You've created me to do. Amen.

Thinking Through Your Life Choices

Listed below are four of the biblical principles for life choices we discussed. The fifth is covered at length in the next chapter.

- In the space below each, write your own brief description of what the principle means to you.

224

- Rank the four principles in your own life, giving a "1" to the area you feel you manage the best and a "4" to the area where you believe you could most improve in making your life choices.

                                                              Your Ranking

1. Put first things first—seek the kingdom   _____
   of God.

2. Know your mission.   _____

3. Know your limits.   _____

4. Simplify—aim for balance in your life.   _____

- Below are lists of ideas recommended by our life choice experts—those who have taken our classes before—to help you weave these four biblical principles into your life. For those principles you ranked "3" or "4," which ideas might help you? With your calendar in hand, consider what changes you might commit to in this season of your life as you work to create life choices that more truly reflect the person you are.

1. Put first things first—seek the kingdom of God.

- Use commuting time for worship—with musical or devotional tapes.
- Buy a coffee maker with a timer—knowing that coffee is waiting may help you get up a few minutes earlier for prayer.
- Designate a special place in your home for worship—a chair, a closet, a room.
- Put time with God into your schedule before you plan anything else.
- Commit to a small group for worship or prayer.
- Keep track of the results in your life when you do *not* place God

at the top of your list. Any motivators here?

- Schedule regular retreat times—perhaps even an hour per week that you use as time alone with God.
- If the method you choose isn't working, try another!

What other suggestions might work for you?

2. Know your mission.

- Give yourself several months if necessary to determine your mission (see Writing a Personal Mission Statement, page 251). Write out your mission and keep a visible reminder handy.
- Say no to things that keep you from your mission. Give yourself time to think by not saying yes too quickly.
- Don't set the bar so high that you are doomed to failure.
- As you work to discover your mission, pray that you will "know it." This may take months of thought.
- Schedule time seasonally for reflection and evaluation of your priorities in view of your mission and your changing life circumstances.

What other suggestions might work for you?

3. Know your limits.

- Remember, even God rested on the seventh day!
- Let go of guilt. Take the *shoulds, musts,* and *have to's* out of your vocabulary.
- Leave your date book at home so that you have time to consider each request and determine if it is in line with your personal mission.
- View saying no as giving others an opportunity to develop or to serve!
- Build time for self-care into your schedule.
- Use your mission to set priorities and parameters for your life and thereby know where to draw the line.
- Ask not only what you can do for others, but what they might be better off doing for themselves.

What other suggestions might work for you?

4. Simplify—aim for balance in your life.

- Look at your activities, possessions, etc., as "overhead." Can you reduce or cut anything out and thereby be happier?
- Experiment with approaching an event, task, or celebration with simplicity, and discover the joy and freedom this may create.
- Don't give in to the clutter others say is necessary. Discern your own true needs.
- Establish your values so that you can more easily make decisions based on your own definition of simplicity.
- Stay away from stores and other distractions, unless you are shopping for or filling a specific need.
- Focus on what is *really* important for the day, perhaps the *one* most important activity.
- Focus on the eternal rather than on keeping up with the Joneses.

What other suggestions might work for you?

For Journal or Discussion

1. Think over your activities during the past week and figure out what percentage of your time went to the following activities:

	Percentage of time
• Work	
• Personal time	
• Time for God	
• Leisure activities	
• Family	
• Other	

   Ideally, is your time allotted the way you would like? Which area, if any, do you feel you'd like to spend more time pursuing? Which life choice principle is most applicable?

2. Review the four life choices principles listed above. Are there ways you can adjust how you spend your time? Use this space to commit to one or two steps that will help you move your life choices toward those God would have you make.

3. Which area is easiest for you? Describe to others how you make it work. Add suggestions to the lists given for each principle.

4. Consider how the four principles apply not only to you personally but to your workplace or volunteer activities. Are there ways you might help your church, volunteer organization, workplace, or other setting bring balance to life choices for the organization and those who work or worship there?

5. Reflect on Ecclesiastes 3:1–8, which begins, "There is a time for everything, and a season for every activity under heaven" (v. 1). What "time" is it in your life? Are you pursuing the right activities for this season?

LifeKey #8

Fulfillment is making music where God wants you to play.

CHAPTER 8

SERVICE—FOR WHOM WILL YOU PLAY?

There is nothing quite as exhilarating as getting out of bed in the morning, going back into the world, and knowing why. Enthusiasm is derived from the certainty that for this I was born, and I am doing it! It is thrilling knowledge that I am fulfilling God's intended purpose for me.[1]

—Bill Hull

A member of our congregation remarked, "I can easily summarize what it means to be a leader in the church. When I was promoted to the senior management team of my firm, I got a parking space with my name on it right by the door. When I became a church elder, I got to leave my car four blocks away to free up space in the church parking lot!"

Jesus made this point more than once: "'Whoever wants to become great among you must be your servant, and whoever wants to be first must be slave of all'" (Mark 10:43–44).

Servanthood is not a popular image in our society. The word evokes images of people at the beck and call of others, with little time for their own needs. Often this image of the woeful servant is layered onto Christian service until we believe, "If I am to serve, I shouldn't care for my own needs, nor will I be happy, because that isn't *holy*. I'll be a slave to others, belittling myself in the process— that's my fate if I want to be saintly."

We are quite certain that this is *not* the biblical view of servant-hood.

---

[1]Bill Hull, *Jesus Christ Disciple-Maker* (Colorado Springs: NavPress, 1984), 71.

Biblical Servanthood

The apostle John's account of the Last Supper begins, "Jesus knew that the Father had put all things under his power, and that he had come from God and was returning to God . . ." (John 13:3). So what did Jesus, with all the power of the world at His disposal, do next? Summon legions of angels? Perform great miracles that would sustain the faith of His disciples through the tumultuous events of the next few days? No, because He was confident in His own station, Jesus knelt and washed the disciples' feet.

True servants can perform *any* task—not because they are worth little or nothing but because they understand their own worth in God's eyes. Jesus served from a place of power, not weakness. He stands ready to help you serve in the same way. How? To illustrate, let's look at Simon Peter.

We first meet Peter in a fishing boat, his nets empty despite a night of hard work. Jesus does not yet ask Peter to follow Him; He instead asks Peter to row out to deep water and again cast out the nets. Peter, with his fishing expertise, doesn't think much of this idea, but as he obeys, his nets, and the nets of James and John in the other boat, are so full of fish that they begin to break. "When Simon Peter saw this, he fell at Jesus' knees and said, 'Go away from me, Lord; I am a sinful man!' " (Luke 5:8).

Jesus used the bulging nets of fish to show these first disciples not their own powerlessness but the power available to them as servants of God. He first reassures this little band of men that they need not be afraid. From now on they will do more than bring fish into a boat. They will work with Him to bring people to God— they are worthy of this great commission.

THE FIRST PRINCIPLE OF BIBLICAL SERVANTHOOD

*Serve from a place of fullness, not emptiness.
Jesus stands ready to fill your nets.*

If anyone had justification to serve from a place of shame or defeat, Peter certainly did. Even with the incredible advantage of being at Jesus' side for three years, Peter stumbled again and again until he turned his back on the Lord. Read anew how on the night when Jesus was arrested, Peter denied being a disciple even as Jesus looked on:

> Another asserted, "Certainly this fellow was with him, for he is a Galilean."
> Peter replied, "Man, I don't know what you're talking about!" Just as he was speaking, the rooster crowed. The Lord turned and looked straight at Peter. . . . And [Peter] went outside and wept bitterly. (Luke 22:59–62)

Just a few hours before, Peter had sworn that he would never desert Jesus. Imagine him, crushed and broken by his failings, returning to his fishing boat with his old partners. Miserable in their failure to remain loyal to Jesus, they sought something familiar to them. Once again, the disciples fished all night with nothing to show for their labor. A stranger on shore suggested they throw their nets on the other side of their boat. When they did so, they caught so many fish that the nets were too heavy to pull into the boat. As John exclaimed, "It is the Lord!" Peter was so excited that he jumped overboard with his clothes on!

Do you see how Jesus took Peter back to their beginning together, filling his nets with fish as a sign of forgiveness? This Peter, now knowing forgiveness, could proclaim his joy even after being imprisoned and flogged for preaching about Jesus, "rejoicing because they had been counted worthy of suffering disgrace for the Name. Day after day, in the temple courts and from house to house, they never stopped teaching and proclaiming the good news that Jesus is the Christ" (Acts 5:41–42).

Servants who allow God to fill their cup are free to be used for God's purposes. They are secure, solid, and healthy enough to align with purposes that are bigger than themselves. They can confidently pursue their mission in life, those good works God prepared in advance for them to do.

THE SECOND PRINCIPLE OF BIBLICAL SERVANTHOOD

Biblical servants ensure that their own needs are met so they can focus on the needs of others.

In the last chapter about life choices, we learned that God

designed us to take time for ourselves, just as Jesus did. Jesus went to weddings, visited with friends, and took time for personal prayer. He made sure that He was full before pouring himself out to others.

Martin Luther wrote that when he was particularly busy, he found he could spend no less than *two* hours a day in prayer. Luther knew that his spiritual nourishment was crucial if he was to have the energy to serve others. Rest, recreation, and renewing your relationship with God are vital—God designed you to require them. You *deserve* them. Joy-filled service happens when your own needs are satisfied in such a way that you can forget yourself and concentrate on the needs of others. Sometimes joy-filled service even feels like cheating because it is so full of satisfaction.

Servants who continually renew their own souls through the grace of God are ready to take their eyes off of themselves and begin to search out where to use their gifts—those places or settings to which God calls them. Sometimes these service environments are the equivalent of a holiday. The setting is so to their liking that it is as easy as a day at the beach. Other times, however, because God's purposes are often far-removed from the purposes of humankind, it may take some time and practice before the joy surfaces.

The gospel of Mark tells us that as Jesus prayed in the Garden of Gethsemane, He was deeply grieved, even to death (Mark 14:34). The cross was not the road to happiness or self-actualization, but it *was* the road to fulfillment.

There is a biblical difference between self-actualization and fulfillment. As Jesus was being arrested, He said to the disciple who tried to defend Him, "'Do you think that I cannot appeal to my Father, and he will at once send me more than twelve legions of angels? But how then would the scriptures be fulfilled, which say it must happen in this way?'" (Matthew 26:53–54 NRSV). Think of the self-actualization Jesus would have experienced if suddenly the heavenly host had appeared to rescue Him. Picture what Hollywood could do with such a scene!

Yet Jesus chose fulfillment. His prayers before He was arrested make it clear that the choice *was* His—once Jesus was on Earth, He had the same free will that you do to follow God's choices or your own choices. If you think Jesus' cosmic view of the consequences of His decisions gave Him a stronger will to do right than you could ever muster, then consider the disciples. The Gospels make it clear that these were *ordinary* men, just like you and me, with our giftedness and our weaknesses. They *chose* to continue their mission despite dangers of persecution, shipwreck, imprisonment, and death. Yet they were able to claim, as did Paul: "Therefore I am content with weaknesses, insults, hardships, persecutions, and calamities for the sake of Christ; for whenever I am weak, then I am strong" (2 Corinthians 12:10 NRSV).

THE THIRD PRINCIPLE OF BIBLICAL SERVANTHOOD

Finding ways to use our giftedness for God requires conscious commitment. God leaves the choice of serving or not serving in our hands.

Choosing fulfillment over personal happiness was the key to Paul's commitment to serving God, just as it is for you today. If you understand that you are making the choices God wants you to make—choices that will bring fulfillment to you and others—you can more easily turn from using your gifts for perhaps selfish happiness and turn toward using your gifts for God.

We choose our paths and our attitudes, including our attitude toward letting God influence our values and our passions—our choices about where to serve. Sometimes, though, you may not feel immediately that you are in the right spot. Many years ago a mother of three young children was once again at the endless job of cleaning the house. Feeling frustrated as she scrubbed the entryway floors, she complained, "God, I never have time for You anymore. My hours are filled being a nanny and housekeeper."

At that moment she felt the calming presence of God speaking to her, "But you are right where I want you, down on your knees where you can lift to me your prayers of praise and petition." The mother realized that one of God's missions for her life was a prayer ministry for others. Now that her children are grown, she continues daily worship and prayer for others. Down on her knees, working or praying or both, she has shown others the difference a love for Jesus can make—and she has found fulfillment for herself.

You may not find contentment immediately when you follow God's will. Like this young mother, you may be in the midst of your work before you realize what God has in mind. God doesn't promise happiness in every circumstance—but instead offers contentment to those who follow the call.

Does this sound frightening, as if God leads us blindly toward horrendous hardships and battles? Well, what if you choose a different path? What if you choose circumstances other than what God has in mind for you? Corrie and Betsie ten Boom found God's calming answer to these questions. As they faced choices while the German armies overran their country, Betsie remarked, "The center of His will is our only safety—Oh, Corrie, let us pray that we may always know it!"[2]

As humans, we want to ask, "Couldn't we just..." or "Yeah, but..." Time and again, though, people who step out in faith to the center of God's will eventually find that there is no place else they would rather be!

A. W. Tozer commented that God has taken responsibility for our eternal happiness and would willingly manage our lives if we would only allow it.[3] Is this the God in whom you have placed your faith? The One who is responsible for your eternity? The God who stands ready to bring contentment to you in every circumstance—not happiness, which could be superficial, but the deep-seated joy that comes through connecting yourself with the spirit of Christ? If so, answer your doubts with the thought that what God has in mind for you is far better than any other path you could take.

THE FOURTH PRINCIPLE OF BIBLICAL SERVANTHOOD

As we open our hearts to God's purposes, we become available to move to the places God wants us to be.

The paths may not always be obvious. When Jesus heard of the illness of His dear friend Lazarus, He had choices to make. He could have healed Lazarus from a distance—He had done it before in healing the centurion's servant. He could have hurried to Bethany—His agenda was His own. He could have saved Mary and

---

[2]Corrie ten Boom, *The Hiding Place* (Bantam edition, 1974), 67.
[3]A. W. Tozer, *Knowledge of the Holy* (San Francisco: Harper & Row, 1961), 69.

Martha a lot of worry by following their plan and healing their brother. However, He knew that God had another plan. God's purpose in that hour was to demonstrate the power Jesus had over life and death, even His own death on the cross. Jesus knew clearly, "'For I have come down from heaven to do the will of God who sent me, not to do my own will'" (John 6:38 NLT).

Mary and Martha also believed themselves to be servants of God, but as they mourned the death of their brother, God's intention escaped them. Both of them cried out to Jesus that if He had not tarried, Lazarus would not have died. They did not comprehend God's purposes until they heard the words of Jesus at the tomb and saw their brother living and breathing and walking once more.

Choosing to follow God's paths often results in these types of experiences—you believe you've done everything required of you and yet the situation worsens until you wonder if you really did choose correctly. The key to fulfillment is resting in the knowledge that you are within God's will even as you search to understand what God is doing.

THE FIFTH PRINCIPLE OF BIBLICAL SERVANTHOOD

Following God's leading does not always result in the world's approval. What will result is your own fulfillment as an instrument of God.

Paul says, "Am I now seeking human approval, or God's approval? Or am I trying to please people? If I were still pleasing people, I would not be a servant of Christ" (Galatians 1:10 NRSV). Paul's fulfillment came through knowing that he was carrying out purposes far greater than his own. When Paul was still Saul, he experienced self-actualization—he set his own goals and gained the respect of the religious authorities by persecuting the early church. He tasted worldly success. Yet once he met God on the road to Damascus, he chose to find fulfillment by acting for God. And that kind of fulfillment is eternal.

What Does a Modern Servant Look Like?

What are the first things that come to your mind as you think of modern-day servants of God? Someone who is self-sacrificing, away from home, working with the poor? There are many, many people who are *en theos,* acting with God, in these ways, but these are not the only servants. Often, however, the church celebrates this model of servanthood to the point that it is difficult to think of other types of servants. Compare your perceptions to the following people.

Consider what Dr. Diogenes Allen, professor emeritus of philosophy at Princeton Theological Seminary, once told his students: "Why was I chosen out of hundreds of candidates to chair this department? Sure, my Ph.D. is from Oxford, and literally all of the top schools sought me for their staff, but why am I here? Because I was *called.* This is where God wants me. Teaching is my calling, whether or not it perfectly fulfills my own interests—for if I could choose where to serve, it would be in a place like the Athens of ancient times, surrounded with other philosophers, filling my days with discourse and dialogue. But *here* is where God has called me, to influence my students."

Note that he didn't mention his abilities as a philosophy professor but that he has been called to use his life gifts and spiritual gifts in this place, at God's calling—for what God has placed in his heart.

Listen to another servant, a successful businessman: "I don't know why God gave me a talent for making money, but I'm sure this is what I am meant to do. The more I make, the more I can give away. I can sponsor youth programs, send entire missions teams, donate to building efforts—if I left my career to serve the poor myself, I'd only be one set of hands. This way, I can multiply what I could do alone."

Note that his heart isn't ruled by making money but by *giving* it away. He is a servant of God through and through, but in ways that are perhaps more hidden than the missionaries he supports, especially because he would rather give anonymously.

Or consider one family in India. David toured India as part of a missions/education group to survey the progress of various outreaches. The adults in one of the families David visited had attended seminary in the United States, then returned to their native country to serve. They chatted about life in America, and David mentioned some of the foods that he craved and planned to eat as soon as he returned home. To David's astonishment, in a land where American-style bread is almost unheard of, he was served a plate of French toast the very next morning! David was left to wonder at the effort his hosts must have gone through to offer this luxury. The family had applied their ingenuity and their knowledge of David's homeland to serve him, a student, who had come to serve them.

THE SIXTH PRINCIPLE OF BIBLICAL SERVANTHOOD

The right place for you to serve is where God calls you to serve, whether far away or right where you are.

Biblical servants can be found everywhere today, from the board rooms of multinational corporations to pockets of urban decay, from the laboratories of the great research hospitals to the streets where volunteers help children cross safely as they walk to school. Perhaps too many of us tend to confine servanthood to the exotic or unusual—and we know certainly that some of us are called to serve in such ways. But God also calls many of us to have a servant's heart right where we are. Often God is simply waiting for us to lift our eyes to see, really see, all the opportunities to be servants.

How Do I Get From Here to There?

Maybe your journey isn't from here to there at all, but a series of small steps to realign who you are and what you do best. Service isn't necessarily *over there*. It might be *right beside you*. It may take time and effort to discover where God calls you to serve.

The answer, too, may be a process, not a single, life-changing call. Take a look back over your *LifeKeys*—your interests, your gifts, your personality, your passions, your values. You may not see the patterns until you come round the next bend. For Jack, a friend of ours, the pattern in the end surprised him, yet was obvious in hindsight.

Growing up in a church where missionaries were the celebrated heroes, Jack knew firsthand many such servants of God. Family friends, home on furlough from foreign countries, often dined with Jack's parents. As a boy, he loved to hear their stories. He saw his parents restrict their own spending so as to have more funds available to support several mission projects. However, Jack never experienced "a call" to such work and went off to college to major in business.

Jack soon discovered his life gifts for negotiating, selling, and leading. By the age of thirty, he found himself an extremely successful businessman. His career led to settings that truly appealed to his personality. He loved the competitive atmosphere where he worked; information was the key ingredient to his trade, and he enjoyed every minute of the pursuit for the best tips and most current knowledge.

Success, however, did not turn Jack from his upbringing. He continually looked for ways to serve God other than the full-time missionary vocations that had been his childhood models, but he struggled to find ones that fit his gifts. Jack and his wife gave to several mission efforts out of their spiritual gift of giving. Jack also felt himself pulled toward planning teams at his church—especially planning for missions—acting through his spiritual gift of leadership. Serving meals together as a family at the Salvation Army on Christmas Day became a tradition. While he was thus able to be a servant as well as a businessman, Jack still felt disconnected from these tasks. The tasks did not present the interesting challenge that his profession did, nor were the atmospheres ones that really caught his attention.

As his fiftieth birthday drew near and as he reached the top of his profession, Jack realized that he was tired of competing: "It suddenly struck me that in order to be number one, I had to beat everyone else. I no longer wanted to see others lose. I wanted a different set of goals for my life, but I was afraid to leave the job that challenged me so completely. I needed that intellectual stimulation—that's how God made me."

While Jack was grateful for his success, he longed to do something significant—not necessarily in the eyes of the world, but something that would make a difference in the quality of life for other people. One afternoon, Jack ran into an old friend who had just completed an investigative visit to Uganda with an international organization that matched the skills of business leaders with the needs of people and projects in developing countries. As he heard his friend describe the educational, industrial, and financial consulting services these volunteer businesspeople were providing to various organizations, Jack felt an inner excitement—mission work with a business twist! He had never been able to picture himself as a traditional missionary, but this program would put his business-oriented life gifts to work.

This "chance" encounter led to Jack's own first visit to Africa, then to some training to develop intercultural skills that helped him fit into his new "mission" even more precisely, and finally to an early retirement so that he could serve in the places to which God was calling him. Besides a trip to Africa each year, he found new service projects that intrigued him all around his church and community—once he had the time and understood the ways God asked him to use his gifts. "I still use my hands to serve others, but I am confident that God wants me to use my money and my mind even more so.

"And when I travel under the auspices of a business endeavor, I can still do the work of God. Two years ago, because of my position as an 'expert,' I was able to convince a group of wealthy landowners that it made economic sense to pass on their knowledge of advanced agricultural techniques to their poverty-stricken tenant neighbors. When I returned to the area a few months ago, they had actually done so! Now their neighbors can produce enough food to feed themselves. The end of their vicious cycle of poverty may be in sight. The missionaries in the area hadn't been able to convince these farmers to love their neighbors, but in my role as a business leader, I was a part of breaking down that first barrier. Only a handful of people know that I played a role, but my joy in that role is far more significant than any other business deal I ever made."

Your Path to Servanthood

God calls some of you to leave your boats and embark upon a whole new life as a servant. Some of you might stay in your current roles, yet make other life choices that allow you to serve in new ways. Still others of you, like Jack, may find that the next season of your life brings together what God has been placing in your heart all along.

Whatever your own personal path, God has chosen it to fit your way of life, your giftedness, your own *LifeKeys*. Let God fill your nets to prepare you for those good works already chosen for you.

Prayer

Dear God, Help me to be a biblical servant, confident in how You have gifted me so that I can forget myself and become a part of Your purposes. Help me reach the point where it is more comfortable to know I am within the circle of Your will, no matter what that might mean, than anywhere outside Your will, no matter how safe that might seem. Show me the next steps. Amen.

For Journal or Discussion

1. Most of us aren't headed overseas, nor will we take early retirement, but will serve right where we are. Think about your workplace, family, and other arenas. How might you change what you do to reflect a servant's heart?

2. Who has been a servant to you? How?

3. Philippians 2:4 reminds us, "Each of you should look not only to your own interests, but also to the interests of others." To serve from a place of fullness, we need to look to our own interests, yet we still need to look outward as well. Contemplate your own life. Are you finding balance between meeting your needs and those of others? If not, what are some steps you could take?

4. Consider the six principles of biblical servanthood:

   - Serve from a place of fullness, not emptiness.
   - Biblical servants ensure that their own needs are met so they can focus on the needs of others.
   - Finding ways to use our giftedness for God requires conscious commitment. God leaves the choice of serving or not serving in our hands.
   - As we open our hearts to God's purposes, we become available to move to the places God wants us to be.
   - Following God's leading does not always result in the world's approval. What will result is your own fulfillment as an instrument of God.

- The right place to serve is where God calls you to serve, whether far away or right where you are.

Consider how these principles mesh with your views on service. Journal or discuss each one. Which seem true? Which seem difficult to act on? How do these redefine or expand your definition of the word *servant*?

5. Recall the words of the business executive who compared his reserved parking space at work to being asked to park down the street as a church elder. How else might Christian leaders act as servants?

6. The author of *Authentic Happiness* recounts how, after a dispute over whether happiness comes from having fun or from showing kindness, he gave his students an assignment to explore the question. They were to "engage in one pleasurable activity and one philanthropic activity, and write about both. The results were life-changing. The afterglow of the 'pleasurable' activity (hanging out with friends, or watching a movie, or eating a hot fudge sundae) paled in comparison with the effects of the kind action. When our philanthropic acts were spontaneous and called upon personal strengths, the whole day went better."[4] Have you experienced this as well? Give some concrete examples.

---

[4]Martin E. Seligman, *Authentic Happiness* (New York: The Free Press, 2002), 9.

A FINAL NOTE OF ENCOURAGEMENT

Once upon a time in a faraway land lived a young girl named Nalia. In Nalia's country, each person's sixteenth birthday was celebrated with a great feast. At the end of the evening, the parents of the honoree announced the future of the child—the special gifts their son or daughter had and how those gifts would be used.

Being the youngest of four daughters, Nalia watched as all of her sisters heard their futures. The oldest sister was a great musician, destined to beautify the lives of others through song. The next sister was a wonderful teacher who fostered a love of learning in her students. The third sister excelled in leadership and loved sports. She developed a recreational facility that provided rest and diversion to people in their town.

As Nalia's sixteenth birthday drew near, she wondered what her future would hold. "Surely my sisters got all the gifts—what could possibly be left for me? I'll probably end up with something I hate, stuck inside with too many people, instead of out in the gardens I love. Or worse yet, they'll assign me to something I can't do very well, like sales or singing with my sister."

As she pondered what she was sure would be a dismal future, she decided, "Why stay here at all? I'll run away before my party and make my own choices."

And that's just what Nalia did. Leaving her homeland behind, she went to work as a hired girl for a large household, spending most of her time cultivating their vegetable garden. Lonely, she often daydreamed about the beautiful flower gardens of her childhood home. Tears filled her eyes at memories of the first buttercups pushing through damp soil in the spring, roses in a dozen shades of pink, and walkways where she'd skipped and scampered and stopped still at the sight of new buds on her favorite bushes. Patiently, their gardener had taught her about what made each flower grow. "Well," she thought, "at least here I *am* outside, even if vegetables are quite dreary when compared to roses."

Years went by. One morning, as she cleared their breakfast table, she heard her mistress saying, "No, those aqua-tipped flowers are no longer available. The gardener who used to care for them died several years ago and no one else in that land knew how to care for them."

Nalia wondered. *Her parents'* garden had been famous for its aqua-tipped violets. Could they be talking about her old friend the gardener? She just had to find out. Promising to return if she could, she packed her few belongings and caught a ride with a neighbor who happened to be traveling her direction.

Shy after being gone so long, Nalia approached her old home by the back way, not sure how she would be greeted if she went to the front door. To her horror, the beautiful garden was in ruins. What could have happened? Were all the members of her family dead? No, for she could hear her sister singing through the parlor window. And, who was staring at her from the stable entrance?

"Nalia? It *is* you!" her mother cried as she ran toward her. As they hugged and assured each other that all was well, Nalia asked, "But what has happened to our flowers?"

With a sigh of sadness, her mother replied, "They were *yours*, for you to care for as soon as you turned sixteen. Only you had the passion and love of growing things to nurture our garden when the old gardener retired. When you left, there was no one else to take your place. But now that you have returned, we can celebrate your feast, tell you of your path for the future . . . as soon as you tell us why you left."

What could Nalia say? That she had left because she assumed her parents—who had watched her, looking for her natural bent, the way she *should* go, her gifts, her passions, her values—would send her down a path of frustration? "I'm sorry ... I didn't understand ... but now I do and—let's celebrate!"

———— ∞∞ ————

And yes, they did live happily ever after, and the garden flourished as Nalia began the future for which she was designed. Your future can hold the same fulfillment as Nalia's, for yours is more than a fable. While our parents may not have the same insights as those in Nalia's country, God does, and has promised that we are here for a special purpose.

LifeKeys is an individual journey. Very few people complete such a journey in a few days, weeks, or even months; the progress varies greatly depending on where a person starts. As you finish these pages, you may be just at the beginning of your personal discovery. We encourage you to reread what you have learned about yourself several times over the next few weeks. This review helps surface your *LifeKeys* in different ways until you understand what they mean for your future.

As we end each *LifeKeys* class, we hold a short prayer service. We return to the three underlying themes on which this book and the class are based, allowing people a chance to reflect on what these themes mean to them.

- *Do you believe that you are created in the image of God?* For many of our participants, the class has helped them realize for the first time:

  "I am a valuable soul just as I am ... even in the small things I do—God cares and loves me."
  "I now see myself as a person of value because God made me uniquely."

- *Do you believe that God has given you a special blend of life gifts, spiritual gifts, personality type, and values? That you are indeed fearfully and wonderfully made?* Some of our participants learn to celebrate the gifts God chose specifically for them!

  "I'll never see my own abilities or those of others in quite the same way again!"

"I'm no longer afraid to discover my gifts, for whatever they are, I know they are just right for me!"

- *Do you believe that God has planned good works for you to do?* A few of our participants find affirmation for areas of service or ministry that they have long contemplated. Others are ready to begin the search for the good works God has planned.

"Now I am focused. I know my vision, my passions, and how to use my giftedness to ensure God's dream for me."

"I think I am at the point, after a somewhat dormant season, to step out in faith and begin using gifts I've come to understand more clearly."

"I commit to continue the process of discovering where my gifts can be used and having unwavering FAITH in the path I'm on, even as it changes and grows."

During a silent moment for personal reflection, we ask each person to offer up a commitment to God, placing their response to the following in an offering plate:

As I leave this class, I want to make a commitment to action, be it in continuing on the journey of discovering what God has created me to be or carrying out those good works prepared in advance for me.

The commitments range from promising to view themselves as people of value to stepping out in faith to start new ministries.

What is your next step?

Can you say with your heart, in a paraphrase of Ephesians 2:10: "For I am fearfully and wonderfully made by God, created in Christ Jesus for good works, which God prepared in advance for me to be my way of life"?

It is true—you are a valuable soul just as you are! Whatever God has chosen for your good works, they are chosen to fit your way of life, your calling, your mission. May your *LifeKeys* help you find true fulfillment!

For Journal or Discussion

1. Place yourself in Nalia's shoes, and reflect back to chapter 1 where we asked you about childhood dreams you never pursued.

Did you, like Nalia, think such dreams were impossible? What might you do now to act on those dreams?

2. Read *The Tale of Three Trees,*[1] a folktale retold for children but with a universal message about our struggles to understand what God is doing in our lives. If you, like each of the trees, feel despair that God can't work through your circumstances, reflect or journal about the message the story might have for you.

3. What might your next step be? Below are suggestions that others have found helpful:

   • Find a friend or group of people to again work through your *LifeKeys,* using the discussion questions at the end of each chapter.

   • Choose and read a book that will help you dig more deeply into a specific *LifeKey.* A list of suggestions is found on pages 283–285.

   • Work through one of the specific *LifeKeys* applications: Volunteering (page 255), First Career (page 263), Midlife Transitions (page 269), and Retirement (page 277).

   • If you identified growing closer to God as your first priority right now, consider meeting with a minister or spiritual director for suggestions on prayer and study that might help you.

   • Meet with a volunteer coordinator or people involved with specific ministries to understand how you might join with them.

4. Write a letter to yourself. Include what you've learned about your *LifeKeys* and your commitments as to how you will continue the process in the weeks ahead. Mark your calendar with a time to reread this letter six weeks from now.

5. As a group, discuss how you might support each other in continuing the *LifeKeys* process. Other groups have:

   • Spent time in deep discussion over life gifts and spiritual gifts, helping each person discern which ones they have.

   • Chosen a service opportunity to volunteer for together.

   • Read a follow-up book together. Favorites of other groups include:

     · *Finding and Following God's Will* (Kise). An in-depth look, through stories and biblical teaching, at how God guides us.

---

[1]Angela Elwell Hunt, *The Tale of Three Trees* (Batavia, Ill.: Lion Publishing, 1989).

- *SoulTypes: Matching Your Personality and Spiritual Path* (Hirsh and Kise). Understanding how your personality type influences your spiritual practices.
- *Working With Purpose* (Kise and Stark). The five "corporate callings" we have as Christians and ways to influence corporations, without apologizing or proselytizing, to carry them out.
- *The Path* (Jones). A guide to writing personal mission statements.
- *The Life You've Always Wanted* (Ortberg). Understanding and working toward God's vision for our lives.
- *What's Your Type of Career?* (Dunning) or *Do What You Are* (Tieger and Tieger). Both provide career direction, using your personality type.
- *Looking at Type and Spirituality* (Hirsh and Kise). A deeper look at the impact of personality type on one's spiritual practices.

WRITING A PERSONAL MISSION STATEMENT

In chapter 5, we talked about how your values can become the foundation of a mission statement, serving as your "North Star" for life choices. To grasp how important a mission statement might be, imagine that it is the year 1492 and you are standing on the deck of the Santa Maria. Out in uncharted waters, tossed and turned by forces in the sea and air, you are unsure of the direction to head, yet desperate to stay on course.

As night falls, the stars appear one by one until they carpet the sky. Finally you can roll out the maps, pull out your sexton, and hone in on the only thing that allows you to find your bearings. Yes, there's Ursa Major. You follow the pointer stars to Ursa Minor and the North Star. You jot down your measurements and set the ship's course.

For us today, in these rapid waters that are so characteristic of our lives, a thoughtfully written mission statement is as important as the North Star was to Columbus. Especially for vocational choices, your mission statement can help you view yourself as a "business"—outlining what you do best, where you prefer to operate, and for what causes or purposes you will act.

Don't be surprised if it takes you four or five tries—or four or five months!—before you consider your mission statement adequate. Remember, you are creating a "North Star" for your life. Provided are four examples of mission statements to guide your first efforts. Note how *different* the four are. This is not an exact science, but an individual expression of what matters to you.

My mission is to help others reach their full potential, giving them tools and models to successfully continue the process on their own.

My mission is to envision, communicate, and live out a model of a Christian man in America in the 2000s, in order to impact and empower as many people as I can over the longest period of time and to the deepest extent for the gospel and the kingdom of God.

I will do this by following the leading of the Holy Spirit and the following values I hope to model:

A healthy, balanced life	Financial stewardship	Lover of learning
Long-term friendships	Laughter	Organization
Adventure and risk	Beauty and natural	Excellence
Creativity and vigor	things	Family
God and Jesus	Marriage	Self-respect
Integrity and character		

My mission is to become, with God's guidance, the best Christian woman I can possibly be. I will do this by combining my life gifts of creativity and imagination together with my spiritual gifts of encouragement and leadership to effect positive changes in my life and in the lives of others.

I will give of myself and my time to my immediate world and to our larger world by volunteering, being there for others, and spreading the message of God's peace and love.

My mission is to be a creator and builder of things that enrich others' lives and bring beauty and harmony into the world.

To uplift, to celebrate, and to help grow everyone I can through word and deed so that they may better know their own worth and through me know the unconditional love of God.

As a husband, to continually build an ever-growing, nurturing synergistic relationship.

As a father, to always love, nurture, encourage our children to *become growing and contributing human beings who, in achieving their potential, love themselves, God, others, and nature.*

As an executive, to create working environments where all feel they are growing and contributing. To lead my company based upon high principles, thereby affirming those principles to stake-holders and contributing to society.

As a part of the family of humankind, I am an employee of God in the business of transforming lives.

Review your responses in "My *LifeKeys* Notations," as you work your way through the following four steps:

- Write one or two sentences that describe your life gifts and spiritual gifts in order to summarize the things you do well.
- Reread your observations about your personality type (page 147) and your passions (page 211). Write one or two sentences that encapsulate the atmosphere where you would most likely choose to use your life gifts and spiritual gifts.
- From your values summary (page 188), adding from passions if appropriate, write out the purposes that really matter to you and for which you would likely take action.
- Bring your three sets of sentences together into one paragraph.

LifeKeys Applications

Volunteer and Service Opportunities

All of us can temporarily operate out of our *LifeKeys* and may do so for many reasons:

- We want to support a friend or family member's efforts.
- A crisis demands that we take action.
- No one else has stepped forward to help with something we want to see accomplished.
- We need to support an activity our children, spouse, friends, or other family members are involved in (school, sports, scouts, community organizations, etc.).

Often we even find joy in the activities we pursue in these ways. How much time you spend researching a volunteer opportunity will naturally depend on the depth of commitment you plan to make as well as the impact you will want to have on other people.

A first step, though, is considering what you hope to accomplish through volunteering. Sometimes our purposes are purely altruistic; we want to join with God in helping people. At other times, we have other legitimate motives. When that is true, identifying those motives is key to finding fulfilling experiences. Many of these other motives, as well as other criteria for volunteering, come from our *values* such as being of service, location, balance, or personal development. Others come from our *passions* or our *personality type*. These exercises are designed to help you sort through the whys of volunteering before looking at exactly what you might do for God.

1. While we volunteer to be of service to others, often other

legitimate motives are involved. Which might apply to you?

- I'm passionate about using my gift of _____.
- I want to serve while spending time with friends or family.
- I want to develop my gift of _____.
- I want some specific work experiences.
- I want to reinvigorate my spiritual life.
- I want to escape my daily routine.

What others can you think of? Does looking at these alter how/ where you need to serve right now?

2. You can use your life gifts pattern as a guide to understanding whether a volunteer opportunity might be a good match for you. Here are some questions to ask:

Realistic	Investigative
What concrete results might I see in my work?	How flexible are the hours and tasks?
How much would I work independently? With a group?	How much freedom is there in how things are done?
Are there many meetings?	Are there intellectual challenges?
How clear are the lines of duty and responsibility?	What opportunities to learn are available?
Artistic	**Social**
Are there chances to be imaginative, creative, or inventive?	How much emphasis is there on teamwork and social interaction?
How flexible are the hours and tasks?	How would I be helping people?
Are there chances to pursue projects independently?	What is the ultimate purpose of this effort/organization/event?
How structured is the environment?	Do people get to share their feelings or hunches about the work?
Enterprising	**Conventional**
What chances are there for leadership roles, formal or informal?	Are there clear job descriptions?
Are there opportunities to use sales or persuasive talents?	In what ways is the environment well organized and efficient?
How are above-and-beyond efforts recognized?	Are there consistent hours, duties, and systems?
In what ways is this a dynamic environment?	Do those in authority value accuracy and precision?

3. Look through your "My *LifeKeys* Notations." What factors are most important to you when considering volunteer opportunities? Examples might be "I'd like a set schedule," "I want to build relationships as I volunteer," "I need to be close to home," etc.

4. Re-sort your values cards, using the prompt "As I look for opportunities to volunteer, this is how I value _____." Some people find that they have a different mindset around volunteer work versus other areas of their lives.

5. With what kind of organization are you most comfortable volunteering? While churches need active members, it is also true that about 20 percent of the membership can handle 80 percent of the congregation's needs. Look at the list below to consider where else you might volunteer. Which places appeal to you the most? Then follow through and find out how you can help.

- At church, on Sundays or other days of the week
- Christian organizations (non church) such as Young Life, World Vision, YM/WCA
- Hospitals or nursing homes
- Schools
- Large nonprofit organizations (Red Cross, American Cancer Society)
- Local nonprofit organizations (a women's shelter, food shelf, or other small organization)
- As part of a ministry a friend is already involved in
- Where you can help with activities your children/family are part of (scouting, sports teams, camps, etc.)
- Camp or retreat settings
- Your home or another's home
- Playground/recreation center
- Prison
- Hospice

What other settings can you think of?

6. The following are typical volunteer opportunities that people with spiritual gifts in the four major categories often volunteer for. Which might you be interested in? If you aren't sure which fits you best, consider using the interview questions listed above in question 2 to explore an opportunity with someone who has experience in that area.

- Gifts of the Heart (Helps, Hospitality, Mercy, Faith, Giving)

  · One-on-one ministry, such as Stephen Ministries, deacons in some traditions, or other lay care opportunities
  · Volunteer work with local outreaches—child care, Habitat for Humanity, meal preparation and service, home/yard work for the elderly, van service driver, etc.
  · Providing a welcoming atmosphere—new member orientation, event planning, hosting gatherings, greeting visitors, worship planning
  · Fund-raising: leading or assisting with campaigns
  · Administrative tasks: office receptionist, desktop publishing, bulletin assembly, event registration, ushering
  · Maintenance tasks: grounds keeping, paint-a-thons, snow removal, carpentry, electrical work
  · Prayer team and other prayer ministries

- Gifts of Action (Leadership, Administration, Shepherding, Encouragement/Counseling, Apostleship)

  · Ministry or outreach leadership
  · Administrative positions—financial management, event organization, office administration, meal coordination
  · Small group leadership
  · Mission team planning, leadership
  · Support group facilitator

- Gifts of Proclamation (Evangelism, Teaching, Discernment, Knowledge, Prophecy, Wisdom)

  · Elected church leadership or organizational board of directors' membership
  · Advisory positions to ministers and other leaders
  · Teachers: Sunday school, Bible study, adult education, teen leadership, etc.
  · Planning or hosting outreach events, classes for people to explore questions of faith, or servant evangelism projects
  · Social action committee membership or leadership

- Gifts of Inspiration (Healing, Miracles, Tongues)

  · Hospital visitation
  · Planning or participating in healing services or gatherings,

with focus on spiritual, emotional, psychological, or physical healing
- Intercessory prayer teams
- Charismatic worship service leadership or planning/support
- Prayer chain ministries

A Note to Volunteer Coordinators

Teaching *LifeKeys* at various churches and organizations gives us the chance to interact with volunteer coordinators and directors. Often they are the hands and feet of getting congregations excited about gift identification and lay empowerment. For them, there can be tension between helping people discover what God has in mind for them to do and making sure that the church's ministries are well-staffed with volunteers. As we mentioned in our preface, we're quite sure that God has provided enough people with the right combination of gifts, if only everyone took time to unwrap them.

A children's minister we know well, who needs more than two hundred volunteers for her church's Sunday school program, admitted that she was skeptical about using *LifeKeys* to place people in ministry, saying, "When it comes time to fill the last twenty or so slots, as long as they have a pulse I'm not sure I care *how* they're gifted." One summer, though, she agreed to use the *LifeKeys* process to fill all the positions in their very robust Vacation Bible School program. She reported the results at a staff meeting, saying, "Not only was the quality of the program significantly higher than before, but the excitement of the volunteers—before, during, and after—was wonderful. Many already volunteered without being asked to do the same tasks next year—I've already got almost enough volunteers! For me it's proof positive that aligning volunteers with their *LifeKeys* works for me, the programs, and the volunteers."

However, we have also seen that many people seem reluctant to take *LifeKeys* if it is advertised solely as a way to identify gifts for service. Instead, we generally convey that the program is useful for work, volunteerism, and life changes such as retirement. We've found that people who come for other reasons may end up finding new passions for volunteer work as well, but we leave that choice to them.

Here are a few tips for volunteer coordinators that we have

gathered over the years. These have helped churches of all shapes, sizes, and locations use *LifeKeys* in helpful ways.

1. Note that frequently there is a delay between gift identification and volunteering for service.

   As you use *LifeKeys* in your congregation, be realistic about the timing of when people might engage in ministry. Some people will sign up and begin serving immediately. Most, however, need a period of time to internalize and integrate what they have discovered about themselves before they can volunteer. We suggest (as discussed further in the *LifeKeys Leadership Resource*) that you provide follow-up opportunities, perhaps as simple as providing resource references or contact information, for multiple applications, including volunteering, career counseling, and spiritual direction.

2. Not all volunteer needs will be met by *LifeKeys*, but many of the important ones will.

   While gift identification will help with volunteer needs, it won't solve all the problems. What *LifeKeys* does tend to create, however, are the types of volunteers willing to take leadership roles in ministries with larger time commitments, not one-time events or lesser commitments. At the church where *LifeKeys* started, every significant ministry was filled with *LifeKeys* "graduates." The *LifeKeys* process led them to feel a sense of empowerment and meaning in these opportunities.

3. At different stages of their church involvement, people will volunteer for different reasons.

   For new members, the motivation is often meeting new people or gaining a better understanding of their new church's mission and values. Longer-term members might volunteer out of a sense of tradition, the networks they've formed, or a host of other reasons. Don't expect all people, therefore, to volunteer based on their passions or giftedness, although many do. People engage for many different reasons.

4. Permission-giving structures and organizations will get far greater results than permission-hindering ones.

   Because *LifeKeys* encourages people to dream and discover their own passions, our graduates frequently come knocking on the doors of their church's staff, ready and eager to act on what God has put in their hearts. If your structures only encourage placement in existing ministries, those with new ideas may quickly get discouraged or look for another outlet for service. Therefore, expect to review and modify your leadership structures so that laypeople can act on their own callings and carry out the ministry for which God uniquely designed them.

First Career Direction

Few people are anxiety-free about their first career search. After part-time work or high school "McJobs," selecting and then finding a full-time "real" job can be scary. What-ifs abound: "What if I study the wrong courses? Find myself in the wrong career?" "What if I hate the career I choose?" "What if I can't get a job that I want?" "What if the work I'm trained for is something that I really find impossible to do?" "What if my work takes too much from me or takes me away from my other responsibilities?" The list could go on.

We believe that the *LifeKeys* process, at any stage in your life, can minimize the worries and the "what-ifs." The more you know about

- your life gifts (so well-grounded an approach that it is used by the United States government to classify all work);
- your personality type and the places or settings that fit you best;
- your values and those of your prospective career/organization/ co-workers;
- your passions ("I don't want people to know that I'd do this work for little or no pay");
- and your spiritual gifts ("How can I be a force for good no matter where I am?");
- the better your chances of finding a position that feels like the right choice for you. This is true whether you're straight out of high school or college, or entering the work force after raising a family or completing military service.

The season of your life, though, is just as important as you seek employment. Sandra, for example, was an at-home mother until her mid-thirties. She stayed active in church and nonprofit volunteer opportunities, and also served as a board member. Before entering the workplace, she completed a process similar to *LifeKeys* and took a "McJob" at a bookstore so her children could become accustomed to her working schedule. Even though she had a master's degree, she decided to pursue a more marketable degree while teaching at the college level to match her children's schedule. When the season was right for her and her family, she took a position with a large Fortune 100 company that valued her past volunteer experience and was a five-minute commute from where she lived! Providential, we think.

While this first career decision is a big one—in fact, one of the most important ones you will ever make—keep in mind that the average worker in the United States makes as many as five career changes in a lifetime. Most likely, you'll have more than one chance to review your *LifeKeys* and decide where your gifts, values, and passions are directing you next.

Seeking support as you seek career direction is often key to a successful process. Consider the following avenues for support— and share them with your family, friends, or others who are guiding you.

- Invite others who know you and who have special expertise in a career field to mentor you in your process.
- Seek people who have similar life gifts, personality types, seasons of life, etc., to advise you on an as-needed basis about your potential choices.
- Ask your family or close friends to encourage independence of thought and action rather than being too directive of your search. They'll be more comfortable in doing this if they have done their own *LifeKeys* process.
- Be supportive of yourself and seek others who are supportive of you—this can be a very trying time (check chapter 8 on biblical servanthood for suggestions).
- Avoid people who have an "I told you so" attitude when you are trying out new fields of endeavor. Not all of us aim perfectly in our first career move. Especially for Sensing types, experience in the field is the best teacher; and for Intuitive types, matching reality to a dream can be problematic. Give yourself the freedom to try again to find something that aligns with who you are, why you're here, and what you do best.

Remember that one meaning of vocation is "a function or station in life to which a person is called by God."

We do believe that knowing your *LifeKeys* will help you find your calling, as it has for countless others—and the three of us!

Life Gifts

1. The framework we used for life gifts, Holland's Interest Area Hexagon, is widely used for career development. Once you know your RIASEC letters, you can tap into other resources. Visit your library or school career development center and examine the following volumes for the wide variety of careers that match your interests:

   - *Occupational Outlook Handbook* (U.S. Department of Labor). Updated every two years, this volume describes the 250 occupations that cover six out of seven jobs currently most in demand. Learn about working conditions, earnings, employment outlook, and where to get more information.
   - *Selected Characteristics of Occupations Defined in the Revised Dictionary of Occupational Titles* (U.S. Department of Labor). While the title is intimidating, inside are descriptions of thousands of jobs, not just the handful we gave as sample occupations in chapter 2. Each one lists the skills needed so that you can compare them to your life gifts. The jobs are also listed by interest category—such as craft arts or sports. Craft arts, for example, includes engravers, picture framers, fiberglass model makers, sign painters, and many other jobs most of us have never heard of.
   - *Enhanced Guide for Occupational Exploration* (HST Works, Inc.). This book gives data for approximately three thousand jobs, including aptitude and physical requirements, employment outlook, descriptions to help you determine whether you would enjoy the tasks involved, and tips on preparing yourself for the job.

2. Design informational interview questions to use. The sample questions for volunteer positions (page 256) can help you discern whether a setting matches your interest pattern.

   Then spend time observing people working in a job; talk with them, using your informational interview questions; and volunteer in any way you can to explore firsthand whether the position interests you. While these suggestions seem obvious, Sandra in her years of career counseling has met countless people who never explored firsthand the career for which they were training themselves.

Spiritual Gifts

1. Look through the spiritual gifts you recorded in your "My *LifeKeys* Notations." Which ones do you hope to use vocationally? Which ones would you rather use avocationally? For example, some people with the gift of teaching will choose to only use it as a church volunteer. Others with that gift might pursue a degree in biblical studies, Christian education, theology, ministry, or other areas.

Personality Type

1. Pay close attention to the section labeled "Preferred Atmospheres for Work or Service" on your type page. Use it as a checklist: Do the careers or the settings you are exploring honor those aspects of your personality? If not, are you motivated enough to work in that setting in spite of conflicts? While personality type alone isn't enough information for career decisions, the information we provided is based on hundreds of people of each type and their experiences in finding productive work atmospheres for themselves.

2. Three books provide detailed information on using type as a guide for career search. Many libraries have them.

   - Dunning, Donna. *What's Your Type of Career: Unlock the Secrets of Your Personality to Find Your Perfect Career Path.* Mountain View, Calif.: Davies-Black Publishing, 2001. This book provides tips for how each type might best pursue the career search process as well as common pitfalls during the search.
   - Hirsh, Sandra Krebs, and Jean M. Kummerow. *LifeTypes.* New York: Warner Books, 1989. Sandra and Jean describe how each type labors (work settings), learns, pursues leisure, etc.
   - Tieger, Paul, and Barbara Barron-Tieger. *Do What You Are: Discover the Perfect Career for You Through the Secrets of Personality Type.* New York: Little Brown, 1995.

Values

1. Take a look at your top eight values, as you recorded on "My *LifeKeys* Notations," pages 286–287. Write a description of the

kind of work atmosphere that would honor your values. What factors should be present? For example, if you value *independence,* the workplace would honor individual effort and not just team performance. If you value *being of service,* you may be happier in nonprofit environments or for-profit companies that have a mission larger than profitability.

2. Sit down with someone who works in the field you are considering and ask him or her to identify the values most important in his or her workplace. How do these compare to yours? Consider showing the person your list. Where might they predict conflict?

Passions

1. Take a look at the passions you identified. Which might you act on through your career? Which through volunteer work? Which through your daily activities with family and friends?

2. Ask the important people in your life—parents, mentors, teachers, and other friends—what they would do differently. What if they could choose a first career all over again? What would be most important to them? What wouldn't they care about this time around?

Life Choices

1. Look back at the five biblical principles for making good life choices (pages 224–225). Which ones do you struggle with now? Which ones will be the most challenging as you start full-time employment?

2. The choices you make now can affect your ability to make other choices in the years ahead. Think about your attitude toward each of the following areas and make some commitments to yourself about staying in balance.

   • Finances. What are your attitudes toward saving and spending? Some couples commit to living on only one income even if they are both currently working. Some singles commit to never taking out debts other than a mortgage. Still others commit to certain levels of giving or saving. What choices might you make now?

- Service. As you look at first career choices, you have more opportunities now than possibly ever again to combine work and service. Explore ways that you might do so—for example, using computer training at a nonprofit organization, choosing a work location close to a site where you'd like to volunteer, or seeking employment at a firm that gives some time off for volunteer work.

Midlife Transitions

"Midlife Crisis." The term conjures images of forty-something men and women quitting jobs or striking out on momentous adventures, determined to "find themselves" before life passes them by. Yet in our early years of teaching *LifeKeys*, the midlife crises of many of our participants were thrust upon them by downsized industries, the natural milestones in raising children, such as sending the last child to first grade, or sudden health issues.

Often they weren't sure whether their first choices for careers, education, family lifestyle, where they lived, or even their leisure pursuits fit who they were. Yet they wanted to transition without jettisoning what was important to them. *LifeKeys* helped them look at both the challenges and opportunities of mid-life through the lens of what God might be calling them to do. Each *LifeKey* brings specific issues at mid-life. Read through the following exercises, two for each *LifeKey*, and choose the ones that apply best to your situation.

Life Gifts and Spiritual Gifts

In this area, we find good news and bad news. Those who chose their vocation for practical reasons, or based on skills, rather than on their giftedness, find that life is catching up with them. Just like Carla, on page 42, life changes (children, their own health, aging parents, are just a few examples) call for redirecting energy—which naturally declines as we age—that was formerly available for work. Some people's enthusiasm for work and volunteer opportunities diminishes, especially if their careers were mismatched with their life gifts or spiritual gifts.

However, at mid-life many people have had years to develop the gifts they *have* been using into finely tuned instruments. Focus at this point in vocation or avocation can bring effectiveness. Mid-life is time to take stock of what you truly do well, give away those responsibilities that require acquired skills rather than life gifts, and seek more opportunities to use your true life gifts and spiritual gifts.

1. Review the life gifts and spiritual gifts you recorded in "My *LifeKeys* Notations." Which of these are you using currently? Which *LifeKeys* gifts do you want to use in the next season of your life? Are the lists the same or different in some way? It is okay if the gifts you list stay the same. But even if they do, consider which gifts have the greatest pull. Are they in the same interest area or are you shifting among them? For example, from emphasizing your Realistic gifts to emphasizing your Conventional gifts? Or from Gifts of Action to Gifts of Proclamation?

The top life gifts and spiritual gifts I'm using now   *Gifts for my next season*

2. Many *LifeKeys* participants are considering new education opportunities—to change careers, to pick up a skill they're missing, to enhance one of their gifts, for fun, or for personal fulfillment. Opportunities include evening classes, adult degree programs, Web classes, community education offerings, and one-time seminars and classes. One person put it this way: "If I don't start my college degree now, in four years I'll be four years older and still degreeless. . . ."

   Use the chart below to prompt ideas about training or education you might pursue.

- Consider whether you might pursue any of these for career advancement, to explore a possible hobby, or to improve your chances in the job market.
- What blocks are there in your life right now? How might you make room for educational dreams?

Academic Majors and Developmental Courses by Life Gift Interest Area

Realistic
Academic majors
Agriculture
Civil, mechanical engineering
Environmental studies
Forestry
Horticulture
Veterinary medicine

Developmental courses
Creative problem solving
Presentation skills
Strategic planning

Investigative
Academic majors
Anthropology
Astronomy
Economics
Geography
Medicine
Psychology

Developmental courses
Assertiveness and power
Persuasive presentation skills
Project planning

Artistic
Academic majors
Architecture
Art history
Graphic arts
Interior design
Literature/writing/languages
Music/dance/theater

Developmental courses
Financial skills
Public speaking
Time management

Social
Academic majors
Child development/education
Counseling
Cultural studies
Nursing/physical therapy
Religious studies
Social work

Developmental courses
Assertiveness
Conflict management
Business/financial skills

Enterprising
Academic majors
Business administration
History
Hotel/restaurant management
International relations
Political science
Speech communication

Developmental courses
Effective listening
Win-win negotiating
Critical reflection

Conventional
Academic majors
Accounting
Business education
Computer science
Consumer economics
Nutrition
Transportation

Developmental courses
Assertiveness
Creative problem solving
Managing change

Additionally, you might take classes to improve your effectiveness in using your spiritual gifts. A partial list of possibilities includes:

- Church classes
- Financial planning
- Small group training
- Seminary
- Sabbatical opportunities
- Small group study
- Counseling training

- Spiritual direction
- Mission school
- Online courses
- Bible Study Fellowship
- Self study

Personality Type

Type is a dynamic process in a person, not a static reality. In other words, while our personalities are inborn, they continue to develop over time as we mature. At mid-life, many people feel the pull of their third and fourth functions (see the chart on page 169). While these aren't part of our four-letter personality code, all of us need them. At mid-life (although this time frame varies widely among individuals):

- People with a preference for *Sensing*, after years of grounding their information in reality, begin to ponder the future, the parts of life that can't be seen, or see the benefits of trusting their hunches, all the realm of *Intuition*.
- People with a preference for *Intuition*, after years of trying new things, envisioning what might be, and using their imaginations, begin to concentrate on the here and now, the joys of the present moment, and the value of current reality, all the realm of *Sensing*.
- People with a preference for *Thinking*, after years of objective, logical decision-making, begin to tap into personal meaning and values, cultivate close relationships, and consider subjective criteria, all the realm of *Feeling*.
- People with a preference for *Feeling*, after years of stepping into the shoes of others and working out of their values, begin to explore logical thinking, raise doubts and criticisms, search for universal standards or principles, and remain objective, all the realm of *Thinking*.

You may think that your personality is changing, but the process is actually what Jung described as the "journey toward wholeness," or full development of your personality. This makes for new areas of growth, paths to spiritual growth, and deeper understanding of the many issues of life.

1. Have you sensed that the expression of your personality is shifting? What aspects of this part of you seem to want expression today? How is this different than in years past? As Jung put it, "We cannot live in the afternoon of life according to the program of life's morning. For what in the morning was true, will at evening have become a lie."[1]

   You might wish to review the Suggestions for Growth listed on your type page. These are helpful hints for developing your #3 and #4 functions, as listed in the type chart on page 169.

2. Jane and Sandra's research reveals that people experience both rest and richness through spiritual practices and pursuits that use their fourth function. The activities are *restful* because one has to turn off the dominant function to use the inferior (you can't see the forest and the trees at the same time—S and N— nor can you be objective and subjective at the same time—T and F). These out-of-character activities *enrich* our spiritual lives because when we leave our normal practices behind, we in a sense give up control. When we use the spiritual practices recommended for the inferior function, God can get our attention in new ways.

   On pages 216–218, look at the suggested spiritual practices for your opposite type; for example, INFJ would look at ESTP. Which ones might you try now? For more ideas, explore Sandra and Jane's book *SoulTypes: Matching Your Personality and Spiritual Path* (Augsburg Fortress Publishing, 2006).

Values

What we also see in the season of mid-life is a redefining of values. Some of this comes through natural passages and some from a desire to pursue long-buried dreams or neglected adventures.

---

[1]Carl Gustav Jung, *Modern Man in Search of a Soul* (Harvest Book), chapter 5.

Predictably, some values, like financial security and health, may be valued more highly due to circumstances and experiences. Systematically considering how values might shift helps people understand the different pulls of this season of life.

1. Consider the predictable changes that will happen in your life over the next five years. Will you still be taking care of children? Parents? Are there early retirement opportunities? Will your housing arrangements stay the same? Can you stay in your current job?

   How will your priorities shift? What will grow in value? What will diminish? Re-sort your *values* cards, thinking about these transitions. What will be most important to you in the afternoon of life? How do you perceive these shifts? Stressful? Natural? Easy?

My Current Top Eight Values	My "Next Season" Top Eight Values

2. Pretend you have two large trunks in front of you. One is to be filled with things you want to leave behind and one with things you want to keep for the future. Describe what would be the contents of each of these trunks and why.

Passions

At mid-life, many people find that their passions are shifting. Maybe they've accomplished their dreams, or they now know certain things will never come to be, or they've already redefined their goals after years of attempting to live out these early dreams. They may be living with second or third choices, wondering if the dreams are impossible. Mid-life is a chance to dream new dreams, tailoring them for the afternoon, not the morning of life. Our dreams need not be less, for now we have the added wisdom of experience.

Often people have stopped dreaming because of the demands and pressure of everyday life. What we do know, however, is that those who gave themselves the gift to dream new dreams in their midlife years, and acted upon those, became some of the happiest and most fulfilled people in their fifties and beyond.

1. Write down the dreams you had for yourself ten years ago, twenty years ago. How have your dreams changed, if at all? How might you recapture or pursue any of these dreams?

2. Some people at mid-life are concentrating on financial security, perhaps because they've worked in service industries with lower pay. Now they're thinking about paying for children's college tuition, saving for retirement, or decreasing a mortgage.

   Others, though, have perhaps found success and are looking for more meaning. If you could contribute to the next generation in some way, what would that look like? What legacy would you hope to leave behind? How might you empower the younger generation or pass on what you have learned? Through mentoring? Through activism? Through service? Are there issues, local or global, you would like to work on through your job, or avocationally?

Life Choices

At mid-life, you may feel a desire to make the "afternoon of life" trip a lot lighter than the "morning" trip. Letting go of stuff, relationships, past hurts, etc., becomes a major agenda for many as they move into a new chapter of life.

1. On the continuums below, mark how satisfied you are with the way you handle each of the four biblical principles for life choices:

Put First Things First—Seek God

I don't think I
spend enough time
with God.

I'm satisfied with
the spiritual side
of my life.

Know Your Mission

I don't seem to
have found a
clear purpose in life.

I have a
clear purpose
for my life.

Know Your Limits

I am often
worn out in
spirit, mind, or body.

I take enough
time to re-create
myself spiritually,
mentally, and physically.

Simplify—Aim for Balance in Your Life

Possessions
seem to sometimes
rule me.

I'm satisfied with
the way I handle
my possessions.

Now, with a different color pen or marker, mark where you would like to be on each continuum. Where is the biggest gap? How temporary is the problem? What can you control? Look back through the suggestions given for each of the four biblical principles (pages 225–227). Commit to acting on one or two as you make life choices at mid-life.

2. Mid-life brings a chance to reevaluate how you make choices. Consider the above continuums. Are your difficulties in moving toward your ideal views in any way hampered by the career choices you've made? Consider what you might do to make changes to bring things more in balance at work. For example, one physician started her own practice to avoid being pressured by partners with different values. A marketing representative changed firms to one that required less travel.

Retirement Planning

If you're like most people, you've spent more time planning a weekend outing than your retirement. People with a preference for Sensing often find it difficult because there are too many uncertainties, and retirement seems so far off. People with a preference for Intuition often view retirement as the "all things are possible" time of life and may not be realistic about their options.

In truth, with increasing life expectancy, if we are in good health, we need to plan for twenty to twenty-five years of retirement. There's a lot to sort out as we look toward retirement, a time to celebrate who we are yet acknowledge what is lost:

- Yes, we lose some of our vitality, but we've gained a deeper sense of our values and character.
- Yes, we're faced with our own mortality, but we've gained a clearer focus as to what is important in life. We let go of extraneous things.
- Yes, we have less energy available for work or activities we've deemed important, but we've gained wisdom that helps us use wisely the energy we have.
- Yes, we feel inadequate sometimes with our outdated training or lack of knowledge of technical advances, but we've had time to more fully develop our own life gifts and spiritual gifts.
- Yes, we're concerned about the world's deep problems that we're leaving to the next generation, but we've gained a desire to have an impact, to leave a legacy, to focus on things that matter eternally.

With all this in mind, use the following exercises to sort through what matters most to you in retirement. Begin planning ahead so that your life is filled with meaning and purpose.

1. Consider what might be your biggest concerns in retirement. Rate each on a scale of 1 to 10, with "1" being "I'm not concerned" and "10" being "I'm very concerned about this factor during my retirement":
   a. Financial security
   b. Health (your own and that of those close to you)

c. Meaning and purpose

d. Finding rest and balance

As you work through other exercises below, keep your concerns in mind.

2. The following are typical leisure activities often enjoyed by people within the six life gifts interest areas. An exercise follows the list.

Realistic

Activities with physical risk

Gardening

Home improvement projects

Hunting, fishing, camping

Sports, exercise

Animal training

Gourmet cooking

Driving/enjoying boats, planes, ATVs, etc.

Investigative

Attending classes, lectures

Walking, biking

Scientific hobbies

Chess

Computers

Photography

Reading

Continuing with your work

Artistic

Attending arts events

Drawing, painting

Flower arranging

Interior design

Photography

Music

Reading, writing

Yoga, Tai Chi, etc.

Social

Creative hobbies

Outdoor, solitary pursuits for rest

Community events

Entertaining

Friendship groups

Religious activities

Travel with friends

Volunteer work

Enterprising

Organizational leadership	Small entrepreneurial efforts
Competitive sports/cards	Vacations
Entertaining	Golf, sailing
Political activities	Fund-raising

Conventional

Arts and crafts	Traveling, tours or with family, RV
Collecting (stamps, coins)	
Home improvement projects	Volunteer work, especially
Organizing home/office	administrative tasks
Games, crossword puzzles	Vacation home

In strong relationships, people both find things in common and maintain their own identity by pursuing some interests on their own. The following exercise can help you discuss life in retirement.

a. Individually, highlight in one color those leisure activities that are most enjoyable for you.
b. Highlight in another color those that you are interested in trying.
c. Compare your chart with your spouse or friends.

Look for similarities and differences. Discuss together:

- Which activities could take the place of work in your lives?
- Which activities do you prefer doing individually?
- Which activities might you enjoy together?
- Are there new activities that you could pursue together that you hadn't considered before?

3. Each of us has a different tolerance level for taking risks. Further, there are different kinds of risk. How might you rate your comfort level in each area? High, medium, or low?

a. Taking physical risks
b. Taking financial risks
c. Taking interpersonal risks
d. Taking artistic risks
e. Taking entrepreneurial risks
f. Avoiding all risks

In retirement, what is your comfort level for risk in the following areas? High, medium, or low?

- Changing location
- Spending/saving
- Different arenas for volunteer work
- Pursuing new leisure activities
- Dealing with relationships (adult children, remarrying . . .)

4. Sometimes, when a career didn't bring meaning or fulfillment, people look toward retirement with dreams of a twenty-year vacation. However, for most of us, endless leisure activities eventually bring dissatisfaction. If you didn't enjoy your life work, how might you find meaning in retirement?

   a. Look back through your *personality type* (pages 148–163), especially:

   · Preferred Atmospheres for Work or Service
   · Contributions to Workplace or Spiritual Community
   · Typical Responsibilities or Tasks

   What was missing in your work life? How might you find it in retirement?

5. Consider your *life gifts*. Which ones didn't you get to use in your work? How might you use them in retirement? Might you wish to take a class to develop a life gift you never got a chance to use? Refer to question 2 in "Life Gifts," "Midlife Transitions," for ideas (page 270).

6. Think about your *spiritual gifts*. With the precious gift of time that retirement typically allows, which gift can you use or develop more fully?

7. Re-sort your *values* cards, thinking about retirement. What is or will be most important to you? Is there a difference if you think about the first two years of retirement vs. twenty-five years of retirement?

My Retirement Top Eight Values

Write your own definitions for any values that are new for you on this list.

How does this change your priorities of God, family, work, friends? How can you maintain balance?

What areas are under your control for making these changes? What will be difficult to control?

What areas of change might be stressful to you? Are there any potential conflicts?

Are there two or three concrete steps you can take to move toward your "retirement" values? What are they?

Consider the values of those closest to you (have them sort the cards if possible). How can you use your life gifts, spiritual gifts, or personality type to resolve any conflicts or make the most of values you share?

8. For many, rest and restoration is an important aspect of retirement. However, restoration comes through balance, where your use of time includes activities that feed your spiritual nature, your mind, and your physical health. What activities appeal to you in each area?

9. After completing the above exercises, choose one of the following as a way to summarize your goals for retirement:

   a. Make a list of goals for retirement.
   b. Write a letter to yourself about your hopes for ideal retirement years.

c. Share your goals with your family or other people who are important to you in this season of life.

10. Consider writing a new life gifts sentence or mission statement for your retirement.

Suggestions for Further Reading

Chapter 1

Bolles, Richard N. *What Color Is Your Parachute?* Berkeley, Calif.: Ten Speed Press, 2005.

Brand, Dr. Paul, and Philip Yancey. *In His Image.* Grand Rapids, Mich.: Zondervan, 1984.

Buford, Bob. *HalfTime.* Grand Rapids, Mich.: Zondervan, 1997.

Fox, Matthew. *The Reinvention of Work: A New Vision of Livelihood for Our Time.* New York: HarperCollins, 1994.

Chapter 2—Life Gifts

Bolles, Richard N. *How to Find Your Mission in Life.* Berkeley, Calif.: Ten Speed Press, 1991.

Bradley, John, and Jay Carty. *Discovering Your Natural Talents.* Colorado Springs: NavPress, 1994.

Hirsh, Sandra, and Jane Kise. *Strong Interest Inventory™: Resource: Strategies for Group and Individual Interpretations in Business and Organizational Settings.* Mountain View, Calif.: Consulting Psychologists Press, Inc., 1995.

Holland, John. *Making Vocational Choices.* Odessa, Fla.: Psychological Assessment Resources, Inc., 1992.

Chapter 3—Spiritual Gifts

Flynn, Leslie B. *19 Gifts of the Spirit.* Colorado Springs, Col.: Chariot Victor Publishing, 1994.

Murray, Andrew. *Teach Me to Pray*. Minneapolis: Bethany House Publishers, 2002.

Sherrill, John. *They Speak With Other Tongues*. Grand Rapids, Mich.: Fleming H. Revell, 1964.

Swindoll, Charles R. *Flying Closer to the Flame*. Dallas: Word Publishing, 1993.

Chapter 4—Personality Types

Duncan, Bruce. *Pray Your Way: Your Personality and God*. London: Darton, Longman, and Todd, Ltd., 1993.

Dunning, Donna. *What's Your Type of Career: Unlock the Secrets of Your Personality to Find Your Perfect Career Path*. Mountain View, Calif.: Davies-Black Publishing, 2001.

Hirsh, Sandra, and Jane Kise. *Looking at Type and Spirituality*. Gainesville, Fla.: Center for Applications of Psychological Type, 1997.

———. *SoulTypes: Matching Your Personality and Spiritual Path*. Minneapolis: Augsburg Fortress Publishing, 2006.

———. *Introduction to Type and Coaching*. Mountain View, Calif.: Consulting Psychologists Press, 2001.

———. *Work It Out: Clues to Solving People Problems at Work*, 2nd edition. Mountain View, Calif.: Davies-Black Publishing, 2005.

Hirsh, Sandra, and Jean Kummerow. *LifeTypes*. New York: Warner Books, 1989.

Tieger, Paul, and Barbara Barron-Tieger. *Do What You Are: Discover the Perfect Career for You Through the Secrets of Personality Type*. New York: Little Brown, 1995.

Chapter 5—Values

Covey, Stephen R. *The Seven Habits of Highly Effective People: Restoring the Character Ethic*. New York: Simon & Schuster, Fireside edition, 1990.

Chapter 6—Passions

Chang, Richard. *The Passion Plan*. San Francisco: Jossey-Bass, 2000.

Jones, Laurie Beth. *The Path*. New York: Hyperion Books, 1996.

Kise, Jane. *Finding and Following God's Will*. Minneapolis: Bethany House Publishers, 2005.

Chapter 7—Life Choices

Covey, Stephen R., A. Roger Merrill, and Rebecca R. Merrill. *First Things First*. New York: Simon & Schuster, 1994.

Foster, Richard J. *Celebration of Discipline*, revised edition. New York: Harper & Row, 1988.

Ortberg, John. *The Life You've Always Wanted*. Grand Rapids, Mich.: Zondervan, 1997.

Chapter 8—Service

Kise, Jane, and David Stark. *Working With Purpose*. Minneapolis: Augsburg Fortress Publishers, 2004.

Seligman, Martin E. *Authentic Happiness*. New York: The Free Press, 2002.

Warren, Rick. *The Purpose-Driven Life: What on Earth Am I Here For?* Grand Rapids, Mich.: Zondervan, 2002.

My *LifeKeys* Notations

My Life Gifts (Write your top 8-10 gifts in the corresponding area.)

R———I

C   A

E———S

My Life Gifts Sentence

NAME:

DATE:

My Spiritual Gifts

1.

2.

3.

4.

5.

My Personality Type is __ __ __ __

Factors important to me as I choose places to work or serve:

My Top Values

1.

2.

3.

4.

5.

6.

7.

8.

My Passions

For whom, where, or for what causes do you hope to use your gifts? Be as detailed as you can about what God is putting in your heart.

Note: Use the last tear-out card in this book to summarize your *LifeKeys* Notations. Then tear it out and put it in your day planner, on your desk or dresser, or someplace else where it will remind you of all you have discovered during your *LifeKeys* journey.

Accuracy
Being true or correct
in attention to detail
Psalm 147:4

Artistic Expression
Expressing self through the arts—
painting,
drama, literature, etc.
1 Kings 6:29–32

Achievement
Enjoying a sense of
accomplishment or success
Ecclesiastes 2:24–25

Authenticity
Ongoing desire to honestly
express who one is
James 1:22–25

Advancement
Striving to move ahead rapidly,
gaining opportunities
for growth or seniority
Proverbs 22:29

Balance
Giving proper weight to each area
of a person's life
Ecclesiastes 3:1–8

Adventure
Seeking new and exciting challenges,
which may
include taking risks
Genesis 12:1–2

Challenge
Attracted to new problems,
difficult tasks
Hebrews 10:35–36

Aesthetics
Appreciating what
is beautiful
Philippians 4:8

Competency
Wanting to meet or exceed
standards or expectations
2 Corinthians 3:4–5

Competition
Matching efforts or abilities
with self or others
1 Corinthians 9:25

Creativity
Being imaginative
and innovative, going
outside the norm
2 Chronicles 2:13–14

Conformity
Preferring to be like others,
not standing out
Romans 12:2

Efficiency
Working to accomplish tasks in
comparatively little time
Proverbs 13:4

Contribution
Giving or making a difference
for others
Ephesians 2:10

Fairness
Giving everyone
an equal chance
Luke 6:38b

Control
Being in charge or wanting to have
influence over outcomes
Proverbs 25:28

Family
Placing importance on maintaining
familial relationships
Ephesians 6:2–3

Cooperation
Striving for congenial relationships
and teamwork
Colossians 3:12–15

Financial Security
Being free from
financial worries
Luke 12:16–20

Flexibility
Coping easily with
change and surprise
James 4:13–15

Independence
Wanting control of own time,
behavior, tasks
Galatians 6:4–5

Friendship
Placing importance on close,
personal relationships
Ecclesiastes 4:9–10

Influence
Capacity to affect or shape people,
processes, or ideas
Matthew 5:13–16

Generosity
Giving readily or liberally
2 Corinthians 9:7–8

Integrity
Maintaining congruity
between what one claims to be
and how one acts
Proverbs 11:3

Happiness
Finding satisfaction,
joy, or pleasure
Psalm 37:3–4

Learning
Lifelong commitment to
growing in understanding
Proverbs 1:5–7

Humor
Enjoying the witty
or amusing
Proverbs 17:22

Leisure
Appreciating unstructured or
unscheduled time
Ecclesiastes 8:15

Location
Preferring a specific place,
neighborhood, or area of country
that matches lifestyle
Psalm 139:7–10

Peace
Desiring tranquility, serenity,
lack of discord
Philippians 4:6–7

Love
Cherishing oneself
or others
1 John 4:7–8

Perseverance
Sustaining momentum,
having fortitude
James 1:2–4

Loyalty
Seeking to be faithful,
constant, and steadfast
Proverbs 18:24

Personal Development
Wanting to use one's potential
and grow to the fullest
1 Timothy 4:14–15

Nature
Finding joy and renewal
in the out-of-doors
Psalm 19:1–3

Physical Fitness
and Health
Healthy regard for one's body,
enjoying sports involvement
1 Corinthians 6:19–20

Organization
Being in control of time,
priorities, possessions,
and processes
Exodus 18:19–22

Power
Seeking to sell to, persuade, lead,
or influence others
1 Peter 5:2–4

Prestige
Having or showing success, rank,
wealth, or status
Matthew 20:25–28

Self-Respect
Having pride or a sense
of personal identity
Psalm 139:14

Recognition
Desiring the respect of others
or credit for achievements
Proverbs 22:1

Service
Helping others or
contributing to society
Isaiah 58:6–8

Religious Beliefs
Sustaining faith in
a higher power
Psalm 119:35–37

Stability
Maintaining continuity,
consistency, and predictability
over a period of time
Psalm 57:7

Responsibility
Being accountable
for outcomes
John 15:10–11

Tolerance
Accepting or remaining open
to the viewpoints and
values of others
Ephesians 4:32

Security
Feeling safe and confident
about the future
Psalm 91:1–2

Tradition
Treasuring customs and
links with the past
Psalm 79:13

Variety
Desiring new and different
activities, frequent change
Genesis 1:31–2:1

Prompt Card

"As I work to make major decisions,

this is how I value _____."

These are very valuable to me.

These are valuable to me.

These are not very valuable to me.

LIFE KEYS of _____

LIFE GIFTS

```
        C
    R       I
  E           D
        S
```
(hexagon shape with letters R, I, C, D, S, E at vertices)

ISTJ	ISFJ	INFJ	INTJ
ISTP	ISFP	INFP	INTP
ESTP	ESFP	ENFP	ENTP
ESTJ	ESFJ	ENFJ	ENTJ

VALUES

1. _____
2. _____
3. _____
4. _____
5. _____
6. _____
7. _____
8. _____

SPIRITUAL GIFTS

1. _____
2. _____
3. _____
4. _____

PASSIONS

LIFE GIFTS SENTENCE: _____